ANTI-SEMITIC STEREOTYPES WITHOUT JEWS

BERNARD GLASSMAN

ANTI-SEMITIC STEREOTYPES WITHOUT JEWS,

IMAGES OF THE JEWS IN ENGLAND
1290-1700

Lamar University Library

WAYNE STATE UNIVERSITY PRESS   DETROIT   1975

Library of Congress Cataloging in Publication Data

Glassman, Bernard, 1937-
  Anti-Semitic stereotypes without Jews.

  Bibliography: p.
  Includes index.
  1. Antisemitism–England.   2. Jews in England–History   3. England–Civilization.   I. Title
DS146.G7G56   941'.004'924   75-16391
ISBN O-8143-1545-3

4

TO SUE, ARTHUR, and VIVIAN

CONTENTS

PREFACE

There is certainly no lack of competently researched material dealing with the history of the Jews in England from early times through the modern period. The pioneering work of Joseph Jacobs, Lucien Wolf, E. Nathan Adler, H. S. Q. Henriques, and Cecil Roth has been supplemented by a number of articles and studies in *Transactions of the Jewish Historical Society of England* and other learned journals. My prime concern in writing this book is not to repeat the facts of Anglo-Jewish history, but to explore how the Jew was viewed by the Christian community during the centuries after the expulsion of 1290 through the time of the resettlement and why these attitudes developed. During a large part of this period (up to 1656) England was virtually *Judenrein* (without Jews); and except for a small group of Crypto-Jews, there was no real Jewish community in the country. Yet anti-Jewish sentiments continued to be spread by the preacher, the playwright, the writer, and the storyteller. If flesh-and-blood Jews were not present in any significant numbers, the molders of public opinion kept a shadowy image of them alive in the minds of the English people. It was this medieval stereotype, cultivated during the Tudor and early Stuart periods, that ultimately forced Cromwell to give up his plans to formally readmit the Jews into England. It was to plague Anglo-Jewry even after a small community was unofficially reestablished in the second half of the seventeenth century. Enlightened social

9

philosophers and religious leaders were to find that this hideous image from the Middle Ages, though not as extreme as anything found on the continent, could not be passed over lightly.

In this book I have touched upon various religious and literary sources of history that have either been neglected or only partially utilized in the examination of attitudes towards the Jewish people. Many of the original sources cited in this work are representative samplings of a vast amount of material that has yet to be fully studied and evaluated. Perhaps a few comments on the nature of the works cited will aid the reader in appreciating the scope of this study and indicate to him various avenues for further research.

It is unfortunate that the students of this period of history have failed to appreciate the importance of Christian sermonic material in understanding the image of the Jew in the mind of the English people. Throughout the period of time covered in this book, sermons were an important means of shaping public opinion. Handbooks containing source material for preachers were very popular among the clergy, and they present a very good picture of the official attitudes of the religious establishment as well as the ideas to which the common man of the era was exposed. These sermons preserved and popularized some of the crudest forms of anti-Semitism that were found in the folklore of the times. In addition, they perpetuated the centuries-old stereotype of the Jew that originated in the pages of the New Testament and which was an important part of Christian theology. The effect of sermons upon popular attitudes should not be underestimated in studying the development of anti-Semitic sentiments. For several centuries, Jews appeared in numerous popular stories that were used for sermon illustrations. It was this portion of the religious instruction that remained in the mind of the faithful for the longest time. In addition, the written sermon became a popular form of literature, and quite often the preacher's words reached a much larger audience than those who were present at his religious services.

In presenting dramatic and nondramatic material, I have tried to avoid the simplistic procedure of using literature as documentation for the writing of history. Some early Jewish scholars who were guilty of this have distorted the significance of several of the great

10

works of English literature. Although there is no reason to believe that the dramatists and poets were not guilty of the same prejudices that were echoed from the pulpits, it is wrong to assume, for example, that Chaucer and the Prioress speak with one voice. As I have pointed out in chapter 2, there are complex ironies in the *Canterbury Tales* which should not be overlooked. The same can be said for Marlowe, Shakespeare, and the other Elizabethans. In amassing diverse materials which include, in addition to the works mentioned above, religious drama, mystical literature, ballads, folklore, travellers' accounts, political tracts, and conversionist literature, I have tried to evaluate each source in its own literary and historical context, appreciating that their value in shaping public opinion varied greatly.

The student of public opinion and propaganda can argue that the mass media may reflect rather than shape the thinking of the people. This may be true in a society where Jews have made their presence felt and where popular attitudes toward them are the result of a combination of real and imagined experiences. Since there were so few Jews in England during this period, the average Englishman was obliged to rely upon what he heard from the pulpit, saw on the stage, and absorbed from the wandering minstrel and storyteller to form his opinions. This oral tradition, which was supplemented by various tracts and pamphlets, was an important source of information about Jews, and there was virtually nothing in society to counterbalance these forces that had the weight of centuries of Christian teachings behind them.

Unfortunately, there is little reliable data to accurately determine what the common man actually thought about the Jews. Almost all of the material presented in this book reflects the attitudes and prejudices of the religious establishment, the court, and the intelligentsia. Certainly the expulsion of 1290 did meet with the approval of the masses. Subsequent public expressions against individual Jews like Rodrigo Lopez, personal physician to Queen Elizabeth, and the readmission controversy concerning the right of the Jewish people to return to England in the middle of the seventeenth century, betrayed an anti-Semitism that affected all strata of society. This is not to say that the English quality of "live

11

and let live" did not permit a very small number of Jews to live unmolested in the country as long as they did not openly practice their faith or focus undue attention upon themselves. The lack of hard facts prevented me from determining if there really was any significant gulf between the attitudes of the religious and political establishment and those of the average man. There is no lack of evidence, however, to show how anti-Semitic sentiments in a society almost devoid of actual Jews reflected deep-seated irrational responses to the Jewish people, rooted in the teachings of the church and exploited by men who needed an outlet for their religious, social, and economic frustrations. I leave it to men of good will to ponder the sentiments of Nicholas Berdyaev:

> For us Christians the Jewish problem does not consist in knowing whether the Jews are good or bad, but whether we are good or bad. For it is more important that I should consider this question with reference to myself rather than to my neighbor, since I am always inclined to accuse him. [1]

I would like to express my sincere gratitude to all those who were of assistance in preparing this book. Warren Spencer and Joseph Tyrrell were responsible for guiding my early research in British history. Abraham Halkin continued their work, and also directed my doctoral studies in this area at the Jewish Theological Seminary. Gerson Cohen's invaluable comments crystallized some of the analyses found in this book, and I deeply appreciate the advice and encouragement that he gave me throughout the writing of this work. Gavin Langmuir read the chapters dealing with the medieval period. Jacob Neusner was most generous with his time, and his advice was always welcome. His encyclopedic knowledge of Jewish history and his sense of style and organization was a great help to me. I am particularly grateful to B'nai Brith and the Merrill Trust for providing a research grant to do work at the British Museum. I also received help from the staffs of the libraries at Brown University, the Jewish Theological Seminary, Old Dominion University, Southeastern Massachusetts University, and Union Theological Seminary.

This book was written while I served as rabbi at the Gomley Chesed Synagogue in Portsmouth, Virginia, and at my present pulpit, the Tifereth Israel Synagogue in New Bedford, Massachusetts. I consider myself most fortunate that my congregants have appreciated the need for their rabbi to be allowed time for scholarly pursuits, and I am deeply indebted to them for their many kindnesses.

B. G.

ONE

GENESIS OF A STEREOTYPE

For almost four centuries the English people rarely, if ever, came into contact with flesh-and-blood Jews. Yet they considered the Jews to be an accursed group of usurers, who, in league with the devil, were guilty of every conceivable crime that could be conjured up by the popular imagination. To fully appreciate these attitudes towards Jews and Judaism from 1290 to 1700, one must understand the place of this alien people in English society prior to the expulsion of the Jews. Just as historical studies of any particular period cannot be neatly confined to certain blocks of time, any analysis of prejudice must also go beyond the period in question. In the case of Anglo-Jewry, Christian attitudes formed prior to 1290 were to continue for several centuries. Although in later years other factors influenced public opinion, both religious and secular literature contained remembrances of the pre-expulsion community.

William the Conqueror brought the first group of Jews over from France in 1066. From the beginning the Jews were protected by the king, and in return they provided a small part of William's wealth. Because of the church's policy of forbidding any Christian from indulging in money-lending or virtually any form of commercial speculation, the Jews were given free rein in this lucrative area. In a relatively short time, some of them were able to multiply the funds that they had brought with them from the continent, and by the middle of the twelfth century, Aaron of Lincoln, a Jewish financier, was supposedly the wealthiest member of the commercial classes. The king used his Jewish subjects as a kind of sponge to absorb the wealth of his people. It was, after all, a simple task to squeeze the money out of the Jews after they had diligently acquired it through their money-lending activities.

In England, as in other countries in Western Europe during the late Middle Ages, legal recognition and the support of the right of the Jews to maintain their own separate religious and communal organizations were in direct proportion to their fiscal contributions to the crown. As long as the Jews could supply the king with money in the form of fines, special taxes, and loans, they were allowed to maintain what amounted to a privileged place in society.[1]

The special position enjoyed by the Jews aroused the ire of the church, and both the hierarchy and the lower clergy found the apparent wealth and position of the Jews to be a source of constant annoyance. Through the centuries the church fathers had viewed the Jews as an accursed people, who by rejecting Jesus were condemned to be wanderers and fugitives over the face of the earth. These clerics never advocated that the Jews be physically harmed or restricted in the practice of their faith. However, they wanted the Jews to be kept on as lowly a level as possible to support the theological contention that the Christians were the true elect of God and that the Almighty had rejected the Jewish people. For example, Robert Grosseteste (1175–1253), Bishop of Lincoln, firmly believed that the Jews, "being guilty of murder in cruelly killing by crucifixion the Savior of the world,"[2] were condemned to bear the mark of Cain and live a wretched life among the Christian people. Though cursed by God to be eternal wanderers, like Cain, they were to be protected from being killed and they were to be allowed to remain "witnesses of the Christian faith against the unbelief of the Pagans."[3]

In an attempt to reduce the influence of the Jews upon the Christian people and to keep them on a lower social and economic level, the popes and councils issued various proclamations. They reflected a growing intensity of the church's discriminatory and segregationist policies towards the Jews, which began at the end of the twelfth century and became progressively harsher through the next century. Stephen Langton (? –1228), Archbishop of Canter-

15

bury, was one of the leading spirits at the Fourth Lateran Council that was called by Innocent III in 1215. Partially through his efforts, attempts were made to limit Jewish commercial and social intercourse with Christians. Owing to his zeal and that of other clerics in the country, England was the first nation in Europe to adopt the infamous Jew Badge in 1218.

The official church policy of degrading the Jews and alienating them from Christian society had little influence on those Englishmen who had profitable commercial dealings with them or who knew them on a personal basis. However, by taking advantage of the fears and superstitions of the masses, most of whom rarely if ever had any contact with Jews, the church built up a diabolical image of the Jew that was to persist for centuries. Many accusations against the Jews came from the overzealous local clergy and not from the hierarchy of the church. But the people accepted these slanderous remarks as being the official church teachings. [4]

The prejudice that the lower clergy felt towards the Jews can be found in the manner in which the chroniclers treated the details of the notorious ritual murder accusations that first shook the Jewish community of England in the middle of the twelfth century, and which continued to affect Jewish-Christian relations for many years to come. Thomas of Monmouth's [5] gruesome description of the supposed tortures inflicted by the Jews upon William of Norwich in 1144, and Mathew of Paris's [6] account of the alleged ritual murder of Hugh of Lincoln in 1254 followed a certain stylized pattern and revealed an underlying theme. The villains were not merely nonbelievers in the same category with Moslems or heathens; they were actually antagonists of Jesus, who knew he existed and yet crucified him rather than accept him as their king. [7] Many Englishmen, influenced by the stories in the gospels which vividly depicted the Jewish role in the Crucifixion, needed no proof of Jewish guilt for alleged crimes committed in contemporary society. If the Jews had crucified Jesus, they readily believed that Jews also tortured and killed young children before Passover and committed other such fiendish acts.

It is easy to understand how such stories of Jewish treachery were readily believed in a society that did not have any empirical verification of such incidents. However, it is more difficult to

16

explain why they persisted for so many centuries. Perhaps the blood libel was a means of transferring onto their victims the guilt that the Christians felt for their own acts of oppression. By making the Jews guilty of the very crimes that Christians had committed, the Christians' burden of guilt was shifted. Also, any acts taken against the Jewish community could be conceptualized as just punishments for previous crimes.[8]

On a somewhat deeper level, the Jews became the scapegoats for the repressed desires of Christian society. In the stories of the alleged ritual murders, the Jews were invariably pictured as being the members of the older generation who inflicted pain upon innocent children. Here is a continuation of the theme of the Crucifixion where the "Son of God" was put to death by the Jewish elders who worshipped "God the Father." In later literature, plays, and sermons, Christian attitudes towards the Jews were to be tied up with this conflict between the generations and the oedipal fantasies that resulted from it.

The ritual-murder accusations pointed out another important aspect of the anti-Jewish sentiment of the time and of the centuries that followed. They reflected the deep-rooted belief that the Jew, as the sorcerer, needed Christian blood for magical purposes. Human blood, preferably from a child, was believed to be a necessary ingredient in various witches' rituals, in preparing poisons, and in writing compacts with the devil. Therefore, it was not too difficult for the masses to accept the idea that the Jews kidnapped children and slaughtered them in some demonic rite. The pagans, in ancient times, had leveled this same charge against the early Christians, and in the mediaeval period they in turn made the same accusations against both Jews and heretics.[9] It was a simple but effective means of showing the faithful that, with the enemies of Christendom lurking about, the church and its stronger magic were needed to protect them. The more sinister the Jews appeared, the greater role the church could play in defending good Christians from their devilish attacks.

The English clergy was the first to fabricate the ritual-murder accusations against the Jews and the first in Europe to spread the myth of the "Wandering Jew."[10] In these stories, as well as in those that centered around the Crucifixion, the Jews were closely

17

associated with the devil. Through the years they were to play interchangeable roles as the eternal adversary of God, the Antichrist, as well as the usurer and the sorcerer. The devil was needed as an object for the projection of hostilities, and the Jew served equally well in this capacity.[11] The teachings of the church which echoed from the pulpit and which appeared in the drama and in the secular and religious literature of the country reflected these themes clearly.

After the Lateran Council of 1215, the sermon became an important means of teaching church doctrine and of spreading some anti-Jewish prejudice as well. At this time the friars began to circulate among the people and preach to them on a regular basis. Instead of delivering sermons four times a year, these men went out as often as they were able to the market places, the private homes and castles, the cemeteries, the churches, and the preaching crosses, both to entertain and instruct the people.[12] Through songs, poems, and stories the friars presented their messages to people who could not comprehend the subtleties of the usual church teachings. They drew heavily upon the *exempla* and other legends of their time to hold their listeners' interest. *Mariales* or anecdotes that described miracles attributed to the Virgin were particularly popular. In keeping with their general tone, many of these selections contained unflattering and often slanderous references to Jews.[13]

These sermon illustrations were further developed after the expulsion, and they continued as an anti-Jewish tradition through the fifteenth century. In the church's early years missionaries had used miracle stories to convince the masses of the superiority of Christianity over the powers of paganism, and the mediaeval church furthered this tradition. That some of the villains in these stories were Jews did not disturb the clerics. They were disturbed by many of the grossly superstitious folk beliefs that were to be found in the stories. However, the clergy did not want to disparage any attitudes that might encourage greater piety on the part of the masses. If, for example, the stories of the wondrous powers of the Host would elevate the power of the church in the eyes of the faithful, the clergy were willing to tolerate such beliefs.[14] Thus, for the sake of strengthening Christian beliefs and enhancing the image of the church the wonder tales along with the wicked Jews who were so often found in them remained. In chapter 2 I discuss how the germ of many of the great narratives in secular literature appeared first in these naive and sometimes crude stories that were of such interest to the mediaeval English community.

The sermon illustrations that portrayed the Jew as the crucifier of Jesus, the devil's agent, and the enemy of good Christians left a deep impression upon the minds of the general population both before and after the expulsion. The same can be said for the early religious pageants and plays that were popular forms of instruction and entertainment. In the summer festival of Corpus Christi, founded by Pope Urban IV in 1264, for example, Judas was portrayed by a person wearing a red beard who was bent beneath the weight of his money bags. He was closely followed by someone dressed as the devil to remind the spectators of the kinship that existed between the two of them. The masses who witnessed the spectacles and who had no contact with Jews in their personal lives, accepted the distorted, diabolical stage Jew as the real thing.[15] In the next centuries, the crude productions of the Corpus Christi pageant began to evolve into modern drama, and the characterization of the Jew was to become more complex and more grotesque.

In addition to the effects of anti-Jewish sentiments in the official and unofficial teachings of the church and the effects of various attempts to segregate them from society, the general population tended to distrust them because they considered the Jews to be strangers in their midst. They were separated from the English people not only by their religious beliefs but also by their national and ethnic origins.[16] Although there was no official ghetto in England, the Jews were set apart from their neighbors because they were considered to be part of a displaced nation living in a foreign land. Thus, when Edward found it expedient to expel the Jews from England, after they were no longer of economic value to him, he was overwhelmingly supported by public opinion. As Trevor-Roper has noted:

Edward I

no ruler has ever carried out a policy of wholesale expulsion or destruction without the cooperation of society. To think otherwise, to suppose that a ruler, or even a party in the state, can thus cut out part

19

of the living tissue of society without the consent of society, is to defy the lesson of history. Great massacres may be commanded by tyrants, but they are imposed by peoples. Without general social support, the organs of isolation and expulsion cannot even be created.[17]

The expulsion of 1290 fit into this pattern, and this anti-Jewish sentiment was deeply ingrained in the fabric of English life throughout the next several centuries.

TWO

EMBELLISHMENT OF
A STEREOTYPE

From the time of the expulsion of
the Jews to the reign of Elizabeth, the crude sermonic homilies of
the past were embroidered with vivid imagery and with new
anti-Jewish themes. The increasing popularity of the drama as a
means of teaching religious lessons created the stage Jew, a figure
who acted out his role as the adversary of both Christians and
Christianity. He added a touch of reality to the image created in the
ballads and in the folklore. Secular writers also began to use the
Jew for their own literary purposes and to make him an infamous
figure in their works. During this period the growth of interest in
Hebraic studies brought a small number of Jews who had
converted to Christianity to England to teach at the universities.
Additional secret Jews also settled in the country. However, the
stereotype of the Jew as the accursed usurer, the Host desecrator,
and the murderer of innocent children was to continue in a society
where the absence of a significant number of practicing Jews
prevented any possible means of disputing these irrational accusations. The popular image of the Jew had developed out of the need
for Christianity to show itself superior to Judaism and to justify its
claims that it was the new Israel. Thus, Christian anti-Judaism
continued to be a central and an essential element of the daughter
religion's system of beliefs. Out of the theology of the church, a
focus was provided for those individuals, religiously motivated or
not, who had the need to displace and project guilt and hatred

21

through a socially accepted outlet.[1] Dramatists, preachers, writers, and folk singers were to share in this inheritance and to enhance it as well.

Landa claims that "in no department of human activity has Jew baiting been more persistent and popular than in the realm of drama."[2] This form of anti-Jewish propaganda affected both the performers and viewers of the productions. For the actors and the audience, the physical representation of sacred events was proof of their reality. "The play was a spiritual force superior to the material world and able to transform it, enoble it, or even to ward it off," Sieferth notes.[3]

Although the earliest examples of English drama appeared prior to the expulsion, it was not until the end of the thirteenth century that drama broke away from the confines of the church and attracted the general populace. The use of the vernacular and the direct involvement of the guilds in the various productions brought the drama to the masses. The Jew was "fair game for the merciless sport of the ignorant people whom the ecclesiastical writers of the mysteries and the miracle plays were anxious to impress," according to Landa.[4] The image of the Jew, as it appeared on the stage, was widely accepted by the people and lasted for centuries. Even when the drama developed various secular themes, the Jew with all his grotesque attributes remained. In the more enlightened centuries that followed, the Jew remained the villain, for he was far too popular with the masses to be cast aside.

In the years after the expulsion, the simple Corpus Christi pageants grew increasingly complex. The mystery cycles developed from these annual productions, and they became a regular part of the life of the larger towns in England. The size and scope of these productions varied in different localities, but their treatment of the Jew was consistent. There was little, if any, deviation from official and unofficial church policies. In *Christ's Passion*, one of the Chester mystery plays, virtually the entire guilt for crucifying Jesus was placed upon the heads of the Jews. The work reflected the spirit of other Passion plays that were written before and after the year 1375, when this particular cycle was first performed.

The unknown author of the play described how the Jews brought Jesus before Pilate for punishment. Pilate, pictured as a just and merciful ruler, could find no reason for harming Jesus, and he protested to the Jews:

Fault in him I find none.
Therefore it is best that we let him be gone
And out of these doors let him go yon
Wither he will to take his way.[5]

The Jews were not satisfied with his decision and loudly protested that Jesus should be put to death on the cross. Pilate decided to wash his hands of the whole matter, and the Jewish community immediately took the initiative in punishing Jesus. It was the Jews who stripped Jesus of his cloak and beat him. They were the ones who tormented him and who cast dice for his clothes. The Roman soldiers were not mentioned once in the Crucifixion scene, and the author portrayed the conflict as between the Jews and Jesus. Pilate was just an innocent bystander.[6]

In the York mysteries, the Jews were depicted with powerful realism. Judas was given perhaps a fuller treatment here than in any other production of the time, and he became a very real character to the audience. In the scene in which he offered his services as the betrayer of Jesus and in another where he implored the High Priest to take back the thirty pieces of silver, Judas was an impressive figure who was filled with villainy. The Jew in general became associated with Judas's treachery and also with his flaming beard.[7] Traces of both Judas's inner and external nature were to continue to be part of the portrayal of the Jew for centuries.

The various authors of the mysteries treated the Jews of the Old Testament in a positive manner. In plays like *Abraham and Isaac*, *Jacob and Esau*, and *Joseph*, the main characters were portrayed as good Christians. However, the Jews of New Testament times were totally different creatures. They followed closely the diabolical image that began in the Epistle of Paul to the Romans and which was perpetuated and embellished through the centuries. What was true of the authors of the mysteries was equally true of those playwrights and authors that came after them.

During the fourteenth century virtually any subject of religious significance could be made into a play. Thus, it is not surprising that the legends that Jews desecrated the wafer of the Eucharist would eventually be put on the stage.

In 1378, such a work, *The Play of the Sacrament,* appeared. Before the actual performance of the play, Banns, or public announcements, were made in the neighboring towns and villages by men known as vexillatores (banner-bearers). The Banns of this work described the cruelty of the Jews and the way they mistreated the wafer. Thus, anti-Jewish sentiment was spread to many who did not see the actual performance. Through the Banns the people heard how the Jews "grevid our Lord gretly on the grownd and put him to cruell passyon" and how they "Nayled hym to a pyller; with pynsons plukked hym doune" (Banns, 36–40).

The plot of the play centered around Syr Arystory, who was bribed by the Jew Jonas to steal a consecrated wafer. The motive for the sacrilege was the Jew's curiosity over the Christian belief that it actually contained the blood and the flesh of Jesus. Perhaps the most horrible scene in the play occurred when the Jews, having gained possession of the wafer, pierced it with their knives and nailed it to a post. They were portrayed as hateful people who symbolically wanted to re-crucify Jesus. The audience likely associated the Jews' dialogue in the play with that which was uttered in Jerusalem at the time of the Crucifixion. One of the Jews in the play drew his knife and proclaimed:

> Now am I bold with batayle hym to bleyke,
> This mydle part alle for to prene;
> A stowe stroke also for to stryke,
> In the myddys shalbe scene!
>
> [396–400]

After the Jews had tried to mutilate the wafer with their daggers, they threw it into a cauldron of boiling oil and then placed it in a redhot oven. Finally, the bleeding image of Jesus appeared and pleaded with his tormentors. The Jews, stricken with remorse for their deeds, then asked for forgiveness and prepared themselves for a penitential pilgrimage and ultimate conversion.

Miracle plays such as *The Play of the Sacrament* gradually gave way to the moralities, works that dealt with the personification of such abstract qualities as Beauty, Strength, Gluttony, and Mammon. The stage Jew was very much a part of this transition. For example, in the play, *St. Mary Magdalen*, Infidelity portrayed Mary's lover. He boasted that at the time of the Crucifixion his name was Moysaical Justice and that he was so much a part of the Jews that he prevented them from believing in Jesus. Infidelity played the part of some of the Jews, especially Judas, in the play. Alongside of him were other Jewish characters, one of whom was Simon the Pharisee, a sly criminal character who was able to commit crimes without being caught.

Another effective means, in addition to the drama, of shaping the religious attitudes of the masses during this period was the sermon delivered by the parish priest or the friar. In a society where the ability to read and write was limited to a select few, the spoken word assumed great importance in reminding the faithful what the church expected of them. The content of these discourses, preserved in various sermon manuals, reveals what the clerics were preaching and, assuming that the listeners were attentive, what the average churchgoers were digesting.

References to Jews were most numerous in sermons delivered during the Easter season. The rituals of Holy Week provided the preacher with a volume of material to fix in the minds of the faithful the enormity of the crime that the Jews had committed against Jesus. For example, part of the Shere Thursday ritual was the snuffing out and then the relighting of a candle. The anthem and the psalms that were sung at this point in the service were to be "with an hye voice and as a ferddeful sowne," which was to represent the cries of the Jews who came to seize Jesus. The altar was not to be covered so as to serve as a reminder of how Jesus was naked before the Jews in his Passion. On Good Friday there was to be no bowing during the service "because of the scornes that they [the Jews] scorned Crist with here bownge."[8]

The supposed role that the Jews played in the Crucifixion, as described in the New Testament, embellished in legend, and portrayed on the stage was familiar to both cleric and layman, and it was a good starting point for moral teaching. One of the richest sources of sermonic material dealing with the last days of Jesus was *The Northern Passion*,[9] a collection of various legends that were

25

designed to appeal to the emotions of the masses. The author portrayed the Jews as the chief villains in the Crucifixion. He made it clear from the beginning that their leaders feared him and that they believed that if Jesus would be allowed to continue to preach to the people, they would leave their faith and follow him. At a banquet they remarked, "If we lat hym thus forth gone/ Oure folk wyll all turn hym tyll/ And all will tha follow hys wyll" (26–28).

Thus, it was the Jewish leaders, headed by Caiaphas, who decided to put Jesus to death. They gave Judas thirty pieces of money to betray Jesus and seized him and brought him to Pilate. Along with these stock accusations, the author included a legend about Judas which further blackened the image of the Jew. After Judas had done his deed, he was stricken with remorse and told the Jews that it was a mistake to betray Jesus. The Jews insisted that the bargain stand. They had paid him, and they refused to free him from his obligation to them. Judas then threw the money at the Jews and, filled with guilt, went off to hang himself. The Jews picked up the silver and started to argue over it. Because the money was "full of felony," they determined that it was not fit to be placed in the treasury and decided to use it to buy a field for the burial of wicked Jews and strangers. Thus, not only did the Jews use money to bribe Judas, but they were also responsible for the purchase of the infamous place where Jesus was put to death.

The author included the usual story of how the Jews persuaded Pilate to allow Jesus to be put to death by assuring him that they would accept full responsibility for the act. They proclaimed, "Al hys blode be on vs sene/ Cryst leue that it be falle/ On vs And oure children alle" (1136–39).

Other legends which added to the Jews' guilt for the death of Jesus and further tarnished their image dealt with the great lengths the Jews went to to persuade a smith to make the nails that were to be used in the Crucifixion. There was a tradition that after the cross had been made, three nails were needed to crucify Jesus. The Jews then went to a smith and told him, "Make thre nayles stif and gude/ At naile the prophet on the rode."[10] The smith, who believed in Jesus, refused to follow their orders and claimed that he could not fashion the nails because his hand was sore. Just as the Jews were about to leave the shop, the smith's wife came and offered to make them. The Jews helped her to strike the iron, and when the nails were finished, they cheerfully went off to Pilate. Thus, the very steel which pierced the flesh of Jesus was fashioned by the Jews.

A major work that dealt with this theme and supplied additional sermonic material for the preacher was *The Siege of Jerusalem*, which was completed in the last decade of the fourteenth century.[11] It began with the story of Jesus' torture on the cross. Revenge for this act took place during the time of Nero, when the emperor sent Vespasian and Titus to Judea to subdue the Jewish people. The Romans sent twelve knights to Jerusalem to tell the inhabitants of the city that they had come to avenge the death of Jesus and to ask for their immediate surrender. The Jews, in ungentlemanly fashion, disfigured the messengers and prepared to defend themselves. In a fanciful description of the war with Rome, the author related how the Jews, equipped with elephants, were ultimately defeated after a bloody siege. The Romans were victorious because they had been told by Vespasian that they had come to avenge the Crucifixion. In the early stages of the battle, Caiaphas, the High Priest, was captured and condemned to a painful death. This was "In tokne of tresoun" that he had committed against Jesus. When the city was finally in Roman hands, Titus asked Pilate about the details of Jesus' death. When he learned that the Jews had sold Jesus for thirty pence, he immediately made a decree that the Jewish captives should be sold thirty for a penny. Pilate, for his part in the crime, was put into prison, where he later died.

In this story the blame for the Crucifixion fell upon both Pilate and the Jews. Yet, the Jews, as individuals and as a people, suffered much more than Pilate. The Roman conquest of Judea was turned into a holy crusade; the destruction of Jerusalem and the slaughter of the city's inhabitants were portrayed as a pious act. The Jews were pictured as the villains in the struggle, a people who did not fight fairly, as when they mutilated messengers sent under a flag of truce to ask for their surrender. The Romans, filled with noble motives, punished them measure for measure. The author showed that the temple was destroyed because of the Jewish involvement in the Crucifixion.

The Jews, their hands stained with the blood of Jesus, were evil incarnate, a perfect example of a debased people who could be contrasted with those enlightened individuals influenced by the church's teaching. Thus, Bishop Brunton of Rochester used in a sermon the example of Jewish behavior at the time of Jesus' passion to denounce the corruption of justice in his own day. After quoting a passage from the book of Proverbs, "the vows of the just are acceptable with God" (15:8), he noted:

> But these things notwithstanding, to speak solid truths, it is the same with the Justice of the English as it was with the Justice of the Jews at the time of Christ's Passion. For, just as Christ had manifold testimony of his own justice from his opponents, namely from Pilate, Pilate's wife, Judas the Betrayer, the thief and the centurion, yet contrary to all justice was betrayed to death, and Barabbas, the famous thief and murderer, was freed from the death of Christ, in these words—"Come, let us oppress the just man, who is contrary to our doings," so also is it with the powerful men of the world to-day and the leaders of the realm.[12]

Preachers often used references to the Crucifixion to attack those things that the Jews stood for and which the church opposed. For example, Thomas Wimbledon, a fourteenth-century cleric, denounced the Jewish practice of accepting the binding authority of Mosaic Law: "Wo to the Iewe, that tristed so moche in the olde/ lawe; than schal he see Marie sone demynge the/ world, whom he despised and sette on the Cros."[13] It is significant that the preacher associated the Crucifixion with those who follow "the olde lawe." For him, such an outlook was reserved for those who despised Jesus and who put him to death and was something which no self-respecting Christian would accept as part of his religious philosophy.

In the sermons of post-expulsion England, the image of the Jews varied from that of a people who were morally neutral but blind to the "true faith" to one of outright villains who were enemies of the church and the Christian people. Even in what appeared to be contemporary stories, the guilt of the Crucifixion often seemed to hover over the Jews, and there was the inference that this type of crime was something that they were capable of repeating if given the opportunity.

The need to convert the Jews, save their souls, and enable them to merit the rewards of heaven appear in numerous sermon illustrations of the period. The clerics were convinced that if only the Jews would be exposed to the truth of Christian doctrine, usually through some supernatural occurrence, they would renounce their faith and accept Christianity. The fact that there were no Jews in England who openly practiced their faith did not seem to deter the preachers. The stories containing references to Jews, which in many instances were carried over from earlier centuries, could be used to point out the superiority of Christianity over Judaism and to strengthen the faith of Christians who questioned the teachings of the church. The Jews, shrouded in legend, were an excellent foil, and the clerics used them often in their sermons. Thus, if they did not exist in the flesh, their imaginary spirits were resurrected to enhance the power of the church in the eyes of the faithful.

Mirk's Festial, one of the more popular sermon collections, contains a story of a Jew and a Christian who were discussing the "comyng of our lady." The Jew refused to believe in the supernatural powers of the Virgin unless a lily, the symbol of Mary, sprang from a wine pot that stood between the two. When the lily immediately appeared, he converted.[14] In another story in this collection, a Jew who came to England from France was captured by thieves. After the thieves had robbed him, they bound him and placed him in an abandoned house. While he was there, the Virgin appeared to the Jew and announced, "I am Mary that thou and all thi nacyon despysythe." She then unbound him and showed him the "paynes of hell" and revealed to him places of "gret ioye and blysse." After this experience, the Jew, impressed with the powers of the Virgin, converted.[15]

A more complicated tale of a Jew who learned of the power of the cross and then was converted to Christianity appeared in another collection of legends which made up another sermon handbook. It tells of a bishop who was tempted by the devil to have sexual relations with a woman until he finally decided that he "wolde hafe a do with hur." One night a Jewish traveller who was passing through the area could not find a place to spend the night and was obliged to sleep in the temple of Apollo. At midnight, a company of fiends appeared with their chief and started to discuss their treachery. One of them boasted to his comrades how he had tempted the local bishop with a woman. He was commended by the chief of the group and told to continue his work. The leader also advised the fiends to search the temple and to make sure that no one had overheard their conversation. When the Jew saw the fiends approaching, he made the sign of the cross and they promptly disappeared. The next morning the traveler went to the bishop and told him what had happened. The cleric repented for his misdeeds and sent the woman away. The Jew, who was now duly impressed with the power of the cross and of the Christian faith, converted.[16]

In these tales, Jews were pictured as basically decent individuals who were receptive to the power of the church. These stories, however, were not the most common ones in the preacher's repertoire. More often than not, the Jews were depicted as brutal individuals who appreciated Christianity as the true faith only when confronted with dramatic proof. This portrayal is understandable. The more stubborn and cruel the Jew appeared to be, the greater were the powers of Christianity that brought about his conversion. There is, for example, the story of the Jewish storekeeper who made an image of Saint Nicholas and set it in his shop along with his goods. He asked the image to protect his property while he was away on a trip. When the Jew returned, he found that someone had entered and stolen his property. He became angry and began to beat the image, threatening to continue until his goods were returned. The saint went to the thief and showed him his "sydes all blody." He explained that he had received this beating from the Jew because he had failed to guard his property. The next day the goods were returned and the Jew, out of gratitude and amazement, became a Christian.[17]

But even this story about a particularly brutal Jew converting to Christianity was restrained in comparison to one that centered on an attempt by a group of Jews to steal a consecrated wafer. A Jew who was friendly with a cleric agreed to meet him after the good Christian had participated in a mass on Easter Sunday. After the Christian had received the sacrament, he went to the meeting place only to find that he was surrounded by a group of Jews who seized him and cut him open to steal the wafer that was lodged in his intestines. When the band finally got at it, the wafer shone so brightly that it blinded the Jews and attracted a crowd, who released the cleric. Immediately, all the cleric's organs returned to their former positions, and he was healed. As a result of the miracle, many thousands were converted to Christianity.[18]

In the contexts of the sermons, the purpose of this story was to remind the faithful that God looks after those who believe in him. To mediaeval men, the church was pictured as a vast storehouse of magical power. Tales about the powers of the Host and the miraculous punishments that were meted out to those who tried to steal it reinforced this image in the eyes of the faithful at the expense of the Jews. No doubt the vivid portrayal of the Jews' cruel attempt to steal the wafer remained in the minds of the people longer than the lesson that was to be learned. At least one mediaeval preacher complained that his flock missed the main points of his sermon. "When they should be like glass windows letting in the light, excluding tempests they are only wretched sieves retaining, while steeped in the waters of preaching, nothing from without but the filth."[19] After hearing these types of sermons, the masses likely remembered the earthy stories about the Jews far better than the Christian teachings associated with them.

The brutality of the Jew, coupled with a narrow and erroneous religious outlook, was another popular theme of the mediaeval preacher. A story that must have aroused the interest of many a half-dozing congregant centered around a clerk who got a Jewish girl pregnant. Fearful as to how her parents would react, he concocted a plan to remove any blame from himself and from the girl as well. He took a long hollow reed, placed it next to the elders' bedroom, and told them that their virgin daughter had conceived the Messiah. The parents, convinced that they had heard a divine call, went to their daughter's room, examined her, and found her to be pregnant. The girl, who had been rehearsed by the clerk, said that she was still a virgin. The parents were overjoyed. When the time for her delivery drew near, a large group of Jews assembled anxiously awaiting the birth of the Messiah. The baby turned out to be a girl, and the crowd filled with rage, killed the child by throwing it against a wall.[20]

Another assumption perpetuated in the sermons was that when a Jew saw the light and converted to Christianity, he became a new person and left his supposedly "Jewish" traits behind. In one particular sermon illustration, the preacher was not fully convinced that this was true. This story was supposed to illustrate the problem of temptation. However, the cleric's choice of subject matter reflected a deep hostility to the Jew who had converted but, who in the eyes of the cleric, was still a basically untrustworthy, conniving person. The story centered around a Jew who became a Christian and who studied with some monks. When the monks could teach him nothing that he did not already know, he went out into the world to seek more knowledge. During his travels, the devil appeared to him in the likeness of an angel and urged him to learn quickly because he would soon become a bishop. Later, the devil appeared again and told him that the local bishop had died and that on the next day he would take his place. The converted Jew had been spending the night at a priest's house when the message came to him, and, anxious to make a good impression on the people whom he would soon meet, he stole his host's horse and cloak. His act was soon discovered, and the converted Jew was brought before the authorities and sentenced to death. Thus, the preacher pointed out, he ascended not as a bishop upon a throne but as a thief on the gallows.[21]

In the previous story, the Jew succumbed to temptation, but a more common theme portrayed him as associated with the devil, acting as an agent who led others astray. The best example can be found in the legends that centered around Theophilus, who was described as the clerk of the Bishop of Cizile.[22] Theophilus was a good man, beloved by the people. When his superior died, they urged him to take his place. Theophilus was influenced by a fiend not to take the bishopric, and so another cleric was chosen. Theophilus retained his previous position until malicious reports circulated by the devil forced his superior to put him out of his administration. For a while Theophilus continued to live a humble life, but after a time he began to brood over his lost power. Finally, he went to a Jew who was a known agent of the devil and who had sent many souls to hell to seek help in regaining his former position. The Jew led him to the devil and told his master of

Theophilus's plight. The rest of the tale centered around the hero's return to power, his life of honor, and ultimately his repentance to the Virgin for the pact that made him, like the Jew, the devil's man.

The Jew was the devil's man not only because he brought Christians into the clutches of Satan but also because of his practice of usury. On the continent as well as in England, preachers reminded their flocks that God had created farmers, priests, and soldiers, but that the usurers were invented by the devil. Satan was the Jew's partner in all his financial transactions; the two of them were closely identified with each other.[23] Although the English preachers never approached the continental clerics in the intensity of their scorn of the Jewish usurers' devilish practices, they did include some biting references to them in their sermons.

A popular legend, adapted for sermonic purposes, told of how Constantine saw the original cross in a vision and sent his mother and two messengers, Benciras and Ansiers, to search for it. The queen had with her a goldsmith who owed a large sum of money to a Jew. He had agreed to surrender an equivalent weight of his own flesh to the Jew if he could not repay the debt on the day that it was due. When the time for repayment came, the goldsmith was unable to satisfy the Jew's claims, and the case came before the queen's court. Benciras and Ansiers, who served as judges, asked the Jew how he intended to claim his bond. The Jew replied that he would first put out the Christian's eyes, then he would cut off his hands, and lastly, he would cut off his tongue and nose. The judges agreed to allow him to proceed, but they warned him not to take any blood because this was not part of the contract. The Jew protested that this was impossible and cursed the judges. They then acquitted the Christian and condemned the Jew to forfeit his goods to the queen and to lose his tongue. The rest of the tale dealt with the Jew's plea for mercy and his offer to show the queen where the original cross was buried if she would pardon him.[24]

As agents of the devil, Jews were not considered to be fully human. They also were subject to some very peculiar maladies. According to legend, both Jewish men and women menstruated, and they also suffered from hemorrhoids and other similar ailments that required the therapeutic use of Christian blood. They bled abnormally because they were devil-like and also because their ancestors had promised Pilate that if he would allow Jesus to be killed, his blood would be upon them and their children. There were several references to the idea in sermonic literature of the time, and perhaps the most popular story used by the preacher was the one of "the canon and the Jew's daughter." In this tale a young cleric fell in love with a Jewish girl whose parents were very strict with her. Because they watched her so closely, the lovers could only meet on Good Friday night, a time when, according to the author, "alle iewes bledyn benethyn for wreche of cristes death."[25] The next morning when the bleeding had stopped, the father of the girl discovered her in bed with the canon. The Jew gathered his neighbors together and went to the church to complain to the local bishop about the young man's behavior. The canon, realizing that he had sinned, repented in his heart and promised to do penance. When the Jews came before the bishop, they found that they could not speak, and they could not accuse the young man of having committed any misdeeds. The canon then entered a stricter order, and the Jew's daughter was baptized and became a nun. The story was used in the sermon to show the power of contrition and to demonstrate how a penitent individual was saved from shame. However, it was another reminder of how the "bloody Jews" were defeated by the stronger magical powers of Christianity.

As agents of the devil and as heretics, the Jews were a physical threat to both Christians and Christianity. Preachers found any number of instances in the past where Jews persecuted the early followers of Jesus and attempted to suppress their teachings. They told, for example, of how after the Crucifixion, Stephen preached against those who did not believe in Jesus. The Jews "stoppid here eres" so that they should not hear him and finally took Stephen outside the city and stoned him.[26] Another legend focused on an incident that supposedly occurred when Mary's bier was being carried toward its final resting place. "A prince of prestes of Iewes" was filled with wrath against her and attacked the funeral procession of the woman whom he claimed had "trowbelyd vs and alle oure kynde." Miraculously, his hands stuck to the bier, and all those who were with him were blinded. Only when they all accepted Jesus did the torment end.[27]

In the latter case, the superior magic of Christianity again

34

prevailed. This was not limited to the distant past, but it was an ongoing process that spanned the centuries. Belief in the powers of the Christian faith, particularly in those of Mary, was good insurance against the designs of the devilish Jews and of all other sources of harm.

One of the oldest miracle tales of the Virgin that found its way into the sermons of the time served as a reminder of the protection that Christianity offered the faithful. The story related how a Jewish youngster enjoyed playing with his Christian friends, who accepted him and treated him as an equal. One day he went with them to church where he admired the image of the Virgin and observed the mass. When he returned home, his father flew into a rage over his visit to the church and threw the boy into a fiery furnace. The child's mother was shocked by what her husband had done, and she immediately ran out of the house to summon help. When she returned to her house with several townspeople, they found that the fires in the oven had not harmed the boy. They stood in amazement as he told them how the Virgin Mother, whose picture he had seen in the church, had protected him from the fires. At the conclusion of the tale, the youngster's mother converted with him to Christianity, and the wicked father was condemned to death in the same oven into which he had thrown his son.[28]

The sermon was not the only part of the church service and ritual that perpetuated the anti-Jewish sentiments of the time. The various statues and images viewed by the faithful each time they came to pray also contributed to these negative attitudes towards Jews and Judaism. In England, as on the continent, the synagogue was often represented as a woman with a broken spear who had been cast down from her once exalted place. She was subservient to the image of the church that was now chosen by God to represent him on earth. Such statues were constant reminders of the sins of the Jews, their rejection of the true faith, and the punishment that they so rightfully deserved. Illuminated works like *The Holkham Bible Picture Book*, which was probably painted during the reign of Edward II, depicted among the scenes of the Crucifixion the legend of the smith's wife who fashioned the nails that were to be used by the Jews to pierce Jesus' flesh.[29] Although such books were the property of the privileged few, the common people could learn their Bible stories from wall paintings that reflected similar themes. "To see such pictures is to understand how simply and entirely mediaeval people accepted Christian teaching, and how the gospel stories, elaborated by some legendary traditions, early became an indelible factor in every person's life."[30]

Various forms of devotional and secular literature influenced by the teachings of the church also perpetuated anti-Semitic stereotypes. In the fourteenth century, mystical literature was a popular means of fostering religious feelings and furthering lay education. Very often in these works, hatred of the Jews was presented as an appropriate companion to Christian devotion. For example, Juliana of Norwich, an anchoress who was filled with love for God's creatures, did not include the Jews in this category. Those Jews who had put Jesus to death, and their descendants as well, were "accursed and condemned without ends";[31] they were not worthy of Christian compassion. The Jews served as a perfect object for her hostilities, and they allowed her to be that much more charitable and understanding to those worthy of her concern.

Other mystics used the Jews as a means of aiding them in their quest to rid their bodies of sin. In the "Orison on the Passion," the author began his work by expressing his hope that Jesus would write in his heart the remembrance of the Passion. By reviving Jesus' agony, he hoped to find a certain measure of self-purification. Accordingly, he recounted the story of the Crucifixion, sparing none of the grisly details. To further dramatize the effect of the deed, the author asked Jesus to describe his suffering, how he felt as he was tortured by the Jews.

> Write how douneward thou can loke
> Whan Iewes to the crosse betook;
> Thou bare it forth with newly chere,
> The teres ran dound by thy lere.
> [37–40]

Those who read this devotional piece, like the author, yearned to relive the Passion for the sake of their own purification.

Margery Kempe, another religious enthusiast and mystic of the

36

time, wished to recapture the pain and the suffering of Jesus so that she could deepen her own spirituality. Her diary provides a good insight into the inner workings of the minds of the devout, and it reflects the effect of the church's teachings upon them. During her pilgrimage to Jerusalem, she had a vision of the Crucifixion which became a very real and moving experience for her.

> And then anon she saw Judas come and kiss Our Lord and the Jews laid hands upon him full violently. Then had our lady and she much sorrow and great pain to see the Lamb of Innocence so contemptibly hauled and dragged by his own people. . . . The Jews beating him and buffeting him on the head and jogging him on his sweet mouth, crying full cruelly unto him: "Tell us now who smote thee."[32]

Margery Kempe also saw in her vision how the Jews gave Jesus his cross to bear, how they tore off his garments, and finally how they nailed him to the cross. These supposed deeds of the Jews increased her religious sensitivities while more firmly establishing the Jews as Christ killers.

Perhaps the most popular remembrances of the Jews that were perpetuated in both religious and secular post-expulsion literature were their involvement in usury and their practice of ritual murder. In Geoffrey Chaucer's *Canterbury Tales*, for example, the Prioress, who reflected the religious teachings of the four-teenth century clerics and the general intolerance of the time, portrayed the Jews as murderers, parasites, devils, and usurers. Her tale of the "litel clergeoun," who was redeemed by Mary after having been brutally murdered by the Jews, was a synthesis of various legends and belongs to the cycles relating to the miracles of the Virgin.[33] It was a story that she could very well have learned in the course of her religious training, one that she would naturally share with her companions on their pilgrimage to the shrine at Canterbury.

This "gentle" lady's intense hatred of the Jews and her distorted image of them is evident in the opening verses of her tale.

Ther was in Asye, in a greet citee,
Amonges Cristene folk, a Jewerye,

Sustened by a lord of that contree
For foul usure and lucre of vileynye,
Hateful to Crist and to his compaignye.
[1678–82]

For the simple-minded Prioress, believing the legends of Jewish involvement in the murder of innocent children, a crime of such magnitude could only have been committed by a people, who like Judas, were agents of the devil and were easily influenced to do his bidding. She reminded her companions of the close bonds between Satan and the Jews when she graphically described how these accursed people were persuaded to seize and ultimately to kill the child:

Oure firste foo, the serpent Sathanas,
That hath in Jues herte his waspes nest,
Up swal, and seide, "O Hebrayk peple,
    allas!
Is this to yow a thyng that is honest,
That swich a boy shal walken as hym lest
In youre despit, and synge of swich sentence,
Which is agayn youre lawes reverence?"
[1747–54]

The Jews, with their fanatical beliefs and blind hatreds, allowed Satan to dwell within their hearts and were easy prey for his diabolical schemes. In line with the tradition of Judas, they took the life of an innocent boy whose only crime was to sing the *Alma redemptoris* as he walked to and from school. In pious indignation, she cried out:

O cursed folk of Herodes al newe,
What may your yvel entente yow availle?
Mordre wol out, certyn, it wol not faille,
And namely ther th'onour of God shal sprede;
The blood out crieth on youre cursed dede.
[1764–68]

The Prioress had great compassion for the mother who searched in vain for her missing son and ultimately learned of his tragic fate. However, the Jews who were brutally tortured and put to death for their part in the crime were not to be pitied. They simply received what they deserved. As subhumans, their torment was stated in a very matter-of-fact way that was devoid of emotion. At the conclusion of her tale, the Prioress mentioned the well known story of Hugh of Lincoln, who had also been murdered by Jews. Although the incident had taken place some 130 years before, she treated it as something that happened "but a litel while ago." She no doubt used the story that was so familiar to her travelling companions to add credibility to her own tale. Her child-like faith and her naive acceptance of the legend of the famous boy saint transformed what had allegedly occurred in Lincoln into an almost contemporary event.

Critics note a definite irony in "The Prioress's Tale" and in her own spiritual makeup as well. In the Prologue she appeared as a very sensitive person who "wolde wepe if she saugh a mous kaught in a trappe" and who "sore wepte" if one of her pampered pets would die. Yet, she could calmly report the torture and massacre of the Jews with calm detachment. Although the Prioress compared the boy's mother to Rachel, who wept for her children in captivity (Jer. 31:15), she had no compassion for the more contemporary wandering and oppressed Jew. Her tenderness and charity was limited to small animals, little children, and bereaved mothers. In light of the horrible punishment suffered by the Jews, the Prioress's final prayer for mercy is ironic.

R. J. Shoeck takes the position that "in the tale which Chaucer assigned to the Prioress, the widely circulated ritual murder legend is held up for implicit condemnation as vicious and hypocritical." He believes that the disparity between the Prioress's professed piety and religious devotion and her bigotry would have been recognized by the more sophisticated people of the time. While he realizes that not everyone could appreciate the extent of this disparity, those who could recognize in the other tales the Pardoner's hypocrisy or the Shipman's knavery and deceit could also detect the Prioress's pious hypocrisy.[34]

Many admirers of Chaucer would like to believe that he shared some of the post-Auschwitz sympathies towards oppressed minority groups. However, for the clergy and the laymen of the time, the

Jew was a creature who stood outside of the pale. From the time of the Crucifixion, he had been involved in usury and in the murder of innocent children, and since he was hardly human, he did not merit Christian compassion. Florence Ridley believes that, considering the spirit of religious intolerance of his age, "it would have been most unlikely for a fourteenth century English poet to satirize a nun and a legend of the Virgin in order to attack anti-Semitism." Chaucer, she believes, "intended to satirize her simplicity, emotionalism, and frustrated feminity with an air of mild amusement—but not her religious prejudice."[35]

From a literary standpoint, Chaucer's use of "The Prioress's Tale" rounded out the image of her limited mentality, sentimentality, naivete, and trusting nature. It was a story that in so many ways perfectly matched her description in the Prologue. Yet, at the same time, he unwittingly placed before his readers a beautifully written piece that raised the miracle tales of the Virgin to the level of great literature. When these crude legends would lose their popularity and be pushed into the background, "The Prioress's Tale" would continue to perpetuate the old stereotypes of the Jew and negatively shape the attitudes of future generations.

Another literary figure who mentioned Jews in his works was John Gower (1330–1408), a contemporary of Chaucer whom Chaucer referred to as "moral Gower." Gower was a didactic poet who used stories to make his teachings more palatable for the readers of his day. In this regard, he resembled the mediaeval preachers. One of his tales concerning the Jews is very similar to those that appeared in the sermons of the time.

In *Confessio Amantis*, Gower related the story of two travellers going through a desert together. Each asked the other about his religious beliefs. The first said that he was a pagan and that his faith dictated that "I ought to love all men alike and do to others as I would they should do to me." The second said, "I am a Jew and by my faith I ought to be true to no man, except he be a Jew as I am." It was a hot day, and the Jew, who was on foot, asked the pagan if he could ride on his donkey. The pagan agreed, and the two changed places. After a while, the pagan asked for his donkey back, but the Jew refused to return it, claiming that he was following the precepts of his faith. As the Jew rode on, the pagan prayed that God would judge between them. Later on he found the body of the Jew torn to pieces by a lion. His donkey was standing nearby unharmed. From this Gower concluded that:

> Lo, thus a man mai knowe at ende,
> How the pitous pite deserveth.
> For what man that to pite serveth,
> As Aristotle it berth witnesse,
> God shal hise foomen so represse.
> [7. 1724–29]

Though the lesson of the story had nothing to do with either Jews or Judaism, the image of the crafty Jew getting his just reward likely remained in the mind of the reader.

Gower's approach to the Jewish people was rooted in the teachings of the church, and he did not deviate from the standard doctrines of the past centuries. For example, in his discussion of ancient religions, Gower presented a brief history of the founding of the Jewish faith. He noted how God had chosen the Jews to be his own special people and how he had delivered them from bondage and brought them to the Promised Land. When they rejected Jesus, they lost this special relationship, and they were dispersed throughout the world.

> So that thei stonde of no merit,
> Bot in truage as folk soubgit
> Withoute properte of place
> Thei liven out of goddes grace,
> Dispers in alle londes oute.
> [5. 1724–29]

Gower used examples from ancient Jewish history to illustrate divine justice in the world. He noted in his *Vox Clamantis* that when the Hebrew people sinned and worshipped idols, the Lord handed them over to their enemies. When they repented and returned to God, he helped them to overcome their adversaries. From this, Gower concluded that whatever happens to the human race is based on merit. Thus, the wretched state of the Jews throughout the world and their virtual absence in England resulted from their rejection of the Christian faith.

Gower's positive statement about Judaism was used to point out certain weaknesses in Christian practices:

> For we are so bent upon money at all hours that scarcely one festival day now remains for God. O how the Jew preserves the sacred Sabbath of the Lord, neither buying nor selling nor seeking for gain.
> [5. 11. 687–88]

There were some Jewish practices, like the observance of the Sabbath, that impressed him. But on the whole, Judaism was superseded by Christianity, and its followers were rejected by God.

During the latter half of the fourteenth century, there was a revival of interest in alliterative poems, the most important of which were works of social and moral protest. William Langland's *Piers the Plowman,* a work based in part on some of the sermons of the time, was probably the greatest of these poems, and it graphically expressed the attitude of the common man towards the evils of society. The poem contains several references to Jews worth considering as illustrations of contemporary attitudes toward them.

Modern critics, who want to show the author's liberal spirit, invariably show how he believed that there must somehow be a place in heaven for the good Jew and for the good pagan.[36] They also point out that he mentioned how, in contrast to the Christians, the Jews practiced true charity towards each other.

> If the prelates did their duty, no Christian man would ever stand at the gate crying for alms, or be without bread and soup. For never would a Jew see another Jew go begging, if he could help it, not for all the riches in the world! Alas! that one Christian should be unkind to another, when the Jews, whom we class with Judas, all help one another in need! Why cannot we Christians be as charitable with Christ's gifts as the Jews who are truly our teachers, are with theirs?
> [9. 81–87]

On the surface these statements seem to indicate a liberal spirit and a strong admiration for the Jews. However, the author's lavish praise was primarily intended to point up the corruption of the church and not to modify the anti-Semitic prejudices of the reader. The Jews were an accursed people who could only attain a place in heaven if they would accept Jesus and undergo baptism.

Langland, like so many writers who preceded and followed him, dwelled on the Crucifixion of Jesus. Although he admitted that "Jesus Christ chose as His Mother a Jew's daughter" (chap. 11), he blamed the Jews for accusing Jesus of being a sorcerer and for bringing about the Crucifixion. He pictured them as malicious people who plotted against Jesus and who took delight in their actions. Langland described how they forced a blind knight to pierce Jesus with his lance while he was bound to the cross. For this they were cursed with the words:

> May God's vengeance fall on the lot of you, cowards that you are! For this vileness you shall be accursed for ever . . . never again shall you prosper, never have land or dominion or plow the soil again. But you shall lead barren lives, and make your money by usury, a livelihood condemned by God in all His commandments.
>
> [chap. 18]

During the period following the expulsion, several ballads and folk legends that defamed the Jew were spread among the people and supplemented the work of the dramatist, the preacher, and the writer. It is difficult to date this oral tradition; many of these works were composed before 1290 and were further embellished during the next centuries.

The Jew's Daughter was a popular ballad that existed in several different versions and was circulated for many years. It told of a Jewish girl who enticed an innocent Christian boy to dine wtih her. When the youngster entered her house, she stabbed him, dressed him like a swine, rolled him in a cake of lead, and dropped him into a well. The boy's name was Hew, and it is rather obvious that the authors of the legend used the story of Hugh of Lincoln as a model for their tale.

Judas, the symbol of the supposed Jewish involvement in the

43

Crucifixion, was a popular figure in folklore. The more diabolical he appeared, the better he served as a scapegoat for Christian hostility. *The Legend of Judas Iscariot* was one of many that reflected "a pious intention of blackening the name of Judas,"[37] for it claimed that he was guilty of parricide and incest as well as betraying Jesus. *The Ballad of Judas Iscariot*, another well known piece, related how Jesus sent Judas to Jerusalem to buy food for thirty pieces of silver. On the way, his sister persuaded him to go to sleep with his head on her lap. When he awoke, the silver was gone. In despair, he made a bargain with a rich Jew named Pilate to sell Jesus for the amount of money that had been taken from him. By associating Pilate with a wealthy Jew, the ballad deepened the Jewish involvement in the act.

Jewish usury was another theme that was perpetuated in the folklore of the period. *The Ballad of Geruntus*, for example, dealt with a Jewish usurer who lent a Christian merchant a hundred crowns on the condition that if he could not pay the amount by a set date, the Jew would cut a pound of flesh from his body. These ballads and legends persisted for centuries among the people of England. Their legacy of anti-Jewish sentiment is probably as rich as any other form of expression.

Although the distorted image of the Jew did appear in the drama, the sermons, the literature, and the folklore of the people, there was no concerted effort in England, as there was on the continent, to foster anti-Semitic attitudes.[38] The English people harbored various degrees of hatred towards the Jews; however, there was no official attempt on the part of the church or the government to bring it to the surface. By and large, the English people adopted a "live and let live" approach to the few Jews who trickled into the country after the expulsion. With the exception of a few scattered incidents, only many years later, when there was talk of officially readmitting a large number of Jews, did anti-Semitic sentiments come to the surface.

In the years immediately following the expulsion, individual Jews had some dealings with the English government and with the people of England, but they exerted little influence upon the course of Anglo-Jewish history.[39] These few individuals are significant only as a kind of barometer to measure the intensity of feelings that existed among the general populace toward a group of people who were condemned by the church and banished by the crown.

In 1310, six Jews came to England to negotiate for the readmission of members of their faith to the land that had expelled them twenty years earlier. Except for the announcement of the mission, nothing else appears in the records of the time. They obviously were unsuccessful in their quest, and permission to resettle was denied to them. Although the Jews as a people were forbidden to settle in England, certain individuals in both an official and unofficial capacity managed to enter the country. During the reign of Henry IV, certain Jewish doctors received royal permission to enter London to take care of Lady Alice Whittington, the wife of the Lord Mayor. In 1410, an Italian Jew, Elias Sabot, was allowed by the king to settle in England and to practice medicine. Other Jews, who could be of service to either the crown or the nation, were also allowed to live in England.

In addition to these few known Jews who were entering England with government permission, there were probably more who came unofficially. Proof of this can be found in the records of the *Domus Conversorum,* or Home for Converts, that had been built by Henry III. Before the expulsion there were some one hundred Jews who had entered the home at one time or another. Immediately after the events of 1290, eighty men and women were on the rolls of the institution. Fifteen years later, there were twenty-three men and twenty-eight women in residence. In 1450 there were five converts in the home, and as late as 1500, four individuals appear on the rolls. [40] The fact that there were residents in the home for centuries after Edward's decree suggests that there was a small influx of Jews into England from Europe. The Spanish-sounding names of the residents of the home indicate that the immigrants were originally from the Iberian peninsula. The records of *Domus Conversorum* indicate that at least seven Jews from Spain and Portugal used the facilities of the home between 1492 and 1581. [41] This is rather a small figure, but it is probable that others entered England from these countries and quietly took up residence.

Duarte Brandao, or Edward Brampton as he was later called, is a good example of one of the Portugese Jews who lived in the home. Brampton was a man of many talents who achieved considerable fame and fortune after he was converted to Christianity. Edward IV was his godfather at the conversion ceremony, and Brampton used this personal contact to develop a close relationship to the king. Through the years he served the crown in various capacities. He was knighted and later made governor of Guernsey. After Edward's death, he temporarily fell out of royal favor and returned to Portugal. Later Brampton returned to England and regained his former prominence.[42] Somewhere in his wanderings Brampton met Perkin Warbeck, a pretender to the English throne who proclaimed himself Richard IV, and told him of his experiences at court. It is believed that Warbeck used these stories to good advantage in fabricating a life history that would convince the people that Warbeck was the rightful heir to the throne. The following excerpt from Warbeck's confession is proof that Brampton indirectly aided him in his pretensions:

> Whatever I told you so readily of bygone signs or times, I kept all that in mind as a youth when I was in the service . . . of a certain Edward, a Jew, godson of the aforementioned King Edward: for my master was on the most familiar terms with the said king and his sons.[43]

The excerpt suggests that Brampton's Jewish origin was well known, and yet it did not stand in the way of his many successes at court. The fact that a converted Jew could achieve such prominence is not surprising, since proselytes were viewed with favor and were no longer associated with a cursed or rejected people. As living proof of the superiority of Christianity, they were often given special privileges.

Of greater significance were the attitudes of the English people towards the few professing Jews in their midst. These attitudes can be inferred from several incidents which took place in the beginning of the Tudor period. These occurrences, and others during the reign of Elizabeth, show how there was little correlation between the church's attitudes towards the Jews and governmental practices in situations where the welfare of the country could be furthered by ignoring the Jews' presence.

The Spanish State Papers of 1493 contain, for example, a brief

46

account of an action brought by several Jewish refugees in the city of London against a Spanish merchant, Diego de Soria. It was for the recovery of some 428,000 *marvedis* that was due to them on a bill of exchange. Although the case was an open affair, nothing was done to disturb these Jewish refugees.[44] They seem to have lived in London unmolested by the law.

Five years later Ferdinand and Isabella sent a special envoy to England to negotiate a marriage between Arthur and Catherine of Aragon. The envoy carried with him a complaint registered by the king and queen of Spain that the Jews of England were becoming an "infesting scourge." Henry VII responded to the note by promising to "prosecute without mercy any Jew or heretic that the King or Queen of Spain might point out in his Dominions."[45] Despite the reply, there is no record of any actions taken against the Jews of his realm. The Spanish Jews who settled in London after the expulsion from Spain in 1492 were a small and fairly insignificant group. It was the exiles from Portugal in 1496 that had the greatest impact upon the Jewish communities in England.

The Jews of Portugal had been prominent in international commerce for many years, and they had established agents in various countries. These agents were usually relatives or close associates of the heads of the firms in Portugal and served a valuable purpose in providing information for those Jews who wished to leave the country for safer havens. Many Portuguese Marranos were anxious to settle in the Low Countries. Because conditions were changeable, ships carrying immigrants from Portugal would stop off at Southampton or Plymouth to learn whether or not it was safe to proceed to their destination. On several occasions, when warnings would be posted, the Portuguese Marranos would temporarily settle in London, where there was the nucleus of a Jewish community. Several of the permanent residents were connected with the financial house of Mendes of Antwerp. This was a Marrano firm that conducted considerable business with Henry VIII. The increased value of the Jews in the mercantile trades of England brought about an attitude that was unknown in Spain and Portugal. The Bristol community is a classic case of this spirit of unofficial toleration of the Jews that was felt in England during the reigns of Henry VII and Henry VIII.

As early as 1492, the Jews of Bristol were involved in the cloth trade. Although they professed to be practicing Christians, there is evidence that most of them were observant Jews with strong traditional ties. For example, Dr. Henrique Nuñes had a secret synagogue in his home in which the local Marranos gathered to worship on the Sabbath and festivals. His wife conducted a school in basic customs and ceremonies for Marrano immigrants from Spain and Portugal. She was strict in her observance of the Jewish dietary laws, and she boasted of her zeal in keeping the customs and ceremonies of her people. On the Passover, *Seder* services were held and she personally baked the *matzoth* that were used for the holy day rituals. In a small city such as Bristol, the Jewish practices of these Marranos must have been known to the authorities. Yet, it was not until 1553, when Mary Tudor came to the throne, that the Jews of Bristol encountered any difficulties. The restoration of papal power and the reenactment of the penal laws against heresy caused many of the Marranos to leave the country.

During the reigns of Henry VII and Henry VIII, the small colonies of Jews in London and Bristol were untouched by the authorities. Although Henry VIII "sware to persecute without mercy any cursed Jew in his domain," he found it to his advantage to ignore their presence.[46] Interestingly enough, his matrimonial problems focused considerable interest in Judaic studies and helped to acquaint the learned Christians of the time with the Hebrew language and the works of the rabbis. Henry became so desperate to find some support for his claim that his marriage to Catherine should be annulled that he sought out the opinions of Italian Jewish scholars. He hoped that their interpretation of Leviticus 18:16 and Deuteronomy 25:5[47] would support his arguments that he should be released from his marriage vows. Henry insisted that rabbinical opinion be submitted to him personally, and he had Marco Raphael, a recent apostate to Judaism, brought to England. (Ultimately, most of the Italian rabbis denied the validity of his claims, and he found that he could hope for little support from Jewish sources.)

Henry's quest for a solution to his marital problems that was based on rabbinic sources focused attention on the study of the

Hebrew language that was being pursued by the humanists in Europe. In Germany, men like Johanan Reuchlin (1455–1522) were interested in learning Hebrew so that they could study the Old Testament in the original and also master cabbalistic (mystical) literature. Reuchlin's conflict with the Cologne Dominicans, who had placed a ban on Hebrew studies in 1509, led to a serious split between German humanists and scholastics. It also strengthened the revival of interest in rabbinic literature.[48]

New developments in Italy also affected English attitudes towards Jewish studies. By the end of the fifteenth century English scholars had already started to draw close to the Renaissance spirit of Italy. Pico della Mirandola (1463–1494) and Marsilio Ficino (1433–1499) had introduced humanist scholars to the study of the Hebrew language and rabbinic literature along with other classical subjects. During the period of Henry VIII, humanism in England spread rapidly, and in the latter part of his reign (after 1520) Renaissance ideas in any number of areas poured into the country.[49] Under the influence of the northern and southern humanists, the Hebrew language developed considerably during the reign of Henry VIII. Medals struck in 1545 to commemorate his recognition as head of the church contained Hebrew inscriptions. In addition to this, the Act of Uniformity that was passed in 1549 authorized its use in private devotions.

The interest in this ancient language ultimately brought Hebraic scholars to England to teach at the universities. One of them was John Immanuel Tremellius, who was born in Ferrara of Jewish parents in 1510. He was converted to Catholicism by Cardinal Pole and later became a Protestant. In 1549, he became the King's Reader of Hebrew at Cambridge and achieved considerable recognition as a first-rate scholar. Tremellius was but one of many Jewish scholars who gravitated to England. For example, there was Philip Ferdinand, a Polish Jew, who later was converted to Christianity and taught Hebrew at both Oxford and Cambridge. He published a Latin version of the 613 precepts found in the Mosaic Code. The book, which contained various selections from rabbinic literature, was the first serious piece of Jewish scholarship to appear in England since the expulsion. Ferdinand was a poor teacher, and he was forced to leave the university to find a teaching position elsewhere. Joseph Scaliger, a renowned scholar at the time, was able to secure for him a position in Leyden, where Ferdinand taught until his death. Scaliger often praised his friend, and in a letter to a colleague he wrote the following: "Two years ago I was the means of procuring a Professorship in this University for a Jewish convert, my teacher in the Talmud, but he died and left my studies barren and desolate."[50]

The Jewish scholars who came to England during the time of Henry VIII set a trend that was to continue for several generations. They "familiarized the Englishman for the first time in three centuries with the existence and the appearance of the authentic Jew (albeit in most cases converted)." Certainly, they were able to alter only to a very limited extent the mediaeval image of the Jew created by the church and perpetuated in the literary works of the time. Their greatest contribution was in the teaching of the Hebrew language, as they were responsible for training native-born scholars who would be able to study the Bible in its original form. Indirectly, they brought the spirit of their age-old tradition into the translations of the Bible that were soon to appear, which, in turn, were to create new interest in "the People of the Book."[51]

The progress made in both the general and the academic communities of England during the reigns of Henry VII and Henry VIII come to a standstill under Mary. Little is known about Jewish life in England at this time, but it has been established that the community in Bristol was disrupted and that its leader, Henrique Nuñes, fled to France.[52] In addition, these few Jews who outwardly were Protestants and who secretly practiced their faith suffered the same fate that the genuine Christian members of this group experienced. When Mary was deposed, conditions improved somewhat for these Jews. However, the returning clerics who were forced into exile during her reign and who now were given high positions in the church had been exposed to the witch-hunting and Jew-baiting that was so popular on the continent. This influence, along with hatreds inherited from the past, was to shape the attitudes of the Elizabethans towards the Jews as well as other groups which they deemed socially and religiously undesirable.

THREE

THE NEW JEWISH VILLAIN

The reign of Elizabeth marked an age of conquest and discovery, an era when the people of England expanded their horizons through their travels over the face of the globe and through their interests in the classics. Commerce and industry provided many Englishmen with wealth, and with this increased prosperity came an ever widening audience for literature and drama. However, along with the changes in eating habits, in dress, in morality, and in commercial and leisure-time pursuits, there was a general acceptance of the religious doctrines of the past. It is not surprising, therefore, that Elizabeth translated Boethius, that Raleigh was, among other things, a theologian, and that sermons were as much a part of Elizabethan life as bearbaiting.[1]

As far as the Jews were concerned, the old prejudices of the mediaeval world continued. In the sermons of the time Jews were the Christ killers, the eternal adversaries of Christianity. This theme was repeated in the Protestant religious drama that continued in the tradition of the Passion plays. The most significant changes in the image of the Jews occurred in the secular drama, where the stage Jew evolved into a three-dimensional figure who was a living, breathing, character and not simply a cardboard cutout. Although remnants of the earlier morality tradition were found in these productions that highlighted Jewish wickedness, the Jewish villain now became more human than his predecessors

51

had been. His evil qualities did not diminish, however, and he was equally hateful.

Although the number of Jews in Elizabethan and Jacobean England was small, and most Englishmen had little contact with them, travelers came across Jewish communities that were scattered throughout Europe, Asia Minor, and along the coast of Africa. Englishmen often viewed Jews as curiosities. Although lengthy descriptions of Jewish customs and ceremonies were to be found in the accounts of their travels, they preferred to view the Jewish people at a distance and not too close to home. During this period, interest in biblical studies and in ancient Jewish history also brought Christian scholars into contact with their Jewish counterparts on the continent. These contacts generated some sympathy for the Jewish people, but it was limited to a very few people who, more often than not, were interested primarily in converting the Jews.

In England, as on the continent, the general attitude of Christian society towards Jews "resulted from the trends, the contradictions and the contrasts which characterized the thinking of the leaders of the reformation in their attitude towards heretics and nonbelievers generally."[2] True, the reformation in the church that had started under Henry VIII had put an end to the use of wonder tales with their assorted Jewish villains in the preaching and teaching of religious values. But old prejudices were to continue in new garb, a bit more refined perhaps, but cut from the same cloth. The theological need to prove Judaism inferior to Christianity was not limited to Catholicism; it was readily made a part of Anglican and Puritan doctrines. In addition, pent-up hatreds continued to seek socially acceptable means of expression. The Jew, long associated with the devil, would now be linked together with witches and Catholics, and would become part of the general "Menace" of that age, like the "Red Menace" of the 1950s.

In spite of the increased interest in humanistic studies that marked the Elizabethan Age, the world view of most of the intellectual and religious leaders continued to rest upon what had been inherited from mediaeval Catholicism. The writings of Saint Paul and Saint Augustine continued to influence the thought of the

52

new age. The Elizabethans, though living in an age of rapid change, accepted that the world was so constructed that nothing could be omitted and that everything had a definite place in the scheme of things.

Lord Burghley (1520–1598) expressed the underlying ideal of order and harmony when he noted that "Every degree of people, in their vocation, calling and office, hath appointed to them their duty and order. Some are in high places, some are in low. . . . Remove this divine order and there reigneth all abuse, carnal liberty, enormity, sin and Babylonical confusion."[3] In the Elizabethan world view, everything came from God in a definite descending order. After God came the angels, followed by man, and then the beasts. The Jews had their place in this great chain of being, and they were placed somewhere between the third and fourth orders. True, they had the form of men, but they were the personification of evil, and they, therefore, had to be separated from the rest of mankind. Nevertheless, they were more than beasts since they did have the potential of converting to Christianity and could thereby achieve redemption from their sins.[4]

Although the unconverted Jew was evil incarnate, the Elizabethans, like their mediaeval predecessors, drew a line between those figures in the Bible who came before Jesus (who they believed would have accepted him had they lived in his day) and their descendants who rejected him and were doomed to eternal damnation. By placing the Israelite and the Jew in separate categories, the Elizabethans could deepen their interest in the study of the Bible while at the same time castigating the contemporary Jew. This can explain why there is no contradiction between the Elizabethan interest in ancient Jewish history and the delight they took in booing the stage Jew, a popular dramatic figure of the period.

Although the place of the Jews in the theoretical general order was fairly well determined, there was no real attempt to either punish or segregate them in the real world. As in the years immediately following the expulsion, the few Jews who resettled in England were left alone as long as they did not make their presence too obvious because of the commercial benefits that they brought to the country and the skills that they as individuals possessed. A handful of Jews who practiced their religion in secret were no real threat to society, and they were generally ignored.

During the Elizabethan period, England's foreign relations underwent important changes. English merchant ships traveled to all parts of the world, and foreign merchants flocked to London and other important cities. England at this time had also become the champion of Protestantism in Europe, and persecuted Protestants from Italy, France, Holland, and Germany were welcomed by their English co-religionists. At first the newcomers were accepted by the people. However, the growing numbers of immigrants eventually alarmed the native population, and anti-foreign sentiments began to appear. Native artisans and merchants complained of foreign competition, but there were no legal barriers raised against the entrance of these immigrants. In 1593 the subject was debated in the House of Commons when a bill was introduced to limit the commercial activities of aliens. It was at this time that Robert Cecil asserted that the relief that England offered to the strangers to her shores: "Hath brought great honours to our kingdom; for it is accounted the refuge of distressed nations, for our arms have been opened unto them to cast themselves into our bosoms."[5] Certain minor restrictions were placed upon aliens. They were taxed more heavily than native Englishmen, and at times exceptional duties were placed upon their imports and exports. However, they suffered few real disabilities and, on the whole, occupied a secure place in English society. Cecil's statement reflects what ultimately became an official government point of view, which indirectly benefited the Jews from Spain and Portugal.

This tolerant spirit towards aliens is well illustrated in a case tried in the Court of Chancery in 1596 between Mary May, the widow of Richard May, an English merchant, and Ferdinand Alvares and Alvaro de Lyna, two Portuguese Jews who had supposedly been converted to Christianity. During the proceedings, Mrs. May claimed that her deceased husband's partners, the above mentioned defendants, had spent a great deal of his money paying blackmailers who had discovered that they were really secret Jews. (This was a serious crime in the eyes of the Portuguese authorities and could be punishable by death). Alvares and de Lyna, however, told the court that considerable sums had been spent in bribing certain Portuguese officials who were suspicious about the ownership of the cargo that they were transporting to Portugal. During the trial, witnesses were called who described various Jewish rituals that were practiced in the homes of the defendants. A former servant of Alvares told the court how his master's family had maintained their ancestral faith in England "because they have not been troubled about their relygyon or use of superstycyous ceremonies since they come to dwell there as they now do." The testimony was recorded, but no action was taken against the defendants for their religious practices.

Perhaps the most significant conclusion that can be drawn from this generally insignificant court case is the attitude of the legal authorities towards the Jews of England. The court displayed scrupulous concern for the fair treatment of both parties. To ensure that justice would be done, a foreign merchant worked with two aldermen of London to assist the court. Finally, the court "being moved with the losses and troubles which the poore straungers indured persuaded Mrs. May being present to deal charitably with Alvares in regarde thereof."[6] It pressed for relief to be given to the two men beyond the limits of pure equity, and tempered justice with mercy. The decision that was reached shows how, in at least one instance, the alien Jew was considered to be worthy of the court's full protection.

Gradually, over a period of several years, Jews from Spain and Portugal posing as alien merchants established an unofficial community in England. Lucien Wolf, the first historian to study the period thoroughly, has concluded that there were at least ninety known Jews in the country at the time of Elizabeth.[7] They were sustained spiritually by a secret synagogue in Antwerp that existed between 1579 and 1583 and also in 1594. Members of the congregation kept in close touch with their co-religionists in England, and their brethren in London reciprocated by raising funds for the maintenance of the Antwerp synagogue. This close relationship is documented in a letter addressed to Rodrigo Lopez dated February 18, 1594. Although the text is vague, the author of the note acknowledged the receipt of money sent to him from

London for the upkeep of the synagogue in the Netherlands. He mentioned the generosity of the donors and also reminded them that they had not, as yet, fully paid their pledges.[8]

Evidence exists that the Jews of London were sometimes able to hold religious services. For example, when Solomon Cormano was in the city in 1592 as the envoy of the Jewish Duke of Metilli, he used his diplomatic privilege to hold services in his home. Edward Barton, in a letter to Lord Burghley dated August 19, 1592, mentioned that Cormano was boasting that "he and all his trayne used publickely the Jewes rytes in prayinge, accompayned with divers secrett Jewes resident in London."[9] If such statements were circulated, the presence of an active Jewish community must have been an open secret.

Though the existence of practicing Jews was known to the authorities, nothing was done to outlaw them. Only when there was a public scandal did the government take action. A good example of this can be found in the story of Joachim Gaunse of Prague, who was invited to England to help develop the mineral resources of the country. He lived openly as a Jew for eight years while conducting mining operations in Keswick and in South Wales. In 1589, while in Bristol, Gaunse met Richard Curteys, a Protestant minister who was anxious to converse with him in Hebrew. In the course of their conversation, Gaunse vehemently denied the divinity of Jesus. When he was summoned before the mayor and the aldermen, it was recorded that he defiantly proclaimed that he did not "believe any Article of our Christian faithe for that he was not broughte uppe therein."[10] This created a public scandal, and he was sent to London to appear before the Privy Council. It is not known whether Gaunse was punished for his avowal of Judaism, or whether his friend Walsingham was able to secure his freedom.

As long as Jews did not break the law or outrage public sentiment, they were allowed to live in peace. One very prominent member of the Jewish community, Dr. Rodrigo Lopez, the personal physician to Elizabeth, was tolerated as a secret Jew until he was involved in a case of treason. Only then did he experience the bitter hatred of the nobility and the mob as well. His life illustrates the conditions under which the Jews of Elizabethan

England lived. Lopez was one of the Jews who fled from the Inquisition in Portugal and who settled for a short time in Antwerp. From Antwerp he came to London and obtained the appointment of household physician to Robert, Earl of Leicester, a favorite of the queen. Although he was a convert to Protestantism, he was always referred to as a Jew by friend and foe alike. A letter to Lord Burghley in 1594 by Waad, the clerk of the Council, showed that the two of them had known for years that Lopez was not merely a new Christian but a practicing Crypto-Jew.[11] In any event, Lopez received support from Leicester, Walsingham, and Essex, favorites of the queen, and through their recommendations he was appointed as personal physician to Elizabeth. Lopez's religious beliefs did not hinder him from achieving considerable wealth and social prestige; he was granted a monopoly for several years for the importation of sumac and aniseed into England. This special privilege ultimately generated great hatred against him. By the end of the sixteenth century, monopolies, which were a reward for service to the crown, were the single most aggravating issue in Parliament, and they became a wedge which widened the split between the court and the country gentry. As England's economic situation worsened, the sight of a few court favorites enjoying what seemed to be an unfair means of amassing wealth antagonized a great many Englishmen faced with economic struggles.[12] Lopez, the Jew and the man of special privilege, made many enemies who hoped for his fall from power. They were not to be disappointed for very long.

As court physician, Lopez became involved in some intrigue involving Don Antonio, a pretender to the throne of Portugal. Lopez apparently divulged some secrets that were entrusted to him by Essex, and it is believed that Essex tried to absolve himself by finding Lopez guilty of treason. Some fairly convincing evidence suggests that Lopez was innocent of any attempts to poison the queen (as charged by Essex), and that any confession that he might have made was done under the threat of torture.[13] The trial itself brought to the surface the anti-Jewish prejudices of the times. The prosecution, led by the Solicitor General, referred to the accused as "that vile Jew" and described him as being "mercenary, wily and covetous and corrupt." The economically struggling gentry and the general population avidly followed the proceedings. They rejoiced when Lopez was convicted, and they flocked to see him executed. Lopez was hanged at Tyburn on June 7, 1594. The affair created so much excitement that no less than five official accounts, in addition to numerous private ones, were published. The Lopez incident indicated just how deeply all classes of Englishmen disliked the Jews when their existence was brought out into the open. Although Lopez was not punished for being a Jew, his trial and subsequent execution revealed the anti-Jewish sentiments of the time.

The hatred generated by Lopez lingered on for many years. Early in the reign of James I an illustrated sheet entitled *Popish Plots and Treasons from the Beginning of the Reign of Queen Elizabeth Illustrated with Emblems and Explained in Verse* was published. One of the drawings was labeled, "Lopas compounding to poyson the Queene," and it was followed by the inscription:

> But now a private horrid Treason view
> Matcht by the Pope, the Devil and a Jew;
> Lopez a Doctor must by poison do
> What all their plots have failed hitherto:
> What will you give me then, the Judas cries:
> Full fifty thousand Crowns, t'other replies.
> Tis don—but hold, the wretch shall miss his hope,
> The Treason's known and his Reward the Rope.[14]

The association of the Jew with the devil was nothing new. Now, however, he was lumped together with the Catholic, and he was considered to be a subversive element in society.

While Jews had long been considered to be sorcerers, their powers were limited to effecting good or evil upon single individuals and not to influencing the stability of an entire community or nation. In popular tradition, the biblical heroes had been magicians. Adam's knowledge of all natural things had been lost when he was expelled from Eden, but somehow it was transmitted through Noah, Moses, Solomon, and other biblical figures. Moses, in particular, was famous for the magical powers that he had learned from the Egyptians, and he was portrayed as a sorcerer in some of the mediaeval mystery plays.[15]

In England a tradition held that even the converted Jew had certain magical powers that were at the disposal of individuals in need of them. In 1390, for example, John Berkyng, a Jewish convert to Catholicism, was approached to use his powers to find the person who had stolen two silver dishes from the Duke of York's house in Fleet Street. (He falsely accused the duke's servant of the crime and was subsequently punished for his fraudulent claims.) In 1546, Harry Lord Nevell, son and heir of the Earl of Westmoreland, engaged a man named Wisdom to help him win at gaming and also to hasten his father's death so that he could collect his inheritance. Wisdom told Sir Harry that he had mastered certain magical powers from someone who had learned them from "a blind man which was a Jew born and a practicer of the same art."[16]

Astrological almanacs were very popular in the sixteenth century, and one of the most famous was the *Prognostication of Erra Pater*, the author of which was allegedly "a Jew out of Jewry." It contained a table forecasting the weather according to the day of the week on which the New Year began and also a list of unlucky days. The religion of the author obviously helped to sell copies of the almanac, for as a contemporary jingle proclaimed, "If one affirm he learned it of a Jew, the silly people think it must be true."[17]

The Lopez incident with its deeper overtones of treason went beyond the stock accusations that the Jews practiced sorcery or that they possessed certain occult powers. Overtones of the continental approach to witchcraft which considered such practices to be a crime against society were evident. The Jew in the wonder stories of the mediaeval preacher had been in league with the devil and had led good Christians astray. He was the natural person to be branded as a subversive, and, along with the witch, he could now become the focus of the irrational fears of the multitudes. Thus, the church's teachings which portrayed the Jew as the devil's man could be used to turn him into a scapegoat for social frustrations as well. Trevor-Roper has noted: "In its periods of introversion and intolerance Christian society, like any society, looks for scapegoats. Either the Jew or the witch will do, but society will settle for the nearest."[18] Lopez, the Jew, was right at hand, and he paid the price for being so accessible.

How widespread this hatred was during the period of James I is difficult to determine. At least one adventurer thought that the time was ripe to have the Jews readmitted to England. In the early part of the seventeenth century Sir Thomas Sherley[19] schemed to bring a group of Levantine Jews into England, and he promised them, no doubt for a substantial fee, to plead their case before James I. These Jews wanted to settle in England, build synagogues, and practice their religion freely and without fear. They were willing to pay an annual tribute in exchange for these privileges. Sherley failed to convince the king of his views, so he directed his attention to settling them in Ireland instead. For the right to enjoy religious freedom, he promised James that Jews would pay two ducats per head. He pointed out to the king that the Jews were experienced merchants who could develop a flourishing trade with Spain in such Irish goods as salted salmon, corn, hides, wool, and tallow. Such commerce would bring considerable bullion into the country, and the customs and excise taxes would enrich the king. Reminding him of the conditions in pre-expulsion England, Sherley pointed out the advantages of having the Jews in the country. They could be subjected to forced loans which would yield a considerable amount of money, and he predicted that they might be able to supply the King with as much as a million pounds. This was compared to the 10,000 pounds James could only hope to exact from the London merchants. To support his argument, Sherley showed how the Duke of Mantua exacted between 300,000 and 400,000 crowns from his Jews once every three years. Certainly, he argued, once the Levantine Jews would settle in the country, the king could do even better.[20]

To fully guarantee the success of such a plan, and to feather his own nest, Sherley suggested that "at first they [the Jews] must be tenderly used for there is a great difference in alluring birds and handling them when they are caught; and your agent that treats with them must be a man of credit and acquaintance amongst them who must know how to manage them, because they are very subtile people."[21] James either ignored or rejected the proposal. Public opinion would have been outraged at the prospect of substantial numbers of Jews returning to England. It is surprising that as shrewd as Sherley was, he failed to realize that the king was not anxious to stir up his people over the official readmission of a sizeable Jewish community. In fact, in the few dealings that James had with the secret Jews of his kingdom, he was less tolerant than Elizabeth had been.

During the reign of James I, a small group of Jews was expelled from England as a result of a quarrel which broke out among them and which revealed their true faith to the authorities. The Tuscan envoy, Ottaviano Lotto, describing the "expulsion" on August 12, 1609, wrote the following: "There are many Portuguese here who are trading, and have lately fallen out among themselves. Some of them have been accused of Judaism and have, therefore, been ordered to leave the kingdom and with much dispatch, for the law concerning the matter prescribes the death penalty." There is the possibility that some of these Jews "might have thrown off their disguise in the hope that England was ready to follow Holland's lead in readmitting the Jews."[22] They obviously failed to appreciate James's narrow-minded commercial policies and the climate of anti-Jewish sentiment that the English people had inherited from the past.

The "expulsion" of the Jews during the reign of James I was only a temporary inconvenience to the secret Jews. Many of them remained in England, while others found various loopholes that enabled them to return.[23] Jewish merchants continued to enjoy the protection of the Privy Council and the courts.

In 1614, Samuel Palache, an envoy of the Sultan of Morocco to the Dutch States General and a distinguished member of the Jewish community of Amsterdam, was arrested in Portsmouth, England, through the instigation of the Spanish ambassador. The Spaniard accused Palache of committing piracy and outrage against the subjects of his nation and demanded that he be punished. *The Acts of the Privy Council* record how "Samuel Palache, a Jew" was taken into custody and given a hearing before the Court of the Admiralty. Three distinguished jurists, Sir Edward Coke, Lord Chief Justice of England, Sir Julius Caesar, Master of the Rolls, and Sir Daniel Dunn, Judge of the Admiralty, after evaluating the evidence submitted, released the defendant. Because Palache was a subject of the king of Morocco, then at war with Spain, they concluded that he could not be prosecuted for any criminal acts.

Several months later the Spanish ambassador was also unsuccessful in his attempt to secure the release of a large cargo of sugar that had been brought to England by another Jew. According to Lionel Abrahams, "The fact that two Jews received the protection of the Privy Council and the Law Courts in England in the reign of James I is of some importance in its bearing on the difficult question of the legal status of the Jews in England before the period of the Commonwealth."[24] The legal authorities were perhaps the most liberal group in regard to the Jews, and if the problem of Jewish rights would have been entirely in their hands, there would have been little problem in readmitting them to England. It was the climate of hatred existing among the people of England that prevented the resettlement. The intensity of this prejudice is revealed in references to Jews in the sermons, the drama, and the literature of the period.

Several references to Jews in Elizabethan and Jacobean sermons reflected the inheritance from the mediaeval preacher, as well as the contemporary attitudes towards them. In keeping with past tradition, Jews were hardhearted blasphemers who were also vain, ostentatious, and deceitful. Miracle tales with their Jewish villains were almost nonexistent, but references to their supposedly evil qualities still remained in the discourses from the pulpit. For example, Miles Coverdale (1488?–1569) pointed out in one of his sermons how at the time of the Crucifixion the earth quaked, rocks split, and the veil of the temple was torn, and yet the Jews, being blind and stubborn, would not accept Jesus.[25] Another preacher linked Jewish attitudes toward Christianity with those of the devil. He noted that in regard to the virgin birth of Jesus, there were those who "most Jewishly or rather devilishly . . . go about to teach or maintain the contrary."[26]

At least one cleric equated Jews with those who dressed in an exceedingly lavish way. In discussing the vain wife he stated: "She doth but deserve mocks and scorns, to set out all her commendations in Jewish and ethnic apparel, and yet brag of her Christianity. She doth but waste superfluously her husband's stock by such sumptuousness"[27]

Other clerics, like their mediaeval predecessors, used Jews as examples of a basically evil people who managed to outshine

Christians in some particular area of religion. One of them, for example, praised the Jews for coming long distances to the temple in Jerusalem while his own parishioners were negligent in attending a church that was so close by. "We abhor the very name of the Jews, when we hear it, as of a most wicked and ungodly people,"[28] he told his flock. Yet, he had to admit that they put Christians to shame. Another backhanded compliment which reflected hostility towards Jews was made in connection with their loyalty to ruling powers. In urging his congregants to give greater allegiance to the crown, one preacher pointed out that even the "Jews whom yet we account as the worst of all people" gave their support to foreign rulers. Certainly good Christians could do no less than this "stubborn people."[29]

Some of the more enlightened clerics of the age did preach that Jesus died for the sins of all of mankind and that the Jews were merely agents of God. One of them, Lancelot Andrewes (1555– 1626), noted:

> It is we, that are to be found the principals in this acte; and those on whom we seeke to shift it, to derive it from ourselves, Pilate and Caiaphis and the rest, but instrumental causes onely. . . . Sinne onely is the murtherer and our sinnes the murtherers of the Sonne of God.[30]

The implications of his teachings were lost to those who heard his message, and the scorn for the Jews that stemmed from their being deicides was to continue.

The good Christians of the time, and in the succeeding generations, wanted to believe that the Jews were responsible for the death of Jesus and for a host of ills that plagued both ancient and modern society. To deny the Jewish role in the Crucifixion would challenge an evil image that had been built up over the centuries by the church—one which fit so comfortably into their scheme of thinking and which served as a focus for so many of their fears and frustrations. This theme is evident in the plays of the period that were popular among all classes of the people.

Any study of the Jew in the drama of Elizabethan and Jacobean England must include the Protestant religious plays, which strongly resembled the earlier works of the church. Between 1530 and 1560 a number of those were produced that were influenced by continental Lutherans. One such play, *The Resurrection of Our Lord*, contained many of the elements of the old Passion plays. The setting of the story was after the Crucifixion, and, as in the past, the blame for the act was placed upon the Jews. At the very beginning of the production, the author described how Pilate, looking back at what had happened to Jesus, protested his innocence to a fellow Roman with the words:

> What he was or shoulde be, that knowe not I but this I knowe, that they accued hym of Envye they layed upon cryme, never to him charge but words of blasphemye, agaynst their God and vsage and you knowe howe I would fayne have delivered hym but that they were so busye on me, for the Death of hym.   [20–26]

Caiaphas, the High Priest, was pictured as an unscrupulous person who convinced Pilate that Jesus was "worthyer death, than any theiffe or murtherer" because "he murthered our people in a faulse beleife and stale them from our lawe like a faulse theiffe" (75–78). Not only were Caiaphas and his followers guilty of instigating Jesus' death, but they also tried to conceal his resurrection by bribing the guards at his tomb, whom they paid to spread the tale that Jesus' disciples had stolen his body and had concocted the story of his return.

The earliest play of the period that featured contemporary Jewish characters was a drama called *The Jew* that was performed at the Bull Inn in 1579. Its plot was defined by Stephen Gosson, a leading pamphleteer and critic, as representing "the greediness of worldly choosers and the bloody murder of usurers."[31] Unfortunately, the play itself has been lost, and scholars can only guess about its contents.

Five years later *The Three Ladies of London*, comedy written by Robert Wilson, appeared. It was actually a morality play with the usual allegorical framework associated with such productions. But in addition to such standard characters as Lucre, Love, and Conscience, the author included in his story an unscrupulous Italian merchant, Mercatore, who was pursued by Gerontus, a Jewish creditor. In order to cheat the Jew out of his just compensation, Mercatore went through the motions of converting to Islam, an act which, according to Turkish law, automatically released him from all his obligations. (He later returned to his old faith and congratulated himself on his treachery.) Gerontus, who was far from being a grasping usurer, asked only for his principal, and he was willing to give up any claim to the interest on the loan. He begged Mercatore to respect his Christian convictions and not to practice deceit. This prompted the Turkish judge who released the merchant from his debts to comment, "Jews seek to excel in Christianity and Christians in Jewishness."[32] The Jew in the play is far from being the mediaeval villain; he appears rather to be a victim of cruel circumstances. However, the playwrights who followed were not as kind to their Jewish characters as Wilson was to his. *The Three Ladies of London* was to be overshadowed by *The Jew of Malta* and *The Merchant of Venice* in shaping anti-Jewish prejudices.

Christopher Marlowe's very popular play, *The Jew of Malta*, which appeared in more than one of the theaters in London between 1591 and 1595, marked a transition from the morality plays to the newer forms of drama.[33] The prologue, delivered by Machiavel, resembled the conventional morality device of heralding the appearance of the evil protagonist. However, instead of introducing such characters as Avarice, Greediness, and Usury, Marlowe prepared his audience to meet another of Satan's lieutenants, the Jew.

> I come not I
> To read a lecture here in Britain.
> But to present the tragedy of a Jew
> Who smiles to see how full his bags are crammed
> Which money was not got without my means.
> [Prologue, 29-30]

Barabbas was the personification of several of the vilest myths inherited from the past. Into his character Marlowe fused the infidel Jew with the ruthless Machiavellian and mediaeval Vice. Thus, he produced a figure who was the incarnation of the "inverse of orthodox Elizabethan virtues and values."[34] Barabbas was the sorcerer and poisoner who went "abroad of nights to kill sick people groaning under walls" (3.3. 177–78). He was the man who showed no particular loyalty to any country and who could boast: "And in the wars 'twixt France and Germany,/ Under the pretence of helping Charles the Fifth,/ Slew friend and enemy with my strategems" (2.3. 188–90).

In keeping with the morality tradition, Barabbas was more a theological abstraction than a flesh-and-blood person. His very name, taken from the pages of the New Testament, was associated with the Jews' rejection of Jesus and their acceptance of the treasures of this world.[35] He was the classic adversary of Christian belief and practice who spanned the centuries and who was a direct descendant of Judas Iscariot. For example, Ithamore, Barabbas's servant, noted, "The hat he wears, Judas left under the elder when he hanged himself, (4.6. 67). Ithamore's seemingly harmless and comic remark, "O' brave master! I worship your nose for this," (2.2. 174) was another reference to the close association between Barabbas and the hooked-nosed Judas of the Passion play who betrayed Jesus for thirty pieces of silver.

In the first few scenes of the play Marlowe invested Barabbas with some decent qualities. Before very long, however, they crumbled away, and his human attributes were overshadowed by the monster image that he ultimately projected. In the final analysis, he was a vile creature without scruples of any kind, a miser who would stop at nothing to accumulate and protect his wealth. His brutal death in a fiery cauldron, symbolic of a descent into the mouth of hell,[36] was a fitting end for Barabbas, who so closely resembled the Antichrist.

Marlowe was not interested in flesh-and-blood Jews, and it is doubtful that he modeled Barabbas in the image of any contemporary figure. He wanted to construct an image of evil incarnate to show the hypocrisy of those who claimed that they were good Christians, but who failed to live up to the ideals of their faith. Among other things, Marlowe wanted to condemn the usurer and to show the great lengths to which his passion for money would drive him.[37] According to G. K. Hunter, "Marlowe has missed no opportunity to use his damned Jew as a means of tormenting and exposing those who pride themselves on their Christianity, but give little evidence of charity."[38] Certainly, the same self-righteous people who condemned Barabbas for his unbridled materialism unscrupulously victimized him at every turn. If at the end of the play they were triumphant, it was only because they outdid him in his own villainy."[39] David Bevington believes that the play "ends where it began, without the establishment of a moral order on Malta." The appeal to divine justice made at the conclusion of the work is a mockery, and the Christian rulers were no better and no worse than Barabbas.[40]

Marlowe's attitude towards the clergy was similar. He portrayed the two friars who tried to persuade Barabbas to join their respective orders (and turn his money over to them) as two greedy and corrupt men who, ethically and morally, were no better than the Jew. Although Marlowe did criticize the hypocrisy of individual Christians, he did not challenge the teachings of the church. Whatever he may have felt about Christianity did not color his approach to the traditional image of the Jew. Barabbas, therefore, was not a tragic hero in the Aristotelian sense because, as a member of a theologically accursed people, he lacked nobility and the ability to learn through his suffering. The Jew, associated with the Antichrist, was more a caricature than a real person, and he could not evoke any really deep emotions from the audience. It remained for other playwrights to make him more human and, consequently, more hateful.

William Shakespeare, the greatest of the Elizabethan dramatists, continued the legacy of the stage Jew that had been handed down through the ages, and he also added some new dimensions to it. In his plays, with the exception of *The Merchant of Venice*, he made only scattered reference to Jews, and only in his characterization of Shylock did he forcefully portray the Jew on the stage. The play in several aspects resembles *The Jew of Malta*. Both plays concern an old Jew, father of a beautiful daughter, who was so obsessed with his wealth that he loved his ducats more than his own flesh and blood.[41] Both Barabbas and Shylock had Christian servants who directed the laughter and the scorn of the audience against their masters. (This was an inheritance from the morality plays where the devil was accompanied by his vice or clown.) In addition, each playwright dealt with the tensions that existed between the Jew and the Christian world that engulfed him. There was the need for the Jew's services, on one hand, and the contempt for his person, on the other.[42]

It must be stressed, however, that neither Marlowe nor Shakespeare were interested in the "Jewish question" in the modern sense of the term. They were concerned neither with fighting nor with encouraging anti-Semitism, and their plays should not be viewed in these terms. The Jewish villain's attitudes and practices served as a contrast to the superior values of Christianity. Shakespeare, in particular, used Shylock to deal with such themes as the superiority of Christian love, the proper value of material wealth, the conflict between justice and mercy, and the contrast between the old law and the new.[43] In addition, like Marlowe, he used the Jew as a means for exposing the absence of Christian virtues in contemporary society.

According to Barbara Lewalski, Shylock was in so many ways the antithesis of Christian love, which involves both giving and forgiving and which "demands an attitude of carelessness regarding things of this world founded upon a trust in God's providence." It also requires a readiness to give and risk everything, possessions and person, for the sake of love and a willingness to forgive injuries and to love enemies. In all but this last respect, Antonio was its very embodiment and Shylock its antithesis.[44] Antonio was willing to practice true Christian love by giving away all his possessions, including a pound of his flesh to help a friend. He dispensed his wealth freely to those in need without the thought of personal gain. In contrast to him, the usurous Shylock tightly clutched every coin that came into his possession. His wealth poisoned his relations with everyone, particularly his daughter. When Jessica stole his money and eloped with her Christian lover, he could scarcely decide whether she or the contents of his strongbox was dearer to his heart. After he discovered her absence, he shouted, "My daughter! O my ducats! O my daughter!" (2. 8. 15).

On an allegorical level, the conflict between Shylock and Antonio represented the confrontation between the old law and the new, between justice and mercy. Shylock reflected the supposedly Jewish approach of narrow-minded legalism when he refused, for example, to provide a surgeon to stop Antonio's wounds, since there was no stipulation for it in the agreement between them. His stunning defeat in the trial scene and his forced conversion was symbolic of the triumph of the new law over the old and the superiority of the Christian value system.[45]

The viciousness of the Christians' attack upon Shylock, their slurs, biting remarks, cruel jests, and the manner in which they finally outwitted and reduced him to poverty "does not celebrate the Christian virtues so much as expose their absence."[46] The fact that Shakespeare portrayed him as a three-dimensional character with feelings and emotions highlighted their inhumanity and their lack of charity. There is a danger, however, in reading too much into Shakespeare's apparent sympathy for the accursed Jew. Bernard Grebanier, one critic who is convinced that Shakespeare "stood like an Everest above his contemporaries," views his portrayal of Shylock as an example of his ability to rise above the prejudices of his own generation.[47] This is an exaggeration with little basis in fact. As a sinner who was also sinned against,[48] Shylock uttered several lines that evoke sympathy for his wretched state. Nevertheless, their importance has often been overstated. Shylock's famous remarks about the miserable position of the Jew are well known to the students of the drama.

> I am a Jew. Hath not a Jew eyes? hath not a Jew hands, organs, dimensions, senses, affections, passions? fed with the same food, hurt with the same weapons subject to the same diseases, healed by the same means, warmed and cooled by the same winter as a Christian is? If you prick us do we not bleed?
>
> [3. 1. 54–60]

Critics have interpreted these lines as a plea for tolerance, and yet if they are viewed in their entirety and put within the context of the play, they become not a plea for charity but for revenge.[49] Sir Arthur Quiller-Couch believes that Shylock has been "over-philosophized and over-sentimentalized."[50] Perhaps this stems from the fact that Shakespeare lovers would like to believe that their idol did not really draw an anti-Semitic portrait. But as Herbert Bronstein notes:

> No critical card tricks, no juggling of lines can obscure the fact that Shylock is a greedy usurer who dreams of money bags and is

implacable in his demands for Antonio's pound of flesh... he is a cantankerous old man who hates music and parties and speaks to his daughter only to issue orders. He is also comic in his parsimony and meanness.[51]

Whatever human qualities Shakespeare invested in Shylock's character, they do not detract from his basically evil nature. As John Russell Brown suggests, our insight into his hatred, frustration, and pain makes his contrast with Antonio and the other Christians that more poignant and lively. He is still the foil for the good Christian, the evil Jew whose devilish practices highlight what is or should be the true practice of Christian love.[52]

Shylock was originally played on the stage as a ludicrous old man, mimicked by his servant Launcelot and made the butt of jokes by his young adversaries. It was only after 1741 that he was transformed by the actor Charles Macklin into the serious villain so familiar to modern audiences. But no matter how Shakespeare had intended Shylock to be played, wittingly or not, he further associated the word "Jew" with usury, cruelty, and revenge against Christians. Shylock's villainies could not be separated from his Jewishness, and his vices and faults were considered to be typical of his people. In essence, Shakespeare transformed the "monster Jew" into a creature of flesh and blood with feelings and emotions. In this regard, he was ahead of his time, but any claim that he actively tried to combat the intolerance of his age cannot be supported in the text of the play. Shakespeare's skill in humanizing certain qualities of the Jew actually fostered anti-Semitic prejudices for years to come. He provided a Jewish character whose evil nature could be accepted by sophisticated people who might normally reject the completely negative image of the mediaeval myths. By being cast in a human mold, Shylock's devilish qualities became more credible and hateful to the Elizabethans and to Englishmen in future generations as well. From that point on, any playwright who wanted a Jewish character in his work had a powerful model to copy.

In the fifty-year period prior to the closing of the theaters by the Puritans (1642), a few plays which featured Jewish characters appeared. In *The Tragicall Raigne of Selimus, Emperor of the*

Turks, written by Robert Greene in 1594, a Jew, Abraham, was engaged by Selimus to poison Bajazet, his father. These verses spoken by Selimus reflected the popular notion of the Jew as the poisoner—the man willing to do anything for money.

> Bajazet hath with him a cunning Jew
> Professing physick; and so skilled therein,
> As if he had pow'r over life and death,
> Withall a man so stout and resolute
> That he will venture anything for gold.
> This Jew with some intoxicated drink,
> Shall poyson Bajazet and that blind Lord;
> Then one of the Hydra's heads is clean cut off.
> [1681–1688]

Jack Drum's Entertainment, written by John Masters in 1601, had a character, Mammon the usurer, whose large nose was modeled after Shylock's Semitic appearance. Thus, the distorted physical features of Judas as they appeared in the Passion plays were reinforced in the portrayal of Shylock and were perpetuated by the imitators of Shakespeare. In the play *The Travels of the Three English Brothers*, by John Day, the Jewish character resembled Shylock in his physical appearance, in his desire to extort money from good Christians, and in his lack of compassion and sympathy. The Jew was a "crucifying hangman" who was filled with a love of money and a thirst for revenge. Once again he was portrayed as the villain who threatened to harm a good Christian if his bond was not paid.

The portrayal of the Jew in Elizabethan drama and in the plays leading up to the Puritan period continued to perpetuate the pre-expulsion image. Montagu Modder stresses how the "monster Jew" was humanized.[53] Although this is obviously true, the dramatist, by updating the Jew and by putting his villainy in a more credible form, also kept alive the hatreds of prior centuries and adapted them to new situations. Jewish crimes were no longer in the dim mediaeval past, but they were real and current. The evolution of the drama encouraged the development of anti-Semitic sentiments, and it was responsible in part for the climate of hatred which encouraged the opposition to the readmission of Jews in the seventeenth century.[54]

In the realm of nondramatic literature there was one relatively important work which contained Jewish characters of any significance. In Thomas Nashe's *The Unfortunate Traveller* (1594), the hero, Jack Wilton, while passing through Rome literally fell into the clutches of an evil Jew, Zadok, who sold him to a co-religionist, Zacharie, for use in some fiendish medical experiments. Through the aid of the pope's concubine, Juliana, he was saved, and his Jewish tormentors were severely punished. Nashe portrayed Zadok as a grotesque person who threatned to wipe out the entire population of Rome by poisoning the city's drinking water and by contaminating its bread supply. In addition, the Jew was pictured as an expert in the art of flagellating Christian women. According to the author, "He had the right agilitie of the lash, there were none of them could make the corde come aloft with a twange halfe like him."[55] Zadok's torture and execution was described with a ferocious glee, and Nashe exulted in every horrible detail. It was one of several examples of his deep attraction for the gruesome and the sadistic, which in this instance was combined with a savage anti-Semitism.[56] The book contained definite overtones of the ritual murder legends, stripped of their religious character, and of the execution of Lopez.[57]

By and large, outside of the drama, Jews occupied a minor role in Elizabethan and Jacobean literature, and they were incidental to the main themes of the works. Sir Thomas North's (1535–1601) translation of *Diall of Princes*, which appeared in 1568, contained the lines, "Let him take heed also, that he do not call his servants, drunkards, thieves, villains, Jews, nor other such names of reproach."[58] John Lyly (1554–1606) in his *Euphues* which appeared some ten years later used the word "Jew" as a curse word of the lowest sort. Thus, old stereotypes were perpetuated by making an entire people a derogatory term in the English language. Jews were identified to a countless number of people who had never seen them face to face, but who were convinced that they knew what they were really like.

One exception to this literary treatment of the Jews can be found in Holinshed's *Chronicles*, which was first printed in 1578.

In this work the author displays a sense of humanity in his description of Jewish life in pre-expulsion England. The story of Hugh of Lincoln, for example, was treated simply and without embellishments. There was no bitterness or hatred in his accounts of what happened, for he merely recorded what he considered to be the true facts. In his description of the expulsion of the Jews in 1290, he felt compassion for the exiles. He described how one particular captain of a vessel that was carrying the Jews out of the country tricked his passengers into leaving the ship so that they would drown in the incoming tide. Holinshed described the anguished cries of the travelers and the cruelty of the captain, who stood by and mocked them. He ended the account with the statement: "These mariners which dealt so wickedlie against the Jews, were hanged for their wicked practice, and so received a just reward of their fraudulent and mischeevous dealing."[59] Other chroniclers did not share Holinshed's sympathy for the Jews, and thus it is doubtful if he was able to modify the prejudices that had been perpetuated in the mediaeval works of men like Mathew of Paris.

The chief source of knowledge of contemporary Jewry came from the accounts of travelers and adventurers who wrote of their experiences in Jewish communities abroad. With rare exception, however, these men brought preconceived notions with them on their travels, and they were far from being objective in their descriptions of Jewish life.[60] Selections from the works, the diaries, and the letters of these men reveal the image of the Jew that they presented to their readers and admirers.

Thomas Coryat (1577–1617) was perhaps the most famous of these adventurers. His description of his visit to the Venetian ghetto reflected many of the prejudices against Jews which were prevalent in Elizabethan society. Coryat, a very proper Englishman, was appalled at what he found in a synagogue that he visited there on the Sabbath.

One custome I observed amongst them very irreverent and profane, that none of them, eyther when they enter the Synagogue, or when they sit downe in their places, or when they goe forth againe, doe any reverence or obeysance, answerable to such a place of the worship of

God, eyther by uncovering their heads, kneeling or any other externall gesture, but boldly dash into the roome with their Hebrew bookes in their handes, and presently sit in their places without any more adoe.[61]

Coryat was annoyed with the constant babbling that he heard during the service—something which he considered to have been condemned by Jesus. He was also bored with the repetition of their prayers and with the length of the devotions. Coryat may have found fault with the services, but he was impressed with the way that the Jews kept the Sabbath. He noted that

they keep their sabbath so strictly, that upon that day they wil neither buy nor sell, nor do any secular, prophane, or irreligious excercise; (I would to God our Christians would imitate the Iewes herein) no not so much as dress their victuals, which is alwaies done the day before, but dedicate and consecrate themselves wholly to the strict worship of God.

[P. 300]

He was also impressed with the physical appearance of the Jews that he observed at the services and throughout the ghetto. The men were quite handsome and well dressed, and he came to the conclusion that the negative English expression "to look like a Jew" was not true. He was a great admirer of the Jewish women whom he met, and he considered them to be as beautiful and as well dressed as English royalty.

But with all his compliments, Coryat still viewed the Jews in the light of centuries of the church's teachings, and he lamented over "the damnable estate of these miserable Jews" who reject Jesus and seek salvation through law rather than through belief in the "Saviour of the World." His negative feelings towards both Jews and Judaism were quite apparent in his description of a seemingly accidental meeting with a "Jewish Rabbin" who was no doubt the famous Leon da Modena. Coryat related how he had asked the rabbi about his opinion of Jesus. What began as a friendly discussion soon turned into a heated debate that attracted considerable attention in the ghetto. Coryat claimed that some forty or fifty Jews gathered around him, and that he, fearing that they would harm him, fled from the scene. Luckily, Sir Henry Wotton was passing by in a gondola and he was able to remove the author from the clutches of these "unchristian miscreants" (p. 304). In the frontpiece of the early edition of his *Crudities,* the author was pictured fleeing from a turbaned Italian rabbi who had a knife in his hands.[62]

Another Elizabethan traveler was William Davies of Hereford, who in 1597 journeyed through Southern Europe and wrote a description of the Jews of Italy, France, and Turkey. Davies was obviously unaware of the small colony of Jews that existed in his native country when he noted that they inhabited all parts of Christendom with the exception of England. He was grateful they did not disturb the tranquility of his homeland. After he had observed their communities on the continent, he exclaimed, "I beseech the Almighty God that this our land of England never be defiled either by Pope, Turk, or Jew."[63]

Fynes Moryson (1566–1630) published in 1617 an account of his many years of traveling through Europe and Asia Minor. When in Italy he came across a number of Jews and noted that the princes of the various localities, for their own profit, admitted them into their cities and permitted them "to use horrible distortions upon their subjects, in the lending of money, and in selling or letting out by the day or week upon use both men's and women's apparel and furniture for horses and all kinds of fripery wares."[64] His readers must have recalled how the Angevin kings used the Jews for similar purposes before the expulsion, and perhaps they also wondered if Jews could ever be engaged in productive labor.

Not all the travelers reacted unfavorably to the Jews that they met abroad. One of these, John Sanderson (1560–1627?), praised a Jewish merchant, Abraham Coen, his traveling companion, with the words, "I cannot speak too much good of him in regard to his great humanity and extraordinary charity, his measure being more in those performances than is to be found in many of us Christians."[65] Another traveler, L. A. Addison (1632–1703) noted that, "setting aside the artifices of commerce and collusions of trade, they [the Jews] cannot be charged with any of those debauches which are grown into reputation with whole nations of Christians, to the scandal and contradictions of their profession."[66]

75

Yet, on the whole, while admitting that Jews did have a few good qualities, the great majority of the reports about them were negative, and the impression was created that such people were indeed a very strange breed that no self-respecting Englishman would want to have in his own country.

As noted previously, the study of the Hebrew language and of ancient Jewish history was quite popular in Tudor England. This trend continued during the time of Elizabeth and in the years that followed. In 1558, *Sefer Yosippon*, a mediaeval work written by Joseph Ben Gorion, was translated by Peter Morwyng. He called it *A Compendious and Most Marveilous History of the Latter Tymes of the Jews Commune-Weale*. It was a very popular book, and by 1615 it had gone through some ten editions. Josephus's historical works were also widely read. Thomas Lodge translated these books into English in 1602, and some five editions and three reissues appeared before 1640.[67]

In addition to the translation of the Bible and other Jewish classics, various Christian scholars began to publish books that dealt with the laws, customs, and institutions of the Jewish commonwealth. One of them, Edmund Bunny (1540–1619), a theological writer and preacher, expressed a warm attachment to the ideals of ancient Israel in three books that he wrote.[68] In each he noted that the practices of the Jews both in the religious and political areas were originally ordained by God and could be a source of inspiration for the Christians of his day. Bunny was interested only in antiquity, and he avoided coming to grips with the problem of the Jew of his time.

For the most part, Christian scholars who showed an interest in contemporary Jewry did so out of a desire to convert them to the "true faith." Hugh Broughton, for example, a student of Hebraica and a zealous Puritan, believed that by translating the New Testament into the Hebrew language and by writing commentaries that reflected Christian ideas, he would be able to persuade the Jews to convert. With this thought, he urged James I to supply funds for such a project.[69] In his various tracts, Broughton mentioned how Jews on the continent were interested in conversion, and how from his wide correspondence he detected that some of the most learned Jews of his day wanted to be taught the gospel.

In his work, A *Require of Agreement*, etc., he listed the names of several rabbis in Western and Central Europe who were anxious to learn more about Christianity so that they might ultimately convert. The author conceded that the Jews were a stubborn people, but he felt that a door was now opened for them to be brought into the fold.[70] One of Broughton's most interesting works was his commentary on the book of Daniel in which he attempted to show the "Thalmudiques" the Christological implications found in this Old Testament work. He hoped that the new insights that he presented would help them to "learne to feare God better lest they fall into the rivers of Eternal fyre which Daniel describeth."[71]

Christian interest in Hebraic studies also brought leading thinkers into contact with Jewish scholars on the continent who directly and indirectly were able to modify their own views about the Jewish people. For example, Sir William Boswell, a noted scholar, politician, and diplomat of his day, corresponded with Leon da Modena and raised various questions concerning Hebraic scholarship. The questions were in Hebrew, and Modena answered them in the form of rabbinic responsum. Of particular interest is one of Modena's letters that touched upon Jewish responsibility for the Crucifixion. The rabbi stated explicitly:

> According to my opinion, the Jews never put any person to death by Crucifixion: For they were not permitted nor accustomed to execute sentence excepting by the four penalties of the Court of Justice— stoning, burning, decapitation and strangling. Crucifixion, however, was the penalty inflicted by the Romans: and even though they were then ruling over Israel, the Jews did not administer their law.[72]

Sir Henry Wotton, ambassador to Venice, was another of Leon da Modena's correspondents. Wotton asked him to prepare a work that would explain the basic tenets of the Jewish faith to James I. Modena's effort, *Riti Ebraici*, was one of the earliest books produced by a Jew in the modern period to explain Judaism to the Gentile world.[73]

This contact between Christian and Jewish scholars persisted for many years and was ultimately an important factor in encouraging the readmission of Jews to England. However, in many ways it

77

proved to be a mixed blessing for the secret Jews of the country. Several good Christians became so attached to Jewish practices that they began to follow certain Jewish rituals, and some of these "Judaizers" went so far as to convert to Judaism. This caused quite a stir among both the civil and religious leadership of the time and hardened their attitudes towards the small Jewish colony in their midst. The most prominent example of this reaction to Judaizing was centered around the practices and beliefs of John Traske.

John Traske was born in Somerset in 1583. He was a zealous Puritan who adopted the Old Testament views of Hamlet Jackson, an itinerant preacher and tailor by trade, who persuaded Traske to follow the rituals and beliefs of the ancient Israelites. According to H. E. Phillips, he passed from "extreme Puritanism to an almost orthodox Judaism."[74] Traske and Hamilton preached about the necessity to keep the Sabbath within the Old Testament tradition, the importance of the dietary laws, and the need to keep the Passover in accordance with the Mosaic code.

Traske attracted several disciples and raised quite a commotion. He was attacked by at least one Catholic priest who challenged his approach to Old Testament practices. The cleric called Traske a "Puritan Minister lately grown half a Jew in his singular opinions concerning the old sabaoth and moysaical differences of meates held by him and many other men and women obstinately professing and practicing the same doctrines."[75] More serious were the charges that the state leveled against him and his disciples, who were considered to be subversive elements. On June 19, 1618, Traske was severely punished for his outspoken views. In addition to a heavy fine and a good whipping, he was imprisoned for life and branded with a large letter "J" on his forehead. Traske was severely punished for two reasons. First of all, he was considered to be a threat to the existing order of the government and the church, and his denunciation of the bishops as "bloody butchers" was treasonous and liable to severe punishment. Secondly, he appeared to be trying to convert Christians to Judaism. Bishop Lancelot Andrewes expressed the official reaction to his Judaizing when he spoke against Traske in the Star Chamber stating: "It is good work to make a Jew a Christian: but to make Christian men Jewes hath ever been holden a foul act, and severly to be punished. . . . he is a very Christened Jew, a Maran, the worst Jew that is."[76]

Eventually John Traske recanted and was released from prison, yet the stigma of his Jewishness remained with him until his death. The Bishop of London referred to him as "an unworthy person and a Jew,"[77] and the letter "J" branded on his forehead was a constant reminder of his former "Judaical tendencies." The case of John Traske reflected the intensity of anti-Judaizing sentiment and suggested that Judaism was now linked with subversive activities against both the crown and the church. As Christopher Hill points out: "Judaizing meant, among other things, looking back to the customs and traditions of a tribal society, still relatively egalitarian and democratic, its standards and myths could be used for destructive criticism of the institutions that had been built up in mediaeval society."[78]

Another small group of Englishmen, dreamers, who spoke in terms of the restoration of Zion, created similar problems. These men, called millenarians, also aroused the anger of the king and the church against those who showed an interest in the Jewish faith. Their message, on the surface at least, seemed harmless, but it had political overtones. From their deep love and attachment to the Bible, which at the end of Elizabeth's reign was perhaps the most popular book in England, these men began to yearn for the establishment of the kingdom of God. They envisioned a time when the Jews, properly converted to Christianity and freed from the sin of having rejected Jesus, would reestablish a perfect theocracy in Palestine. This would signal the end of tyranny and the redemption of all of mankind from political and religious absolutism. Actually, the earliest literary expression of this doctrine appeared in the writings of the thirteenth and fourteenth century Franciscans Duns Scotus and William of Occam. John Wycliffe (1320–1384) also included in his teachings various ideas relating to the role that the converted Jew would play in the ultimate struggle with the Antichrist. However, it was during the later part of the Elizabethan era that the whole question of the restoration of the Jews to their homeland became a serious subject of theological inquiry.[79]

In 1585, Francis Kett (? –1589) published a tract, *The Glorious and Beautiful Garland of Man's Glorification: Containing the Godlye Misterie of Heavenly Jerusalem with a Dedication to Queen Elizabeth.* The author considered the site of the ancient Jewish commonwealth to be the place of the ultimate redemption of mankind and awaited the return of the Jews to their homeland. Kett was burned alive for his supposed blasphemies. His book obviously made an impression on the people of his time because, after his death, the Calvinist theologian Andrew Willet (? –1621) challenged the notion that the Jews could ever hope to reestablish their ancient form of government. Thomas Draxe (? –1618), another prominent theologian, upheld the ideas of Kett and forcefully argued that Christians should pray for the Jews and set a worthy example for them so that they might more readily convert to the true faith. Like Kett, Draxe believed in an earthly restoration of Zion.[80] Thomas Brightman (1562–1607) and Giles Fletcher (1549–1611) also continued this tradition. They paved the way for Henry Finch (1558–1625), who further developed the idea of the reestablishment of the ancient Jewish commonwealth.

Finch was perhaps the most famous of all those who wrote on the subject. His book, *The World's Great Restauration or The Calling of the Jews and (with them) of all the Nations and Kingdoms of the earth, to the faith of Christ*, caused a stir in church and court circles. His work, printed in 1621, began with a summary of the various prophesies in both the Old and New Testaments which dealt with the redemption of the Jewish people. Finch viewed the Jews as a holy people who would soon be redeemed after the fall of Turkey, a country that he associated with the "little horn" mentioned in the seventh chapter of Daniel. Through some involved calculations, he came to the conclusion that Israel's redemption would come about in 1650 after the twelve tribes defeated the Turks in battle. The Jews would then convert to Christianity and struggle for an additional forty-five years until finally the biblical prophesies would be fulfilled. At that point they would restore Zion and become even more powerful than they had been before the destruction of the Second Temple. A theocracy would then be established which would put all other rulers and forms of government to shame.[81]

For James I, the most objectionable part of the book was the author's belief that all the rulers of the world, including the Christian ones, would pay homage to "the most glorious kingdom of Jerusalem." Not only did Finch dare to challenge the doctrines of the church, but he also implied that James's reign was not a perfect theocracy. Finch was subsequently imprisoned and forced to apologize for what he had written. [82]

Finch's views about the future power of the restored Jewish commonwealth also aroused the anger of several members of Parliament. These men feared the Judaizing tendencies of good Christians, and they were also concerned with Jewish world domination. In a debate concerning whether or not Sunday should be referred to as the Sabbath, Lord Canterbury remarked, "We desyre the word Saboth should lefte oute, because many of late times have run to Judaisme, as somm have written for the very day: A booke or two ther is lately sett forth of the Jewes ruling over the world etc."[83] A few days later while the debate still raged, Sir Edward Coke expressed similar sentiments, noting that there were many Christians who were inclined to Judaism and who dreamed of the day when kings would lay down their crowns at the feet of the Jews in their restored commonwealth. [84]

The remarks made in Parliament show how Judaizers and millenarians who were drawn towards Jewish ritual, belief, and national aspirations also created a climate of distrust against the Jews who were in England at the time and their brethren throughout the world. The debates focused unwelcome attention upon the small Jewish community that struggled to maintain its anonymity. Although the Judaizers and millenarians were groups composed of a few eccentric individuals who were intrinsically unimportant, their ideas lingered on for several generations. Their approach to Mosaic law, their belief in the restoration of the Jews with a prior conversion to Christianity, and their messianic hopes appeared in the sermons and religious literature for several decades to come. These religious beliefs ultimately became part of the arguments for the readmission at the time of Commonwealth.

Of greater importance, however, were the ideas generated by another small group of Englishmen who began to think in terms of religious toleration. By and large, the Baptists were the most interested in this area. Having suffered religious persecution, they felt that it was wrong to impose upon any person ideas that were against his will—even if they were correct.[85] But along with this liberal spirit there was a strong desire to convert the Jews. They believed that a more humane attitude towards Jews would result in their quicker acceptance of the fundamentals of Christianity.

One of the leading exponents of this point of view was Leonard Busher, a Baptist who fled to Holland sometime during the religious persecutions that took place at the end of the reign of Elizabeth or possibly at the beginning of the reign of James I. In his book, *Religious Peace of a Plea for Liberty of Conscience*, he stressed the need to teach the message of Christianity to combat the false doctrines of other faiths. He was opposed to the forcible conversion of the nonbelievers and noted:

> And for as much also that the false and anti-Christian religion did come by the spirit of error and doctrine of devils and not by fire and sword: Therefore by the spirit of Christ, and the doctrine of the word of God must it be driven out of the hearts and consciences, both of Prince and people and not by fire and sword.[86]

In listing the evils of religious persecution, he pointed out that Jews and other strangers would thus be kept out of the country. They would be denied the opportunity of being taught the "Apostolique faith" and the rewards that go with it. England, too, would suffer the loss of revenue that they might bring to the kingdom. Tolerating the Jews and allowing them to settle in the country would be to their spiritual benefit, since the Jews would be exposed to Christian teachings and to the profit of the entire country.

> Then shall the Jewes inhabit and dwel under his majesties dominion, to the great profit of his Realmes and to their furtherance in the faith: to which we are bound to seeke in all love and peace, so well as others, to our utmost endeavour, for Christ has commanded to teach all nations and they are the first.[87]

Although by the end of the Jacobean period Englishmen showed a new interest towards both ancient and contemporary Jews, in most instances this new spirit was only a thin veneer that covered the accumulated prejudices of centuries. The general climate of opinion towards the Jews was one of hatred and distrust. The dramatist, the writer, the traveler, and the religious leader had done such a thorough job that the few men of conscience who spoke and wrote had little impact upon public sentiment. Lancelot Andrewes could preach that the Crucifixion was the sin of all of mankind; however, for all intents and purposes, the English people viewed the Jews as Christ killers. While dreamers could envision the restoration of the Jews and a return of all Jewry to their ancient homeland, for all of them the Jews' conversion to Christianity was a precondition for this miraculous event. Some more tolerant religious thinkers could talk about the readmission of the Jews to England but, here again, it was only to hasten their own conversion to "the true faith" through kindness rather than open persecution.

In the next decades, England was to undergo a severe upheaval; the whole structure of the monarchy was to be overthrown, and a new political and religious party was to take control. During these tumultuous times the people tended to retreat to fixed prejudices and old hatreds. The stereotypes offered a kind of stability in a rapidly changing world, something to hold on to in a time of flux, as well as providing a much-needed scapegoat for the people's collective fears. Witches and Papists were the center of attention, but the rich folklore relating to the Jews kept them from being forgotten as villains.

FOUR

THE PERSISTENCE OF
A PREJUDICE

When Charles I ascended the throne, the Jewish community of England was at an ebb; only a small number of Jews remained in the country following the expulsion of 1609. Little is known of their religious activities; they likely tried to be as inconspicuous as possible in the few Jewish rituals that they maintained. As refugees from the Iberian Peninsula, they appeared on the surface, at least, to be practicing Catholics. In 1643 a small group of Jews from Amsterdam, motivated by new commercial opportunities that were developing in the country, settled in London. The Portuguese ambassador at the time was Antonio de Souza, a secret Jew, and the Jewish merchants of London possibly may have gathered in the private chapel of his embassy for worship. Though they were few in number, there were some prominent men among them. One was Antonio Fernandez Caravajal, a wealthy merchant who imported into England bullion that was valued at one-twelfth of the entire national income. He was of such value to the crown that when he was denounced by an informer for failure to attend church services, no action was taken against him.[1] Other lesser merchants such as Simon de Caceres and Antonio Robles were also important to the government.

Even with the influx of new blood from Amsterdam, the entire community consisted of only about 100 to 150 persons, and it posed no threat to the status quo. Charles I had few dealings with them

84

and seemed unconcerned with their existence. Except for a few scattered references to Jewish traders in Asia Minor, Jews were rarely mentioned in any of the state publications and documents. The average Englishman was probably unaware of their presence in the country, and once again it was the "stage Jew," the Jew of history, and the Jew of the Bible who were in the public eye. During Charles's reign, the Jew again appeared in contemporary drama as the villainous usurer and the social outcast. In a typical play produced in 1636, one of the characters exclaimed, "Your English Jews, they'll buy and sell their father, prostrate their wives, and make money of their own children."[2]

Travelers continued to write about their meetings with "exotic" Jews abroad, describing the rituals they had observed. John Evelyn (1620–1706) reflected the persistent prejudice of his age when he recorded in his diary how, while visiting the Roman ghetto in 1645, he witnessed a "barbarous" circumcision. He ended his description of the ritual with the words "so ended the slovenly ceremony."[3] Another traveler, James Howell (1594–1666), allowed his theological biases to color his observations of Jewish people. In his letters he noted that Jews did not live in any one particular place but were scattered all over the world. This, he believed, was a punishment for the sin of having crucified Jesus. He further noted that "This once select nation of God, and the inhabitants of the land flowing with milk and honey, is become now a scorned, squandered people all the earth over, being ever since incapable of any coalition or reducement into one body politic."[4]

The reign of Charles I marked the continued growth of the Puritans and their ultimate political and religious triumph. They, along with the Anglicans, were responsible for keeping the image of the biblical Jew alive in the minds of so many Englishmen. In addition to their common attachment to the narrative portions of the Bible, which described the triumphs and the tragedies of the ancient Israelites, the Puritans' minds gravitated towards the Mosaic laws. These statutes "offered a regimen which answered a genuine longing on the part of many of these people for a more decent, more self-controlled and self-respecting existence," according to William Haller.[5] Not only did the Bible mold their speech, but it also shaped their thoughts and served as an important means of expressing the new social and religious ideals that were spreading through the country.[6]

Both Puritan and Anglican preaching during the reign of Charles I reflected a love of the Old Testament and of the Hebrew language. Sermon quotations were often taken from the original Hebrew, and many of the preachers displayed a good command of the ancient tongue. Very often the men in the pulpit compared their contemporary struggles with those that the ancient Israelites experienced in their day. It was not uncommon for both the Anglicans and the Puritans to label their enemies with the names of the traditional adversaries of the Jews.

One Anglican preacher demonstrated in great detail the similarities between ancient Israel and modern England. Just as God had delivered the Children of Israel when they were threatened, so had the Almighty saved the English people. He had protected English Protestants during the time of Mary, he had shielded them from the Spanish Armada, and he had delivered them from the Gunpowder Plot. God was ever with his people, joining with them in their conflicts with Catholicism. The Almighty had blessed the English people with a land that in so many ways was similar to Israel, and he had established "the choicest Religion, that of Protestants" and had set up Episcopal authority. In addition, he had chosen for his people a wise and kindly king. Quoting the verse from Amos (3:2) "You only have I knowne of all the families of the earth; therefore I will punish you for all your iniquities," the preacher claimed that all those who were rebelling against the king would suffer the fate of Israel's enemies.[7] Several Puritan preachers also preached similar sermons against the Anglicans.

Although the Puritan and Anglican preachers used Hebrew quotations, based their sermons on Old Testament texts, and compared the lot of their congregants with that of the ancient Israelites, they, like the pamphleteers and the Bible scholars of the time, had little respect for the unconverted post-biblical Jew. In this regard they hardly differed from each other, and both camps held the same view of the Jews' guilt for the Crucifixion, their evil nature and accursedness, and their need to be redeemed through conversion. Puritan and Anglican sermons on this topic reveal a common bond of hate that both groups shared.

The pulpit oratory of both groups reflected a preoccupation with the failure of the Jews to accept Jesus. Although the theme was a very old one, the preachers displayed some imaginative interpretations of Old Testament texts to emphasize their messages. In one sermon delivered before the House of Commons the preacher interpreted the verse (Isaiah 2:5) "O house of Jacob come ye and let us walk in the light of the Lord" to refer to those Jews who accepted, and those who rejected, Jesus. Jacob's halting represented the unbelievers who did not receive Jesus, while his going upright referred to those who believed in him. In the same sermon the preacher interpreted Isaiah's vision of the end of days in the same way. The mountain of the Lord was the church, and one day it would truly be "advanced in the top of the mountains" and all nations would flock to it. Isaiah's vision was intended "to persuade the Jews, Abrahams seed, Isaacks posterity, Jacobs house to come in and receive Christ."[8] The Jews were constantly used as illustrations of a people who was blind to the true faith and who failed to appreciate the significance of the coming of Jesus. Usually, this was done to show the Christian listeners how fortunate they were in being able to appreciate the truth. But by pointing out the superiority of Christian beliefs, the preachers concurrently lowered the Jews in the esteem of the listeners. By mocking their appearance and their honesty, preachers also helped to make them the outcasts of society. For example, one minister, in order to show the magnitude of Jonah's accomplishments with the people of Nineveh, told his congregation: "Suppose a weather-beaten wandering Jew (Jonah look'd now like such a one) should come into our chief city, and proclaim that within fourty dayes it should be overthrown. O how ridiculous would men think such words as these, they would certainly take them but for some Jewish fables."[9]

Jewish hypocrisy was another theme which appeared in any number of the sermons delivered during the period. In many instances it was used to point out the corruption in society that existed at the time of Jesus and to contrast the evils of the Jews with the ideals of Christianity. Both Anglican and Puritan preachers also compared their rivals' false piety with that of the Jews during the time of Jesus. For example, in a sermon delivered in Oxford shortly after the surrender of the local garrison in 1646, the preacher, Jasper Maime, who received his theological training at Christ Church, spoke at length about the false prophets who practiced all kinds of hypocrisy. He used the Jews who lived at the time of Jesus as a key illustration and noted:

> Thus among the Jewes in our Saviour Christs time there were some who tithed Mint, that they might withold Justice and some payd Cummin, that they might keepe backe the weightier matters of the law. Some made cong Prayers that they might devour Widows Houses and some wore broad phylacteries that they might swallow orphan goods.[10]

Perhaps the strongest sermon preached against the Jews during this period was delivered on February 4, 1648, by the Bishop of Rochester. It was centered around the old theme of the Jewish involvement in the Crucifixion and contained some new flourishes resulting from the country's political situation. As a loyal subject of Charles I, the preacher added treason to the long list of crimes committed by the Jews. In fact, it was the most serious aspect of the deed that they had committed. The bishop noted that had the Jews taken the life of just any man it would have been bad enough. However, they killed their true king, an unpardonable crime. "And this Sonne of Man the king (their king) is the man whom ye shall find so betrayed, despitefully used and murdered by his owne subjects, the bloudy barbarous and inhumane Jewes."[11] All the Jews of the time were guilty of participating in the act, and all had a share in the guilt. They, with the devil's help, hoped to seize the inheritance of the church, and when Jesus refused to surrender it to them, he was killed.[12]

The preacher pictured Herod as being shocked at the news of the Crucifixion, and he put the following words into his mouth: "O ye Jewes! doe ye believe or acknowledge a God? or nature? or reason? or have you any law? or religion and will ye contrary to all these put your king to death. . . . all people, be they never so heathenish will condemne you for it."[13]

The good bishop, stirred by the events of the time, was primarily attacking those who opposed Charles I and who had made plans to do away with him. The stress that he placed on regicide in the story of the Crucifixion was a powerful sermonic device to stress the message to his listeners. Yet, the sermon also reminded them that the Jews were a people who violated all laws of decency and respect. If they were ever to be allowed to practice their religion openly and to resettle in England, they would be a most untrustworthy group. Whatever the bishop's intentions were, he damaged the image of the Jews and cast doubts on their loyalty to the crown.

Not only were the Jews caught in the middle of the controversy between the Anglicans and the Puritans, but they were also involved in the almost constant battling that went on between the Protestants and Catholics. Directly and indirectly the Jews' religious beliefs, integrity, and patriotism were questioned by both sides. William Lithgow (1582–1650), a noted traveler and writer, lumped the Jew and the Catholic together and condemned them both in the strongest possible terms.

> The Jews and Jesuits are brethren in blasphemies, for the Jews are naturally subtil, hateful, avaricious, and above all the greatest calumniators of Christ's name; and the ambitious Jesuits are flattering bloody gospellers, treasonable tale tellers, and the only railers upon the sincere life of good Christians. Wherefore I end with this verdict, the Jew and the Jesuit is a Pultrone and a Parasite.[14]

A more indirect attack upon the Jews and their attachment to Catholicism appeared in an anonymous pamphlet entitled *A False Jew: Or a Wonderful Discovery of a Scot, Baptized at London for a Christian, Circumcized at Rome to Act a Jew, Rebaptized at Hexam for a Believer, But Found Out at Newcastle to be a Cheat.* The author told how Thomas Ramsey, who was born in London, was instructed by the pope to pose as Jew and come to England to seek baptism. He was then to "take up preaching and cry up notions"[15] and thereby undermine the authority of the Protestant faith. Through clever detective work, the alleged spy was caught and exposed, and his plans came to nought. The work was not an anti-Jewish tract, and its primary purpose was to show the evil designs of the Catholic church upon the people of England. Yet, it may very well have aroused the suspicion in the minds of its readers that the Jews who were entering the country, and those who were already in England, were Catholic spies. It also may have heightened the normal distrust that the people had towards foreigners and suggested that if the Jews would officially be allowed to settle in England, they might bring with them the secret agents of the pope.

The Catholics, along with various Protestants, attacked previously discussed Judaizers like John Traske. Their quarrel with Judaism was more theological than political. They considered Judaism and Protestantism to be inferior religions, and to prove the superiority of their own beliefs, they wrote various tracts dealing with the supposed conversions to Catholicism of leading Jewish figures. In one such work, "Micheas, a learned Jewish Rabine," after much contemplation and study, joined the church and became a priest. His supposed confession of the errors that he made while living as a practicing Jew put Judaism in a poor light and perpetuated the anti-Jewish sentiments of the past. The words put into Micheas's mouth reflected the theme of the Passion plays and the classic teachings of the church.

> I do freely confesse (and indeed with an ineffable griefe) that, that Holy One, whone my Fore Fathers (and in them my selfe) did put to the most opprobious death of the Crosse, was, and is the Sonne of the Highest and the true saviour of the World; and therefore I thinke it the lesse wounder that the stony harts of us Jewes (best discovered by such our cruell proceedings) werin the Law was first given to us.[16]

During this period Englishmen were interested only in historical Jews, and Christians did not feel that the modern-day descendants of ancient Israel who rejected Jesus were worthy sources of religious authority.[17] Yet, they could not fully ignore modern Jewry. One group of Puritans concerned with the Jews of their day were the mystics, who, like their predecessors during the reign of James I, believed that the restoration of the Jewish people was at hand and that it would be tied up in some way with the coming of the Messiah. Another interested group consisted of those Puritans who were anxious to convert the Jews to Christianity and thereby save their souls. There were also some who felt guilty about treatment given the Jews at the time of the expulsion and who wanted to make amends to their descendants. Lastly, there were a handful of far-sighted individuals who during the reign of Charles argued for religious toleration for all men, including the Jews. Mixed in with all of these dreamers and idealists were a small number of Englishmen who viewed the Jews of their day strictly in economic terms and believed that their return to the country would stimulate the economy. It is difficult to separate out the various groups, and at times mysticism and materialism were combined in the minds of individual thinkers. Taken together, the membership of these groups was not very large, and the writers who will be noted here were distinctly in the minority.

During the reign of Charles I, the messianic interest of the Puritans intensified. Both they and the Sectarians became deeply concerned about the "second coming" just before Charles's execution in 1649. "Most of them were looking forward to . . . some new communion of saints, some republic, some peaceful kingdom of truth and justice," Nahum Sokolow observes.[18] The biblical prophesies of the restoration of Zion were combined with the coming of the Messiah, and many of these dreamers looked forward to some miraculous deliverance of the Jews as the signal that the messianic age would begin. According to one of these mystics, Robert Maton, "A most righteous and flourishing estate of the Jewes in their own land" was necessary before the "Second Coming would become a reality."[19] The thousand-year reign of the saints with Jesus would occur in Judea and "concurre with the happy establishment of the Jewes."[20]

Perhaps the best summary of the hopes of the English messianists of the period appeared in the anonymous pamphlet *Doomesday: Or the Great Day of the Lords Judgement*. The author noted that the second coming of Jesus was near and that already most of the prophesies concerning the destruction of the world had been fulfilled. "The Jews who betrayed the Lord of life and crucified their redeemer . . . have been scattered among all the nations." The writer further believed that the Jews had already

suffered the "abomination of desolation" that was prophesied by
Daniel. Before Jesus would appear, it was necessary for Israel to be
restored to its land. The author was comforted by the fact that,
according to certain letters from abroad, the Jews were making
plans to recapture the Holy Land. Already, he claimed, a Jew by
the name of Josias Catzini was gathering an army in Illyria,
Bethinia, and Cappadocia for this purpose.[21] John Sadler (1615–
1674) also believed that the time of Israel's redemption was
drawing near, though he was too realistic a person to pay much
attention to wild speculations of Jewish armies marching towards
the Holy Land. As far as he was concerned, the conversion of the
Jews was the prime prerequisite for their national redemption.[22]

Messianists like Sadler were not the only Englishmen who
were concerned about converting the Jews. As the Puritans
became increasingly powerful, several of their leaders felt that if
the Jewish people were exposed, in a loving and compassionate
manner, to their kind of Christianity, they too would accept Jesus.
Perhaps one of the strongest pleas for Christians to actively seek
the conversion of the Jews through a more kindly approach to them
was expressed by Thomas Calvert (1606–1674) in his introduction
to a work written by a Jewish convert, Samuel Marochitanus.
Calvert's reactions to the mediaeval myths prevalent during the
period, his use of contemporary proverbs, and his approach to
Anglo-Jewish history provide a fairly good picture of the prevailing
attitudes towards the unconverted Jews during the reign of Charles
I. Calvert began his introductory chapter with the statement that
Protestant ministers should spend time in Judaic studies so that
they would be better prepared to debate with the Jews and
ultimately convert them. "Next to Scripture, Jewish state and
Jewish learning is to be sought into, as an help to us, as a weapon
against them." He looked forward to the day when the "Church of
the Jews" would join with the Christians in worshipping "the son of
David." For Calvert this would be "as the Resurrection from the
dead."[23]

Calvert reiterated the classical sins committed by Jews against
the Christians. They ranged from the killing of Jesus to the
rejection of his teachings and the persecution of his disciples. He
also blamed Judaism for being the fountainhead of various

heresies, the most notorious of which was Islam. The author meticulously listed the accusations leveled against the Jews through the centuries and accepted many of the myths that had been spread by the mediaeval chroniclers, preachers, and dramatists. For example, he noted:

> They used by craft or coyne to buy and get of the consecrated bread which was left at a Christmas Sacrament of the Lord's Supper, and prick it, burne it, and very basely and scornfully abuse it, Because they heard Christians call it the body of Christ.
>
> [p. 117]

He was sophisticated enough to reject some of the more vile accusations, and could not accept the popular notion that "Jews yeeld a stinke and filthy favour to them that converse with them" and that this odor could be cured by drinking Christian blood (p. 31). He also doubted that they had "a monthly Flux of Blood or a continuall maloderiferous breath (p. 31).

In his review of Jewish history, Calvert noted that not all the accusations made against the Jews were just, noting that many of them were motivated by a desire to confiscate Jewish property (p. 35). Though the Jews were deserving of punishment, he did not condone the excessive cruelty that the Christians showed towards them and believed that church leaders should have acted more charitably. He concluded his work with the hope that the Jews would discover that the only way they could find peace was to convert. "There will be no end of their misery, till they take hold of the skirt of a Christian and look upon Christ whom they have pierced" (p. 43). To help them along, he urged a greater sense of compassion on the part of the Christian people.

In his zeal for converting the Jews, Calvert refuted two popular proverbs that were current at the time. The first was "Happy is that commonwealth, in which there is neither an Abraham, a Nimrod, nor a Naaman. (A nation that is not troubled by a Jew, a tyrant or a leper)" (p. 23). This was an obvious anti-Jewish remark intended to prevent the Jews from ever returning to England. The second proverb was "There are five things exceed in stubborness and pertinaciousnesse, the Dogge among beasts, the Cock among

93

birds, the Goat among Cattle, the Prickthorn among plants, and the Jew among men" (p. 43). This derogatory statement pointed up the traditional refusal of the Jew to accept Christianity. Although the Jews were few in number in the country, they were part of everyday speech, and they were clearly associated with the outcasts of society who stubbornly resisted any attempts to change their ways. These proverbs that Calvert quoted likely were indicative of the way the average man pictured the Jews, and the maxims probably reflected the attitudes of a good part of the population.

Hugh Peters (1598–1660) was another cleric who advocated that Jews be allowed to enter England and experience Protestant compassion so that they would convert. He combined this theological hope with a practical approach to reviving England's foreign trade, which had suffered during the Civil War. In his tract, *A Word for the Armie and two words the Kingdom,* he listed some fourteen cures for the ills that he found in society. In his tenth section he noted:

> That Merchants may have all the manner of encouragement, the law of Merchants set up, and strangers, even Jewes admitted to trade and live with us, that it may not be said we pray for their conversion, with whom we will not converse, we being all but strangers on the Earth. [24]

In addition to those Puritans who were interested in the Jews because of the role that they would play in the second coming, and for conversionist and mercantile purposes as well, there were others who believed that the readmission of the Jews to England would be a means by which the English people could atone for the sins that they committed at the time of the expulsion. Samuel Richardson, a Baptist, published in 1647 a tract in which he stated that the religious outlook of a person did not prevent him from fulfilling his role as a productive citizen, and that even a non-Christian could be a useful member of society. Any nation that failed to recognize the equality of its subjects and made distinctions among them on the basis of religion was doomed to suffer. Richardson believed that the bloodshed that England had experienced was a result of the country's intolerance of the Jews. "And

94

who knows but this is come upon us for troumbling, undoing, depising and banishing the people of God into so many wildernesses."[25]

Johanna and Ebenezer Cartwright shared Richardson's views regarding the Jews. In addition to their messianic belief that the day of deliverance for the Jewish people was close at hand and that England and the Netherlands had the obligation of transporting the Jews to their ancient homeland, they also wanted the English expulsion order annulled. They promised Parliament that if this would be done "the wrath of God will be much appeased toward you for their innocent bloodshed."[26]

In addition to those clerics who spoke in terms of atoning for the sins of the past, there were others who directed their thoughts towards the problem of religious toleration without touching upon Christian guilt. Leonard Busher's plea that the Jews be allowed to settle in England and openly practice their religion, which was first made in 1614, was echoed by various writers during the reign of Charles I.

In 1636 John Weemse (1579–1636) dealt with the general problem of whether or not Jews could be allowed to live in a Christian country.[27] He believed that the relationship between the Christian state and the Jew should be similar to the one that existed in ancient times between the Jewish commonwealth and its non-Jewish residents. In those days there were three different categories of non-Jews. The first group were those who were non-Jews by birth but who wanted to become part of the Jewish people. The second consisted of those who were by birth and conviction non-Jews and who wished to remain so. The last category was made up of those who were hostile to the Jews. Weemse believed that in ancient Israel the first group was fully accepted and welcomed into the fold as equal members of the Jewish people. Those in the second category were allowed to live in peace as long as they kept the Sabbath and observed the "Seven Commandments of the Sons of Noah." The third group, those who were hostile to Judaism, were not permitted to live in this society.

Using the structure of the ancient Jewish commonwealth as a starting point, Weemse drew an analogy between its laws towards the non-Jew and the Protestant state's relationship to its Jewish

95

minority. Thus, any Jews who wanted to become Christians were to be given full and equal rights with the rest of the citizens. Those who wanted to remain Jewish, but who would be loyal to the state, were to be allowed to live in peace. The state had the obligation of showing them the advantages of becoming Christians and to acquaint them with the values of the Protestant faith. However, Weemse opposed any attempts to convert them by force. He noted that "many of them who have beene compelled to bee baptized have fallen backe againe to their vomit of Iudaisme."[28] Jews resident in a Christian commonwealth were to be allowed to follow all their religious laws and to build synagogues. He justified their right to read the Law in their houses of worship by stating that "the word of God [the Law] is still the word of God, although they abuse it to a wrong end."[29]

Although the Jews were to enjoy full religious freedom, they were forbidden to engage Christian servants, and in cases of intermarriage they were obligated to raise their children as Christians. Jews who were openly hostile to the Christian state, like pagans who lacked affection for the ancient Jewish commonwealth, were not to be allowed to live in society. Weemse was primarily interested in writing a theological treatise, and he failed to touch upon many practical problems of Jews living in a Christian country. He did not discuss, for example, whether or not the Jews would be allowed to possess their own cemeteries. Even though Weemse dealt only in general terms concerning the relationship of the Jew to the Christian state, and not specifically with the problem of the readmission of Jews to England, his work prepared the way for the debates regarding the return of the Jews at the time of Cromwell.[30]

Many of the ideas concerning the toleration of the Jews in a Christian country that were found in the words of Busher and Weemse were repeated by Roger Williams (1604–1683), who was a leading figure in the fight for religious liberty both in England and in the New World. In 1644, William returned from the colonies for a visit and expressed his views in a pamphlet entitled *The Bloudy Tenent of Persecution, for cause of Conscience discussed in A Conference betweene Truth and Peace*. The author vehemently opposed any state religion which would prevent the people from worshipping according to the dictates of their individual consciences. He believed that it was the will of God that "paganish, Jewish, Turkish, or Antichristian consciences and worships, he granted to all men in all Nations."[31] He feared that any enforced religion in a civil state would be to the detriment of Christianity, since it would prevent the Jews from entering the country and being exposed to the teachings of the faith of Jesus. He was convinced that although the Jews were rebellious against the teachings of Christianity, they would still be loyal to the state. If given the opportunity, they would be productive citizens as well as converts to Christianity.[32] Williams's notion, that "to molest any person, Jew or Gentile, for either professing doctrine, or practicing worship meerly religious or spiritual"[33] was evil, was far ahead of his time. His book was publicly burned. Although public opinion was not ready for such radical ideas, other thinkers supported the view that responsible citizens who would not attack the official religion of the state should be allowed to practice their own faith. One was Samuel Hartlib (1599–1670) who expressed the opinion that:

> The duty of the Magistrate towards the Religious Conversation of his Subjects, is in this: That open Contempt of religion and Profanenesse be restrained, That the Publike Ministery be Protected from injury, Preserved from contempt, and Maintained comfortably; and that a just Liberty of Conscionable Profession be not denied to such as walke orderly in the things wherein they differ from others about Religion.[34]

John Vernon,[35] another advocate of religious liberty in England, stated, "I would all Jews or heathens, or what ever ignorants are native, with all such foreign you invite to traffique and suffer to inhabit, as freely to converse as commerce with you, without restraint upon religious causes."[36] Such a policy, he believed, would benefit England commercially and would also establish strong bonds of loyalty among its citizens. Using the example of the advantages that Holland derived from allowing its citizens to worship according to their personal convictions, Vernon wrote that such a policy of religious toleration would enhance the popularity of the English government.

97

Edward Nicholas managed to extract all the positive ideas about the Jews from the writers of the period without including any of their negative attitudes. He, like Samuel Richardson and the Cartwrights, believed that many of the troubles that England had witnessed were a direct result of the way that the nation had mistreated the Jews. The Jews were, after all, God's chosen people, and Nicholas, quoting from Jeremiah, showed how anyone who persecutes them will in turn suffer the wrath of the Almighty.[37] He urged that the English people comfort them and allow the Jews to return to England once again and become involved in productive labor. Unlike so many of his contemporaries, he felt simply that this was the only just thing to do. His plea was not connected with any attempt to convert the Jews through kindness. Nicholas came to grips with the problem of the Crucifixion and treated it in a much more liberal way than most of his contemporaries. He thought it wrong, for example, for Christians to base their anti-Jewish sentiments on the fact that several centuries earlier the Jews had crucified Jesus. The author believed that the multitudes of the Jews had not been involved in the act, and, if the blame should be placed on anyone, it should be directed to the elders.[38]

Although Nicholas's friendly attitude towards the Jews was not motivated by a desire to win them over to Christianity, it may have been rooted to some extent in his great hatred of Catholicism. He noted how the Jews had suffered at the hand of the Catholic church and how they were persecuted because they rejected the church's idolatrous doctrines. Nicholas even urged his countrymen to fight all those who hated the Jews, even if they lived beyond the borders of their country, "that our weapons (When quiet here at home) may be bent against the cruel oppressors of his people in forraign parts, and those mercyless Tyrents so rigorous towards the Jews where they are, vexing them and spoiling them of their lives and livlyhood."[39]

During this stormy period of bitter conflict some men isolated themselves from the world and devoted themselves to scholarship, oblivious of the turmoil that engulfed English society. One such person was Robert Burton (1576–1640), an English cleric whose patron, Lord Berkeley, provided him with a living so that he could spend most of his adult life in semi-seclusion studying mathematics, divinity, astrology, magic, medicine, and the classics. He published only one book, *The Anatomy of Melancholy* (1629), which became one of the most popular works of its time and which contained the collected wisdom of its author. In this ponderous piece of scholarship, Burton made several references to the Jews, and these notations reveal some of the prejudices of the Anglican mind. In many cases he merely repeated the classical anti-Jewish statements of the past; however, he was creative enough to embellish them and also to add some original observations.

Burton's first major criticism of the Jews centered around their seemingly "holier than thou" attitudes towards the Christians. While he admitted that no one could love God in excess, he attacked those who were "zealous without knowledge, and too solicitous about that which is not necessary busying themselves about impertinent, needless, idle and vain ceremonies, to please the populace as the Jews did about sacrifices, oblations, offerings etc."[40] He put the Jews in the same category with "superstitious Idolaters, Hereticks and Divinators" and attacked them for trying to appear "more divine and sanctified than others." Burton criticized all those who felt that they had the only true faith. He was particularly critical of the Jews when he noted:

> The Jews at this day are so incomprehensibly proud and churlish, saith Luther, that they alone wish to be saved, they alone wish to be lords of the world. And as Buxtorfius adds, so ignorant and self-willed withal, that amongst their most understanding Rabbins you shall find nought but gross dotage, horrible hardness of heart, and stupend obstinacy, in all their actions, opinions conversations: and yet so zealous withal, that no man living can be more and vindicate themselves for the elect people of God.

Although he attacked other religions and was equally caustic towards the Mohammedans,[41] for example, he seemed to be more systematic in his condemnation of the Jews than of any other non-Christian group. In his remarks about Judaism he denounced virtually every aspect of its theology and practices. His cutting remarks extended from "the Rabbins ridiculous comments, their strange interpretation of Scriptures" to "their absurd ceremonies . . . their foolish customs." Burton repeated the mediaeval accusation that "the Jews stick together like so many burrs" and the crude stories about them which had been the favorites of mediaeval preachers. His most serious attacks centered around the toleration of Jews and other nonbelievers in a Christian society. Burton believed that "to purge the world of Idolatry and superstition will require a monster-taming Hercules." He realized that some people had suggested that Jews and other idolators be allowed to live unmolested. For him, this was far from being satisfactory, and he came to the conclusion that "a wound that cannot be cured must be cut away . . . In Divinity the fire cures what the sword cannot."

Another scholar who was almost totally removed from the political turmoil of his age and who dabbled in a number of areas was Sir Thomas Browne (1605–1681). Like Robert Burton, his interests varied widely from theology to the physical sciences. He received a thorough classical education at Winchester and Oxford and then went on to study medicine at Montpellier, Padua, and Lyden. For most of his life he was a provincial doctor in Norwich. Except for a few restrained passages in his letters which expressed his disapproval of the execution of Charles I, he completely ignored the political situation in England.[42] In his works, the most famous of which was *Religio Medici* (1642), he mirrored the scientific spirit of his age. However, he evidently could not shake off the anti-Semitic teachings of the Church of England. In the opening pages of his work Browne stated that though he was a Christian and a member of the Episcopal church, he considered himself to be tolerant of other faiths and somewhat sympathetic to superstition. This "tolerance" did not seem to affect his attitudes towards the Jews. For example, he had little respect for the rabbinic interpretation of scripture. This came to the surface when he mocked those rabbis who believed that Adam was a hermaphrodite. Browne scathingly remarked:

> I am amazed at the Rabbinicall Interpretation of the Jews, upon the Old Testament, as much as their defection from the New: and truely it is beyond wonder, how that contemptible and degenerate issue of Jacob once so devoted to Ethnick Superstition, and so easily seduced to the Idolatry of their Neighbors, should now in obstinate and peremptory beliefe, adhere unto their owne Doctrine, expect

impossibilities, and in the face ane eye of the Church persist with the
least hope of conversion.

[Pt. 1, sec. 25]

Although Browne had little respect for Jewish beliefs and criticized
the Jews' stubborn adherence to the tenets of their faith, he did not
believe in forcibly converting them. "The persecutions of fifteene
hundred yeares have but confirmed them their error . . . [it] is a
bad and indirect way to plant Religion" (pt. 1, sec. 25).

In a later work, *Pseudodoxia Epidemica* (1646), Browne used his
crude scientific method to analyze the nature of the Jewish people,
and he devoted an entire chapter to the problem of the odors that
they supposedly gave off. It was sandwiched between an essay
entitled "Of Sneezing" and another "Of Pigmies." Browne demonstrated that it was wrong to assume that foul odor was a
national trait. He noted that the Jews were not a pure race, and that
any scientific generalizations concerning them were not valid. He
attacked the belief that their supposed "ill savour" was really a
curse "derived upon them by Christ, and stands as a badge or
brande of a generation that crucified their Salvator" (bk. 4, chap.
10). In his exploration of the problem, he tried to be objective, and
he examined such areas as Jewish diet and sexual customs. He was
impressed with their moderate diet, their choice of foods, and their
bodily self-control. Yet his overall view of the Jews was far from
kind. After absolving the Jews of any physical guilt for the
accusations leveled against them, Browne noted that the Jews had
received this reputation because "the nastiness of that Nation, and
sluttish course of life hath much promoted the opinion occasioned
by their servile condition at first, and inferior ways of parsimony
ever since" (bk. 4, chap. 10). His study of the odors that Jews
supposedly emitted was designed merely to dispel an unscientific
notion, not to overcome prejudices against the Jews in general. In
this spirit Browne admitted that the story of the wandering Jew as
recorded by Mathew of Paris was "very strange and will hardly
obtain belief." He came to the conclusion that if the tale was really
true, this Jew who had lived through evolution and development of
the Christian religion would condemn "the obstinacy of the Jews,
who can contemn the Rhetoric of such miracles, and blindly behold
so living lasting conversions" (bk. 7, chap. 171).

101

In addition to these general scholars whose interests touched upon so many different areas including the Jews, there were others who were interested primarily in studying the Hebrew language, the Bible, rabbinic literature, and the laws and customs of the Middle East. They persuaded Parliament in 1648 to spend some 500 pounds for a collection of Hebraic books to be housed in the library of Cambridge University so "that the Kingdom may not be deprived of so great a Treasure nor Learning want so great an Encouragement."[43] Both Anglican and Puritan scholars were engaged in this area of scholarship, and political and religious affiliation had little effect upon their attitudes towards the literature or the nation that had produced it.

John Lightfoot (1602–1675), one of the most prominent of these scholars, excelled in both the study of the Bible and rabbinic literature. In one of his earlier works, *Ervbhin or Miscellanies Christian and Judaicall and others,* published in 1629, he revealed his attitudes towards the Jews and their literature. Lightfoot was filled with praise for the Hebrew language and believed that "for Sanctitie it was the tongue of God, and for Antiquitie it was the tongue of Adam: God the first founder, and Adam the first speaker of it."[44] He also found a great deal of wisdom in the rabbinic works that he studied. However, he was narrow-minded and accepted only those interpretations of the Bible that agreed with his own understanding of the text or which were in accord with his own approach to religion. For example, Lightfoot was very much impressed with one observation that the rabbinic commentator, Kimchi, made concerning why Jonah was kept in the big fish for three days. He agreed with the rabbis that it was part of God's plan to show mercy to the penitent and noted:

> Could wee looke for a truth from a Iew, or comfort from a Spaniard? And yet here the Spanish Iew affords us both: Comfortable truth and true comfort . . . When a Iew thus preaches repentance, I cannot but hearken, and helpe him a little out with his sermon.
>
> [P. 38]

He was not so kind when he came across the legend that the fish that swallowed Jonah brought him to the Red Sea and showed him the very place where the ancient Israelites crossed over. Lightfoot believed that "the fabling Iewes must find some sleight to maintaine their owne inventions" (p. 54). Lightfoot headed chapter 20 of his book, "Wit Stollen by Iewes out of the Gospell." He listed several selections from the New Testament that resembled statements found in rabbinic literature and concluded that the Jews had stolen this material from the Christian work and that "By this Gospell which they thus filch they must be judged" (p. 58).

John Selden took a much more enlightened approach to the Jews than most of his contemporaries. His scholarly interests exposed him to a great many Hebraic and rabbinic works, and he admired the legal structure of the ancient Jewish state as well as many of its religious statutes. Unlike most of his learned colleagues, he allowed his admiration of the Jews of the distant past to shape his attitudes towards their modern day descendants. He saw no reason why this group of people who maintained their ancient heritage should be viewed with suspicion and treated as outcasts. "God at first gave laws to all mankind, but afterwards he gave peculiar laws to the Jews, which they only were to observe."[45] He compared this to the legal system that he found in his country, where in addition to the common law that applied to all of England, there were corporations that maintained their own distinct laws and privileges. Selden was well aware of the popular prejudices against the Jews of his time. Although he may have shared some of them, he could rise above the hatreds of his generation and point out some positive aspects of their existence in a Christian society. He wrote:

> Talk what you will of the Jews, that they are cursed, they thrive where'er they come; they are able to oblige the prince of their country by lending him money; none of them beg; they keep together; and for their being hated, my life for yours Christians hate one another as much.
>
> [P. 112]

Selden, in addition to his scholarly pursuits, was a practical man who believed that a modern state should utilize its financial resources to the fullest. He argued that the old prohibitions against

103

lending money that had been maintained by the church and the hatred directed against the Jews as usurers had no place in contemporary society. In his comments on usury, Selden noted that according to Jewish law, "The Jews were forbidden to take use of one another, but they were not forbidden to take it of other nations." Instead of issuing the usual tirade against the Jews' hypocrisy, the author approved of their actions and added, "That being so, I see no reason why I may not as well take use for my money as rent for my house. Tis a vain thing to say money begets not money; for that no doubt it does" (p. 204). Selden further justified the lending of money by Jews by showing that many good Christians, including some noted churchmen, practiced it. "No bishop or ecclesiastical judge, that pretends power to punish other faults, dares punish, or at least does punish, any man for doing it (p. 204).

Another more enlightened scholar of the time was Robert Sheringham, who in 1648 published the Hebrew text of the Mishnaic tractate of *Yoma* with a Latin translation and various comments and annotations.[46] In his preface the author made note of the importance of studying rabbinic literature. He pointed to the intrinsic value of the material, the aid it offered in interpreting the Bible, and the fact that the gospels owed a great deal to the rabbis. Sheringham believed that the New Testament borrowed much from rabbinic literature and that the works of these Jewish sages contained many traditions that were of value to both Jews and Christians.[47]

Although the reign of Charles I and the beginnings of the Commonwealth marked an increase in scholarly Judaic works and in the number of tracts concerning the acceptance of the Jews in a Christian state, the rise of the Puritans did not encourage a radically new approach to the Jews. The prejudices of the preachers, the scholars, and the common people suggest that the modern Jews were still more closely identified with their ancestors who crucified Jesus than with the Patriarchs. The Puritans considered themselves to be the "New Israel," and they had little love for the contemporary Jews, who continued to reject Jesus. The Anglicans shared the Puritans' theological hatreds, and they also associated the Jews with the Judaizers who were anxious to overthrow the monarchy.

Still with rare exception, interest in the Jews, even on the part of those who advocated religious toleration, was related to the hope of their ultimate conversion. The Puritans who stressed the need to bring Jews into the fold likely were sincere in their zeal; in keeping with Christian tradition they wanted to save souls. Most of them believed that the stubborness of the Jews in holding onto their ancestral faith stemmed from their hatred of the Catholic church. If the Jews could be exposed to the Puritan brand of Christianity which did not resemble the idolatries of Catholicism, they would willingly convert. They believed that the Jews should be allowed to enter England and experience this refined and purified faith. And yet there was a strong distrust of Jewish converts to Christianity, especially by Englishmen who had actually come in contact with them. With all that Weemse had to say about the need to convert the Jews, he still accepted the folk belief that neither a baptized Jew nor a tame wolf should be trusted.[48] John Evelyn also shared this view. During his travels through Italy, he was invited to be a godfather to a converted Turk and a Jew. Evelyn noted that the Turk seemed to be faithful towards his new religion. However, he considered the Jew to be a "Counterfeit."[49]

This conflict in the English mind over the desire to bring the Jews to England to convert them and the distrust of all Jews, including those who converted, surfaced when the readmission became a real possibility. Menasseh ben Israel's mission to England, which will be discussed in the next chapter, brought these deeply-rooted prejudices out into the open.

FIVE

THE READMISSION
CONTROVERSY

The establishment of the Commonwealth raised new questions about the place of the Jews in Christian society, and more specifically, it reopened the controversy about whether or not they should be readmitted into England. Despite the efforts of a few men of conscience, the accumulated prejudices against the Jews and their faith were as strong as ever, and those merchants and clergy who feared Jewish economic competition or religious domination resurrected the stock accusations against them. The stories that had been circulated by men like Mathew of Paris in earlier ages appeared once more. Various tracts and pamphlets pictured the Jews as murderers of innocent children, usurers, clippers of coins, and the archenemies of good Christians. Much of the so called philosemitism of the time was limited to Old Testament figures. The contemporary Jews, in contrast, were associated in the popular imagination with the vilest of creatures who were unfit to dwell among God-fearing people.

Although in the theological view the Jews were considered to be rejected by God, the new religious makeup of English society during the period of Commonwealth encouraged their resettlement. The multiplicity of sects, each struggling for recognition, brought religious pluralism that much closer to becoming a reality. For example, the Leveller leader, Richard Overton, criticized the intolerance of the government and argued for toleration of

106

Brownists, Independents, and Anabaptists. He was no less empha-
tic in defending the rights of the Jews.[1] The problem of religious
liberty proved to be embarrassing to the Puritans. They realized
that complete toleration of other groups would enable their
opponents to overthrow the new government. To dodge the issue
the pamphleteers argued that Jews and Mohammedans might be
tolerated. However, Roman Catholics and Anglicans, who had the
opportunity to embrace the true faith and who rejected it, should
not be allowed the privilege. The Jews were not considered to be a
threat to the government, and it was possible that they could
become a recognized religious group.[2]

In 1651, Captain Robert Norwood wrote a pamphlet, *Proposals
for Propagation of the Gospel*, which in essence was an answer to
the charges of blasphemy made against him. He wrote that the
state should not compel any man to accept any specific religious
doctrines because he felt that this was against the teachings of the
New Testament. He followed this idea to its logical conclusion and
claimed that the Jews should be tolerated in England, even though
their religious practices were different from those of the Christians. He felt that this was only fair, since, if the situation were
reversed, those who believed in Jesus would want such a freedom
for themselves. This was a very simple application of the "Golden
Rule," which he believed had escaped many of his contemporaries.[3] From a theological viewpoint, Norwood also hoped that
through religious freedom the Jews would be drawn to Christianity. He was annoyed with the Christian clergy who failed to
appreciate the need to allow the Jews to come to England to be
exposed to the teachings of Jesus, and he believed that the clergy
were unduly afraid of the corrupting influence that the Jews would
have upon the Christian people.[4]

Several similar works were being written at the time, but it
probably was the attitude of Oliver Cromwell towards the Jews that
was the most important factor leading to the readmission. Cromwell was a rare personality who combined practical considerations
with lofty religious idealism. He was a shrewd politician who
appreciated the realities of the times, and he was also a deeply
religious individual who struggled to do the will of his creator. He
claimed to be tolerant of most non-Catholic religious groups,

including the Jews. "I profess to thee I desire from my heart, I have prayed for it, I have waited for the day to see union and right understanding between the godly people (Scots, English, Jews, Gentiles, Presbyterians, Independents, Anabaptists, and all)."[5]

On a practical level, Cromwell had every reason to be friendly to the Jews. From the very beginning, the small community of Marranos who lived in London had supported the parliamentary cause. Their loyalty to Cromwell had prompted a royalist spy to report: "I find the Jews here and at London most malicious enemies to our monarchy, and daily wishing England were a commonwealth like Holland."[6] Cromwell did not hesitate to call upon them or their brethren in Europe for help. He believed in using the services of any people as long as they would benefit the state. "The State in choosing men to serve it, takes no notion of their opinion; if they be willing faithfully to serve it—that satisfies . . . Bear with men of different minds from yourself."[7]

Cromwell's toleration of the Jews was a wise policy decision which proved to be invaluable to him in many ways. Members of the London Jewish community acted as contractors to the government, supplying it with both money and stores. Antonio Carvajal, a successful merchant, served as a secret agent for Cromwell. Through his efforts the government was kept informed about the movements of royalist forces on the continent, and his intelligence also detected one of the plots against Cromwell's life. Furthermore, he relayed to the Protector information which enabled the government to seize royalist shipping at Ostend and thereby prevent a renewal of the civil war.[8] Cromwell was well aware of the commercial implications of the readmission. He hoped to induce the Jewish merchants of Amsterdam, who were trading with Jamaica and Barbados, to establish their firms in London. Also, he was constantly in need of funds, and he no doubt looked on the wealthy Jewish merchants as a dependable source of finance in times of stress.[9] Cromwell's patronage of the Jewish resettlement was motivated by several very different factors. As one modern historian so aptly put it:

> Was this because the Old Testament had taught him to think of them as God's chosen people, or was it for commercial reasons and because

108

they worked for his intelligence service? His mind moved to and fro between the city, Whitehall and the Holy Land without a sense of incongruity; the probability is that all three considerations influenced him.[10]

In addition to those far-sighted men who thought in terms of greater religious toleration, and individuals like Cromwell who combined religious sensitivity with practical considerations, an assortment of mystics continued to put forth the messianic doctrines which favored readmission of the Jews. With the establishment of the Protectorate, they openly preached their doctrines to anyone who would listen. One of these men, John Robins, thought that he was God and that he had given life to Adam. He told his disciples that he would soon gather 144,000 men in England and transport them to Jerusalem, where they would be sustained by manna. He also promised that he would cause the Red Sea to split so that his followers could cross on dry land.[11] Another dreamer, Thomas Tany, appeared in 1650 and claimed that as a descendant of the tribe of Reuben, he had come to proclaim that the return of the Jewish people to Zion was fast approaching. In a one page announcement he wrote the following:

Now unto ye Jewes, my Brethren, am I sent to proclaim from the Lord of Hosts, the God of Israel, your Returne from your Captivity in what nation soever ye are scattered. From thence ye shall be gathered into your own land: and Jerusalem shall be built in glory in her owne land, even on her own foundation.[12]

Although Tany claimed that he was a Jew in the fullest sense of the word, all of his proclamations about the return to Zion were put on a christological basis.[13] Both New Testament and Old Testament prophesies were used freely by the self-appointed "High Priest of Israel."

Ultimately, it was a combination of idealism, commercialism, and mysticism that brought Menasseh ben Israel to England to seek the formal readmission of the Jews to the land that had cast them out three-and-one-half centuries earlier. His trip served as a catalytic agent which aroused the deeper feelings of the English people toward Jews. Menasseh's preparation for the journey, and

109

his experiences in London, can serve as a framework for the study of the many pamphlets and tracts that were written regarding the readmission. These works provide excellent source material for understanding the Christian attitudes toward both the Jews and Judaism during the period of the Commonwealth.

Menasseh ben Israel's parents had fled from the Inquisition, settling in Amsterdam at the beginning of the seventeenth century. It was there that he received his Jewish training. Although he was a diligent student of rabbinic and mystical literature, he never became a first-rate scholar. Much of his fame was derived from his influence among the non-Jews. Most of his pamphlets, petitions, and scholarly writings were addressed to a Christian audience, and he was the first rabbi that many of these scholars had known. [14] As a result of his wide correspondence with Christian scholars, Menasseh knew of events in England. Like most Jews on the continent, he was attracted to the increasing Hebraism of English thought and was impressed with the pro-Jewish tendencies of the Commonwealth. Menasseh, the mystic, was also drawn to those English clerics who were thinking and writing about the redemption of Israel. He, too, was awaiting the coming of the messianic age.

Menasseh, like some of his English contemporaries, viewed the civil war as divine punishment for the expulsion of the Jews from England. As early as 1647, he began to think of resettling the Jews in that country, but not until 1649 did he decide on a plan of action. In that year, John Dury, an English Puritan, wrote to the Dutch rabbi and asked for a copy of a story that Antonio de Montezinos had told Menasseh about his travels in America. Antonio de Montezinos, or Aaron Levi as he was known among his Jewish brethren, believed that he had found a group of natives deep in the jungles of South America who were descendants of the Ten Lost Tribes. He told Menasseh the accounts of his explorations, and the good rabbi believed them. Dury wanted a copy of the story to send to Thomas Thorowgood, who was interested in missionary activities among the Indians. Dury was certain that if the Indians were really descendants of the Ten Lost Tribes, Thorowgood would receive additional financial support for his work. Menasseh sent Dury a copy of the affidavit that Montezinos had signed in Amsterdam, and Thorowgood made good use of it in his work, *Jews in America*.[15] Thorowgood claimed that the Ten Lost Tribes were scattered among the nations of the world to the utmost ends of the earth. Because they had sinned, they were punished by God. However, he believed that in the last days Christ would find the lost Children of Israel and bring them to his kingdom. Thorowgood used Montezinos's story as proof that the tribes were indeed scattered and that the coming of Christ was soon at hand. The support of missionary activity would obviously hasten the process.[16]

Menasseh was at first hesitant about publishing Montezinos's narrative because it seemed to prove the need to support Christian missions, but he gradually realized that it could be used for a Jewish purpose. Daniel had prophesied that the scattering of Israel would be the forerunner of their restoration. It was clear that they had already reached one end of the earth. Let them enter England and they would have reached the other end. In Jewish mediaeval literature the name *Angleterre* had been literally translated into Hebrew as *Ketzeh Haaretz*, the angle or the limit of the earth.[17] Only if the Jews would be admitted into England would God's promise be fulfilled. Then they and all of mankind would experience a truly golden age. It was with this thought in mind that Menasseh wrote *Mikveh Yisroel, The Hope of Israel*.[18]

The Latin edition of the work, translated into English, was dedicated to "the Parliament, the Supreme Court of England and to the right Honourable the Council of State." It began with a flowery preface in which Menasseh stated that he wrote the book to gain favor and good will for the Jewish nation. He expressed his gratitude for all the kindness and understanding that England had already shown his people and prayed for the coming of the Messiah.[19] In the introduction, Menasseh mentioned some theories concerning the origins of the inhabitants of America. He believed that the most reasonable one was that of Montezinos, who claimed that the first inhabitants of America were descendants of the Ten Lost Tribes. Menasseh was convinced that they had kept their ancestral rites through the years and that they and their brethren all over the world would soon be governed by the Messiah, son of David. This coming of the Redeemer, Menasseh

111

maintained, is the hope of Israel. The translator of the Latin edition of the work stated in the beginning of the book that he wanted "to give some discovery of what apprehensions and workings there are this day in the hearts of the Jews; and to remove our sinful hatred from off that people."[20] He seemed sincere in his desire to right some of the wrongs committed in the past.

Menasseh's work made a deep impression throughout England. The Puritans were flattered by his compliments paid to the republican government, and those who waited for the imminent coming of the Messiah were delighted that their beliefs were sanctioned by a learned sage of Israel. Readmission, however, had to be based on something more than messianism. Eventually, Cromwell used his influence to allow Menasseh to come to England to plead for his people. After several delays caused by the war between England and Holland, the rabbi was finally able to prepare for his visit. In the summer of 1655, before leaving Holland, he sent out a printed letter to the leading Jewish communities of Europe telling them of his plans and asking for their prayers and good wishes. He mentioned in his message how he had been encouraged to make the journey by "virtuous and prudent individuals" who had informed him that: "today this English nation is no longer our ancient enemy, but has changed the Papistical religion and become excellantly affected to our nation, as an oppressed people whereof it has good hope."[21]

Menasseh arrived in England in October 1655. He brought with him some petitions from the Jews of various parts of Europe, as well as the English manuscript of his *Humble Addresses*. On October 31 he presented copies of this work to the Council of State. It reflected not only Menasseh's hopes, but also what he thought were the attitudes of the Christians towards the Jews. Menasseh began his work by stating that God puts righteous rulers in positions of power and removes those who are wicked. Menasseh referred to those men who had been good to the Jewish People as righteous and to those who had oppressed them as wicked. Quoting the verse, Genesis 12.3, "I will bless them that bless thee and curse them that curse thee," Menasseh stressed the rewards in store for any ruler who dealt kindly with the Jews.[22] In the name of all that is holy he asked that Cromwell grant:

112

That the Great and Glorious Name of the Lord our God May be extolled and solemnly worshipped and praised by us through all the bounds of this Commonwealth; and to grant us peace in your country That we may have our synagogues and free exercise of our religion.

[P. 78]

Menasseh then directed his attention to the officials of the Commonwealth. He repeated the quotations from Daniel that appeared in his earlier work, *The Hope of Israel*, and briefly mentioned that the resettlement would hasten the coming of the Messiah. He then demonstrated the material advantages which England would receive if Jews were allowed to return. Here the mystical rabbi became a realist, and his message was clear and pointed:

My third motive is grounded on the profit that I conceive this Commonwealth is to wreap, if it shall vouchsafe to receive us; for thence I hope there will follow a great blessing from God upon them, and a very abundant trading unto, and from all parts of the World, not only without prejudice to the English Nation, but for their profit, both in Importation and Exportation of goods.

[P. 79]

Menasseh's new approach evoked a storm of criticism. Those groups who strongly advocated readmission on religious grounds resented the emphasis placed on the economic aspects of the problem. On the other hand, opponents of readmission doubted the validity of Menasseh's arguments. They wondered if perhaps the Jews would benefit more than the English through the readmission.

The most vocal opponent of the readmission was the Puritan zealot, William Prynne. His biographer, Ethyn Williams Kirby, described him as follows:

A versatile man, Prynne combined wide knowledge and violent prejudices, a legal mind and a fanatical spirit. From such a character one would expect his strange writings, crammed with facts, burning with violent likes and dislikes. . . . Dominated by a zeal to propagate the social ecclesiastical, and political ideals which he believed right, he was indeed a typical Puritan.[23]

113

Prynne, who led a life of almost monk-like severity, was devoted to the eradication of evil. He preached against women who wore their hair too short and against men who wore theirs too long. He viciously attacked the theater and dancing as inventions of the devil. Because of his violent outbursts, both his ears were cut off and the letters "SL" (seditious libeler) branded on his cheeks. His punishment only increased his zeal, and it enshrined him as a martyr in the eyes of his followers.

Prynne found the Jews to be a perfect target for his venomous pen, and his pamphlet, A Short Demurrer to the Jewes, became a classic anti-Jewish tract that was copied by many of his admirers.[24] In the preface to the reader he explained how he became interested in the problem of the readmission. Prynne described how, on December 7, 1655, as he walked past Whitehall, a certain Mr. Nye (1596–1672), a Protestant cleric who favored Jewish resettlement, asked him "whether there were any law of England against bringing the Jews amongst us?"[25] Prynne reminded him of the banishment of 1290, which he believed was an edict of both Edward I and of Parliament as well. He also told Nye that it was a most inopportune time to bring the Jews into England, considering how the people "were so dangerously and generally bent to apostacy, and all sorts of novelties and errors in religion." Prynne was afraid that the English people would sooner turn to Judaism than the Jews would turn to Christianity. He also reminded his friend that "the Jews had formerly been great clippers and forgers of mony and had crucified three or four children at least, which were the principal causes of their banishment." Nye challenged Prynne's accusations against the Jews, and Prynne decided to dig into the records to satisfy himself that his judgment was sound. He thus began his work with a preconceived notion and searched for material that would support his conclusions. When he could not find evidence to substantiate his accusations, he fabricated it.

Prynne attacked the readmission on religious, legal, and economic grounds, and he provided a rich storehouse of anti-Jewish material that was to be used by other writers in his generation and in those to come. Like other opponents of the readmission, he tried to show that the Biblical bond that existed between God and his chosen people had been severed when the

114

Jews rejected Jesus. He argued that if the Almighty had viewed them as a stiff-necked people who were incorrigible in their ways, then certainly they would not be an asset to England. Prynne further claimed that if God had chosen to punish them by dispersing them over the face of the earth, it would be against God's will to gather them in England (p. 63). Prynne also pointed out that if the Jews would be encouraged to resettle in England, it would logically follow that the Catholics and the royalists should also be allowed to practice their religion and that the country should throw open its doors to all who rejected the Puritan faith. He challenged the notion that the non-Christian countries were more tolerant to the Jews than England was. In his opinion, they, too, refused to fraternize with the Jews and excluded them whenever possible (p. 78ff).

Prynne also challenged the readmission on legal grounds, claiming that the Jews had been banished by an act of Parliament in 1290 and that they could not be allowed to resettle in the country unless Parliament repealed the decree. Prynne admitted that the "Edict and Decree" was not to be found in the Parliamentary rolls, but he claimed that they had been lost (p. 49). Although the *Instrument of Government,* which was a sort of constitution of England during the period, stressed religious toleration, he argued that it did not include Jews but only those of the Christian faith, excluding Catholics and royalists. Because the Jews were infidels, he believed that they were excluded from the intent of the law (p. 55).

Finally, Prynne attacked the readmission on purely economic grounds (p. 99ff). Although he contradicted himself in his statements regarding the economic value of the Jews, his anti-Jewish sentiments were clear. He first claimed that the Jews only bring profit to the king and to the officials of any country that admits them. Citing the example of pre-expulsion England, he showed how eventually Jews must receive special privileges which hurt the general Christian community. After he admitted the economic value of the Jews, Prynne asked if economic advantage was a proper motive for admitting nonbelievers into England. He compared the situation to the Old Testament story of Hamor, who urged the men of Shechem to accept circumcision for purely

115

economic reasons (Genesis 34:20–23). Prynne later claimed that the Jews did not bring economic profit to a country. Referring back to pre-expulsion England, he concluded that the Jews of the time were of no financial value, and that once they had been banished, trade had immediately increased. Prynne unhesitantly distorted any facts of history that could be used to stir up anti-Jewish sentiments, and he perfected the "Big Lie." He was a master propagandist, and his work embraced many mediaeval myths and half-truths. In addition, he unscrupulously maligned clerics and legal experts who favored the readmission.

Prynne's attack against the Jews was motivated by his antagonism towards Cromwell and government members who favored readmitting them into England. The pain and the humiliation that he experienced at the hands of the authorities increased his antagonism towards the readmission, and his attack was just one of his many outbursts against his enemies or those connected with them.[26] None of his pamphlets either before or after the printing of his *Short Demurrer* dealt with the Jews; and his anti-Jewish sentiments seem to have been only a very brief expression of hatred towards them. But it was significant that Prynne could amass so much anti-Jewish material within such a short period of time. It apparently was readily available and part of the sentiments and folklore of the time.

Prynne's attacks demonstrated how latent hatreds based on events long since past could be activated when the proper situations arose. His attack upon Cromwell, through his opposition to the readmission, showed how the Jews of the time, real and imaginary, were a tool in the hand of the zealot or bigot. They could be summoned, however briefly, for a purpose and then quickly forgotten. Along with the witches and the Catholics, they could be used to achieve political or social goals. The opposition to the readmission went beyond questions of theology. However, the teachings of the church supplied the forces opposed to Cromwell with a basis for their arguments against resettling the Jews in the country. The church had created through the centuries a climate of public opinion receptive to their anti-Jewish tirades, and the zealots found a ready audience for their venomous tracts.

Alexander Ross (1591–1654), like Prynne, attacked Cromwell's plans for the readmission by trying to discredit Jews and Judaism in the eyes of the English people. He began his rather lengthy book with the statement that the Jews would soon be coming to live in England and that he wanted to give the Christian reader an idea of what the Jews believed and practiced. He claimed that he would not draw any conclusions about these newcomers, but his intense prejudice against them quickly became clear. Ross believed that after the English people actually saw Jews practicing their religion, they would better appreciate how fortunate they were to be Christians. He wrote, "That having before our eyes their sensuall stupidity and obdurate incredulity, together with the great wrath and severity of God against them, we may be put in serious remembrance of the wonderful bounty and goodness of God unto us."[27]

Ross heaped scorn upon virtually every area of Jewish scholarship, worship, and ritual observance. He believed that the rabbis should be ashamed of their "grosse stupidity," which they displayed in their distorted interpretations of scripture, and he accused them of bringing the dreams and fancies of mad people into their commentaries (p. 27). Ross viewed Jewish prayer as a means by which the Christian people and Jewish proselytes to Christianity were cursed each morning and evening. He was a very knowledgeable person who had thoroughly researched the area, and, as a result, his slanderous statements about the contents of the liturgy carried great authority. In his detailed description of Jewish customs and ceremonies, he combined some accurate observations with various derogatory statements resulting from his own prejudices. For example, after discussing the ritual obligations that the Jews performed each morning, Ross added:

> Sloth and remisness is no way becoming a Jew, who ought to give constant proof of his alacrity and readiness in rising; and thus to think with himself; if any Christian were at the doore who owed me mony, or would pawn something of value, whose coming might be gainfull unto me; or if I was invited by a prince or some great person, from whom I had expectation of some favour.
>
> [P. 95]

117

Thus, the old stereotyped image of the stage Jew was strategically placed alongside the practices of Judaism that many Christians admired.

To further combat any possible positive attitudes towards Jews and Judaism, Ross attacked the Jewish concept of the Messiah and tried to show how it reflected a desire to subjugate other religious groups. He claimed that the Jews believed that when the messianic age would come "the Christians and those nations whose throats they do not cut, shall build them houses and cities, till their ground, plant their vineyard for no hire . . . even the princes shall serve them" (p. 425). Ross's concluding remarks were very significant. He pointed out that Judaism was "not founded upon Moses and the Law, but upon idle and foolish traditions of the Rabbins" (p. 427). Like so many other Christian thinkers, he sought to show that the contemporary Jews and their religious practices were divorced from the biblical world that many Englishmen admired.

An anonymous pamphlet, *The Case of the Jewes Stated: or the Jewes Synagogue Opened,* which may also have been written by Ross,[28] combined a description of Jewish customs and ceremonies related to home observance and synagogue worship with pseudo-history and anti-Jewish prejudice. After a brief introduction to the rituals of the synagogue, the author recounted how the Jews of pre-expulsion England were guilty of torturing Christian children and putting them to death. He uncritically accepted Mathew of Paris's account of one such incident and summarized the alleged crime and the subsequent punishment.[29] At first glance it appears that the author rather haphazardly arranged his material. The supposed incidents of the blood libels are immediately followed by a description of the rituals of the Jewish people, for example. It is possible, however, that he inserted the selections about the ritual murders to remind the readers not to be too impressed with Jewish customs and ceremonies, because they were practiced by some very devilish creatures. He strategically placed slanderous statements about the Jews throughout this short pamphlet to prevent undue admiration of them and their religious practices. Thus, after he described how the Jews prayed for the restoration of the temple, he noted that they also offered prayers for the destruction of

Christianity. The author also wrote that in their private writings the Jews claimed that "the soul of Esau entered into the body of Christ, and that Christ and Christians are no better than Esau" (p. 4).

Another vehement opponent of readmission was a writer known only as W. H. In his work, *Anglo-Judaeus*, he violently attacked both the Jewish people and their religion. It was a carefully documented refutation of Menasseh's *Hope of Israel* and his *Humble Addresses*. In the preface, the author challenged the contention that the Jews of pre-expulsion England had been an asset to the country and that they had lived in "profitableness and faithfulness." He also questioned, on strictly religious grounds, the wisdom of readmitting them to the country. He noted that among the general population of England there were "too many having already taken up, if not their opinions, yet such as border near upon their hold."[30] He referred obviously to the various Judaizing sects, which the author considered to be a threat to the Protestant faith. The presence of any substantial number of Jews could only cause heresy to increase and further undermine Christianity. He supported these contentions with what he considered to be historical facts. W. H. began with the Bible as a source of proof of the evil nature of the Jewish people. He cited the ingratitude of the ancient Israelites, who had rejected God after he had liberated them from Egyptian bondage, and showed how this became a national trait that continued through the biblical period and the time of Jewish commonwealths. All the persecutions that the Jews had experienced were the result of their sinful and rebellious character, and the Jews were not worthy of the sympathy of the Christians. The author took the same approach when he touched upon the history of the Jews in England. He was objective enough to realize that the Jews had been used as sponges by the Angevin kings to "suck up the English treasure which they [the rulers] then squeezed into their own coffers" (p. 6). Nevertheless, he condemned them for their great zeal in accumulating wealth for the treasury and for "the insolency of their carriage" which aroused the hatred of the general population.

All of this was relatively mild compared to the author's total acceptance of the mediaeval myth that the Jews killed Christian

119

children for ritual purposes. His description of the Norwich blood libel closely followed the accounts of the mediaeval chroniclers, and once again the modern Jews were accused of following the example of their ancestors by cruelly crucifying and murdering innocent Christians. He considered the York massacre to be an act of God, a punishment for the Jews' stubborness and cruelty, and he believed those who perished were not worthy of Christian sympathy. Each succeeding persecution was prefaced with some mention of alleged Jewish crimes, so that all their sufferings appeared to be just punishments for treacherous behavior. The author began his description of one massacre with the statement "By this time their iniquities were grown so high, that they were counted a burden to the earth on which they trod; no rising, no stir, but part of it must fall upon them" (p. 14). By cleverly distorting the facts of history, W. H. concluded that in the years that the Jews were in England, they held the people in bondage. They afflicted the Christian population by murdering their children, clipping their coins, charging them usurous rates of interest, and encouraging those who believed in Jesus to leave their faith. The author wondered how the English people could possibly accept Menasseh ben Israel's statement that the Jews had once been an asset to the country (pp. 39–40). He realized how earnestly the Christians wanted to convert the Jews and bring them into the fold. However, he had strong doubts if such a plan would really work, wondering if it was "probable that this people, which hath now been blinde for above 1600 years, should be restored to sight by any but extraordinary power, by any work but one miraculous" (p. 50).

The pamphlet is valuable not only for the clearly stated opinions of the author, but also for the light that it sheds upon the common man's attitudes towards the Jews. W. H. noted, for example, that although some 365 years passed from the expulsion to the time of the writing of his work, in the popular mind Jews were remembered as a people "either apt to do, or fit to suffer any violence." He stated further that the word "Jew" was used to describe a person who was of the lowest and most despised group in society. Among the people of England, cutthroat dealing was commonly described by the expression "None but a Jew would have done so." Popular expressions to describe a terrible misfortune were "This had been enough for a Jew to suffer" and "I would have done so to a Jew" (p. 47).

In addition to the Protestant writers who opposed the readmission and attacked both the Jews and Judaism, Paul Isaiah, a convert from Judaism (1626–1656), added his voice to those who tarnished their image. He was something of a professional convert, a man who changed his faith three or four times in as many years. Yet his writings about his former religionists influenced public opinion, and they cannot be passed over lightly. They appeared at a time "when the taste of the average Englishman inclined towards religious works, particularly to those concerned with the chopping of texts."[31] Paul Isaiah claimed that he was born an "unworthy superstitious Jew" and that for the first twenty-four years of his life he had practiced Judaism. Then he suddenly and miraculously became aware of the truth of Christianity and left his people. The convert showed his scorn of his former religionists when he criticized them for their stubbornness in rejecting the message that he hoped to deliver to them. He felt that "it may seem more easie and possible to turn an hard iron or stone in an instant into water, as soon as a Jews heart unto Christian Religion."[32] Such a statement from the pen of a converted Jew must have added weight to the arguments of those opposed to the readmission who said that there was little hope that the Jews would accept the Christian faith once they came to England.

Paul Isaiah was particularly critical of the rabbis who, he believed, kept the Jews from experiencing the true faith. He accused them of teaching vicious doctrines that prevented their followers from discovering the blessing of Christianity. This was particularly true in the Jewish approach to the Messiah.

> Here may every good upright and Pious Christian behold and perceive, how this blind and heart-stopped people reject the holy Scriptures, Prophets and Ministers, through their Rabbies ignorant and unfit knowledge; for they have no thought in the least of such Messias as should redeem them from their sinnes and spiritual captivity, but of a Valiant Man, who shall so valiantly fight with the Christians, shall slay them and overcome them, take their houses,

goods and lands from them and give them to the Jews for their inheritance, having no other thoughts in them, but how they may rob the Christians of their goods.[33]

Paul Isaiah was not content to show how the rabbis supposedly taught that one day the Jews would seize Christian property. He also pointed out that in the prayer services, which were conducted twice each day, the Jews were "bound to blaspheme Christ and to curse him, and all true Christians which believe in him."[34]

One of the best rebuttals of the arguments and slanders of men like Prynne, Ross, and Paul Isaiah was offered by a writer known as L. D. In his work, *Israel's Condition and Cause Pleaded, etc.*, the author revealed the effects of some of Menasseh ben Israel's arguments upon a small segment of the English population. He obviously had been won over to many of the rabbi's arguments concerning the readmission, and his pamphlet reflected both an interest in the Jewish people and a strong desire to see them resettled in England. L. D. connected the readmission of the Jews with their ultimate redemption, and he noted:

> For though God in his justice did threaten to scatter them into all Nations, yet he doth not say they shall be cast out of all nations . . . If they should not be amongst all Nations, how should God (as he intends it) gather them out of all Nations? A general collection implies a general casting and if so why not some into England.[35]

Like many other Puritans, he believed that once the Jews would be readmitted, the chance of their eventual conversion to Christianity would depend on the general population's attitudes towards them. The power of Puritan preaching, the manner in which the Jews would be treated by the merchants and bankers, and the love shown to them by the people would all be important facts in bringing them into the fold. L. D. urged his readers "to forgive and forget what is past fully and freely, and to cover all with love and charity." He noted that Jesus himself had prayed that Jews would be forgiven for their sins and "to say he was not heard, and his petition not granted is impious and desperate blasphemy" (p. 60).

The author strongly opposed any persecution of the Jews, viewing such acts as against the will of God. He accepted them as

122

"God's own peculiar People" and admitted that although the Almighty may have punished them temporarily for their sins, it was wrong for the Christians to continue to cause them to suffer (p. 68). L. D. refuted the arguments raised against the readmission by claiming that the Jews would in no way threaten Christian society. He believed that they only wanted the opportunity to dwell in peace without any external pressures. He described them as witty, wise, ingenious, well bred, addicted to curious and neat arts and inventions, pleasing themselves in solitary retiredness (p. 74).

Thomas Collier attempted to answer the attacks made against the Jews by W. H., the author of *Anglo-Judaeus*. In his pamphlet *A Brief Answer to Some of the Objections and Demurs Made Against the Coming in and Inhabiting of the Jews in this Commonwealth etc.*, he pointed out that the Jews were punished by God for their rebelliousness for a just reason. Collier believed that "by their fall the Lord hath taken his way to bring forth salvation to us gentiles, which could not be, but in their fall."[36] Thus, the Jewish crime against Jesus was part of a divine plan designed to provide salvation for the Christians. He argued that the hatred that had been focused on the Jewish people through the centuries was unwarranted, since the Crucifixion was ordained by God. He wrote: "Though it was their sin yet it was Gods counsell; yea it is by Christ crucifyed, that we have life . . . so God hath wrought good to us out of their evill, Let us not therefore envy them, but admire the unsearchable wisdom of God" (p. 31). Collier warned his readers against being excessively cruel to the Jews, and he felt that it was un-Christian to "add affliction to the afflicted."

The author attempted to refute several of the standard objections raised against the readmission. He noted for example, that the Christians as well as the Jews were guilty of usury. He asked, "Is there any more reason to keep out them for usury, then to banish those Usurers that are already amongst us?" (p. 25). Collier noted that those who objected to the readmission claimed that Jews were guilty of crucifying children. He questioned the truth of such statements and reassured his readers that if the Jews were caught committing such crimes, they would be guilty of murder and would be properly punished (p. 30). The author rejected the old argument that the Jews could never be readmitted because they had been banished permanently from England. He pointed out that the expulsion had been ordered by "popish Princes" and that contemporary Englishmen should not perpetuate their sins. Instead, his countrymen should repent and turn from the evils committed by their fathers. Collier was realistic enough to realize that the religious leaders of his generation and public opinion as well opposed the readmission. Yet he was encouraged by those who were waiting for the redemption of Israel and who did not share the anti-Jewish sentiments of the majority of the people (p. 31).

Although much that Collier expressed was ahead of his time, his motives were far from being pure. Perhaps he may have admired the Jewish people and wanted to see that justice was done; yet he was also motivated by a strong desire to convert them to the true faith. This can be seen when he noted: "It is neither honourable to God nor our Profession, nor can we perform our duty to God in keeping out a people from us . . . who might be through the blessing of God converted to us" (p. 34). His interest in conversion detracts from his seemingly idealistic exhortations. Thus, Collier's plea that Christians cannot pretend to love Abraham without showing affection to his descendants, and his strong statements concerning the need to protect both the body and the soul of contemporary Jewry, cannot be accepted on face value. Consciously and subconsciously the conversion of the Jews shaped many of his attitudes and opinions. Like other writers of the time, Collier's interest in the Jews and his desire to see them readmitted into England was linked with their ultimate acceptance of Jesus.

One of the most important historical works that advocated the readmission was written just before Menasseh's visit, and it was available to those who were engaged in the controversy with such writers as Prynne and Ross. The author, who went under the name of Philo Judaeus, was probably one of the Fifth Monarchy Men, who believed that the rule of Jesus was fast approaching. However, he had a great deal of love and respect for the Jewish people that was not often found in similar pamphlets. He stressed the fact that if the Christians had any hope of winning over the Jews to their faith, they would have to do so through a genuine concern for the

124

Jews' welfare. He urged his readers to gird their loins so that "when the Hebrews shall by providence come into this Nation, they may see such a lustre and beauty in your conversations, and such loveliness in your affections, as it may allure them to imbrace your faith."[37] Although theologically the author maintained the usual approach to the Crucifixion, he emphasized that Christians should learn the art of forgiveness. He noted that if a Christian would taunt the Jews over the fact that they crucified Jesus, "he does crucifie the son of God afresh" (p. 99). True, the Jews were guilty of the act. However, one who taunts them for having committed such a deed "keeps the wound open and thereby our blessed Saviour bleeds afresh (p. 101).

The author praised the Jewish people for their contributions to Western civilization and commended them for the patience they displayed in waiting for the Messiah, their zeal in studying the Torah, and their generosity in giving charity to the poor. He also defended the Jews against the accusation that they charged excessive rates of interest. Not only did he point out that they were honest in their business transactions, but he also noted that English Christians were engaged in identical practices. Since England had always opened her gates to the dispersed who wanted refuge, certainly the Jews, who were known to be faithful to the laws of the countries in which they lived, should be allowed to resettle. Expressions of Christian sympathy were not sufficient. The opportunity had come for Christians to demonstrate their feelings through concrete actions. The reader was reminded that this was not a social or economic problem, but one that was tied up with the ultimate redemption of the Jews, through conversion, and the second coming of Jesus. Thus, Christian apathy in fostering the readmission was a direct sin against God. The author noted that "truly in the neglecting of this duty we keep silence, and so become guilty of a hainous crime. For what do any of us know whether they may not be part of that means which God will use concerning their restauration" (p. 90).

Menasseh ben Israel's presence in England and his request that Jews be readmitted gave urgency to the whole problem of Christian-Jewish relations. It inspired more than one cleric to rethink his attitudes towards the flesh-and-blood Jews. In theory,

125

it was not too difficult to talk about extending Christian love to Jews in the hope that they might convert. But when the prospect of a flood of Jews entering the country became pressing, old irrational animosities came to the surface. The change of heart that came about from Menasseh's specific requests can best be noted in the works of men like John Dury.

John Dury (1596–1680), a Protestant cleric, was regarded as one of the most important theologians of his time. While Dury was on the continent, Samuel Hartlib, an English scholar, asked him if it was possible from both theological and legal points of view to allow the Jews to be readmitted into England. Dury answered him in his pamphlet *A Case of Conscience.* He pointed out that it was not only lawful but expedient to allow them to return. He believed that it was a Christian obligation to show concern for the wayfarer, and that no nation needed compassion more than the Jewish people.[38] He beleived, as did other writers, that certain restrictions would have to be placed upon Jews after they entered the country. They would be forbidden to commit blasphemy against Jesus, to seek converts, or to profane the Christian Sabbath. In addition, they would be obligated to attend lectures on the principles of Christianity and to engage "in a friendly way" in discussions of the religion. Dury hoped that the Jews would appreciate the truth that God revealed to the Christians through the gospel and that they would ultimately convert. Other restrictions to be placed on the Jews included their separation from the general community in more "friendly ways" than were currently being practiced in Germany. He hinted that it would be necessary to limit their usury and their unethical practices, but he did not go into detail beyond the suggestion that the officials of the state look into the matter (p. 8).

After Dury's somewhat tolerant opinion was circulated, he received some letters in January 1656 that contained the requests that Menasseh ben Israel had made regarding the readmission. Dury then added a postscript to his pamphlet which reflected his change of heart now that the problem of the return of the Jews was a real one. Those few lines that he added to his work are testimony to the deep-seated hatreds of not only Dury but a great many so-called enlightened clerics.

Our state doth wisely to go warily and by degrees in the business of receiving them. Menasseh ben Israel's demands are great; and the use which they make of great privileges is not much to their commendation here and elsewhere. They have ways to undermine a state, and to insinuate those that are in office, and prejudicate the trade of others; and therefore if they be not wisely restrained, they will in short time be oppressive, if they be such as are here in Germany.

[P. 8]

Thomas Barlow (1607–1691) was another cleric whose theoretical approach to Jews and Judaism was far different from his practical attitudes towards the readmission.[39] When a correspondent of his, Thomas Godwin, asked his opinions concerning the return of the Jews to England, Barlow replied in a pamphlet *The Case of the Jews*. He noted that if the readmission would benefit the country financially, it should be approved. The good of all people was the supreme law of any state, and it was important to decide if the return of the Jews would indeed aid the economy of England. Since Barlow believed that the Jews of pre-expulsion England had been an asset to the country through their financial dealings, he saw no reason why this would not happen again. He did not fear Jewish usury, since he believed that it could be easily controlled in the modern state.[40] In relation to the religious aspects of the problem, he saw no reason why Jews and Christians could not live side by side. Certainly, if British merchants had dealings with Jews in foreign countries, they could do the same thing at home. He did not feel that Christianity would be threatened by the coming of the Jews, because in no country had large numbers of Christians ever converted to Judaism. In fact, the opposite would probably happen; the Jews would convert. In typical conversionist fashion, Barlow felt that the nations should not persecute the Jews, but that they should spread the gospel and try to influence them by allowing them to have a greater contact with Christians (p. 48). Thus, for the sake of financial gain and the possibility of encouraging conversion, Barlow believed that the Jews should be readmitted to England.

When the question arose of what restrictions should be placed upon the Jews once they arrived in England, Barlow changed his tone. He now had to deal with practical matters, and he laid down seventeen conditions which were almost mediaeval in tone and content. He believed that Jews should be prohibited from dressing like their neighbors, that they should be forbidden to employ Christian servants and midwives, and that Jewish doctors should not be allowed to treat non-Jewish patients. In addition, Jews were to be compelled to discuss religious matters with Christian clerics. He even would have forbidden that the Jews leave their homes on Good Friday (pp. 73–77). There was a marked difference between his academic interest in Jews and Judaism, his theoretical tolerance, and his own deep-rooted prejudices.[41]

This change of heart on the part of the Puritan clergy was particularly evident at the Whitehall Conference, which Cromwell called in December of 1655 to settle the matter of the readmission. Although he picked as delegates those clerics and laymen who had openly favored religious toleration, the meetings at Whitehall disappointed supporters of readmission. One of the best accounts of the religious controversy at the Whitehall Conference was written by Henry Jesse, a friend of Menasseh who was present at all of the sessions. In his short pamphlet which described the proceedings, Jesse stated that he decided to put down on paper what had transpired in order to satisfy the curiosity of "many good people in divers parts of this Nation who have often prayed for the Jews Conversion."[42] He noted that many Englishmen had written to their friends in London asking about the proceedings, and he hoped that he could supply them with an accurate eyewitness account of the issues that were raised during the debates.

Jesse was primarily concerned with the religious and moral aspects of the readmission. Except for acknowledging that the lawyers agreed that there was no law against readmitting the Jews and that the merchants had mixed feelings about it, he centered his concern on the views of the clerics attending the conference. He treated the major religious arguments for allowing the Jews to return fully and sympathetically, and he showed how some of the clergy were concerned for the needs of the stranger. It was this sense of compassion for these oppressed people, as well as a definite feeling of guilt for the sins of the pre-expulsion period, that moved these religious leaders to advocate the readmission. But

Jesse also understood how keenly they sought the conversion of the Jews. The author noted how some of the clerics believed that:

> In no nation hath there been more faithful, frequent and fervent prayers for the Jews than in England. None are more likely to convince them by scripture, and by holy life, then many in England: And Gentiles . . . must provoke Jews to jealousie, or emulation; and happy is England, if it be instrumental in so blessed a work.
>
> [P. 4]

The conversionist sentiments of the assembled preachers was reflected in a prayer that was offered at one of the sessions. Jesse recorded it as follows:

> O Lord Jesus, thou indeed justly revengest the contempt of thy self and worship, upon this ungrateful people, whom thou punishest most severely. But O Lord, remember thy Covenant and respect them now in misery for thy namessake. And grant this to us . . . that we going on in thy grace, may not be instruments of thine anger against them; but rather, both by the knowledge of thy word, and by the examples of holy life, . . . we may recall them into the right way.
>
> [P. 4]

The prayer expressed the belief of several of the clerics that although the Jews had been rejected by God for having refused to accept Jesus, they were once "Children of the Covenant" and were worthy of any proselytizing efforts that would bring them back to this special relationship with their creator.

Not all of the clerics at the conference were so ethereal. Though many were interested in converting the Jews, others feared that the coming of substantial numbers of Jews would cause good Christians to turn to Judaism. Unfortunately, Jesse did not go into too great detail concerning the arguments raised by those opposing the readmission, yet, it is clear from his brief work that some of these men feared that if the Jews would be allowed to resettle, they would institute Moloch worship and other idolatrous practices in England. This opposition on the part of the clergy was quite strong, and the author noted that Cromwell "had hoped by these preachers to have had some clearing the case, as to conscience. But

129

seeing these agreed not, but were of two or three opinions, it was left the more doubtfull to him and the Councel" (p. 4).

The clerics were hopelessly divided in their attitudes towards the readmission. As the conference continued, their anti-Jewish prejudices became more intense as they realized the negative effects the Jews would have upon their parishioners. Hugh Peters (1598–1660), who for several years had urged that England emulate the Dutch spirit of toleration, was one who gave in to the prejudices of the times. When he was informed that the Crypto-Jews of London had outwardly practiced Catholicism for many years, he denounced them as a self-seeking generation "who made but little conscience of their own principles."[43]

The supporters of the readmission could hope at best to admit the Jews under certain religious and commercial restrictions. This was unacceptable to Cromwell, and he ended the conference. He was interested, among other things, in bringing commercial prosperity to the country by attracting Jewish capital and Jewish commercial talents. To banish these people to decayed ports and cities and to penalize them by double customs duties, as some of the compromisers had suggested, would defeat his plans. In addition, the Crypto-Jews in London, who had served him so well in the past, would be forced to leave the city.

For the next few weeks many observers expected that Cromwell would decide to readmit the Jews on his own authority. However, he did nothing at this point. The Whitehall Conference had revealed to him the intensity of the bias against the Jews and had demonstrated how even those who in theory favored the readmission opposed it as a practical policy. If the clergy could not fully support such a plan, what could he expect from the merchants in the country whose livelihood would be affected by the arrival of the Jews? Certainly, the rumblings that he heard at Whitehall would reverberate throughout England. When a subcommittee issued a report in favor of a severely restricted policy of readmission, Cromwell promptly suppressed it. Otherwise, he deliberately tried to ignore the problem. A few Jews who accompanied Menasseh to London lost hope and returned home. The general public became apathetic to the problem and directed its attention to more pressing issues.

THE READMISSION CONTROVERSY

Menasseh remained in London to compose a book answering the charges that had been leveled against the Jews during the controversy over the readmission. He was particularly anxious to answer the attacks of Prynne. Menasseh's book, *Vindiciae Judaeorum* or *A Letter to Certain Questions propounded by a Noble and Learned Gentleman, touching the reproaches cast on the Nation of the Jewes, wherein all objections are candidly and yet fully cleared*, was one of the most popular pieces of Jewish apologetic literature ever published. The work was divided into seven sections, each dealing with an area of anti-Jewish prejudice. Menasseh began with a refutation of the old argument that Jews used Christian blood for ritual purposes, and systematically delved into the prejudices of the time. In the last section he told of his mission to England and how his high hopes had come to naught. In spite of his bitter experience, Menasseh naively believed that all of the accusations against his people had been fabricated by only a few individuals and that they stemmed from purely selfish motives. "I can not be persuaded that anyone hath either spoken or written against us, out of any particular hatred that they bare us, but that they rather supposed our coming might prove prejudicial to their estates and interests."[44]

Although the attack upon the Jews by such men as Prynne and Ross stirred up considerable controversy, Cromwell remained loyal to the Jews and gave them verbal permission to maintain a synagogue in London, provided that it did not attract too much attention. This semi-official act on the part of Cromwell aroused some resentment from those at the conference who had opposed readmission. The war with Spain that broke out in 1656 gave these men an opportunity to get their revenge.

The Crypto-Jews were able to live unmolested in England by claiming that they were Spanish subjects. At the very beginning of hostilities, the Privy Council issued a proclamation declaring that property belonging to Spanish subjects could be confiscated as a lawful prize. Shortly after this, at the instigation of an informer, the property and papers of a Marrano merchant, Antonio Rodriguez Robles, were seized. Robles first protested against the confiscation of his goods on the grounds that he was Portuguese and not Spanish. However, it was known that he had lived in Spain and had

131

passed himself off as a Spanish Catholic. Also, he had been employed by the Spanish government. Robles turned to his co-religionists for help, and they convinced him to base his plea of innocence on the grounds that he was a Jew. They promised to support him in his quest for justice and were convinced that Cromwell would come to their aid. After thorough investigation, the council ordered the immediate discharge of the warrants issued against Robles and ordered that his ships and merchandise be returned.[45]

> The case was the turning-point in the history of the London Congregation of Marranos. It brought them for the first time into the light of day as a Jewish community. Thenceforth they were compelled to rely for whatever privileges they might claim in this country not upon their foreign birth, but upon their quality as Jews.[46]

The Robles Case gave the Marranos the courage to petition for the formal right to conduct services and maintain a cemetery. In the words of their request:

> Wee pray with all Humblenesse yt by the best meanes which may be such Protection may be granted us in Writting as that wee may theren meete at owr said priwate deuosions in owr Particular houses without feere of Molestation either to owr persons famillys or estates, owr desires Being to Liue Peacebly under yor Highnes Gouernement, And being wee are all mortall wee alsoe Humbly pray your Highnesses to graunt us License that those which may dey of owr nation may be buryed in such place out of the cittye as wee shall think conuenient.[47]

The Marranos essentially were asking for permission to practice their faith openly and to begin to function as a recognized community. Cromwell willingly granted the request. In December 1656 their presence in England became an established fact when they rented a house in Creechurch Lane as a place of worship and openly practiced their faith. But the small colony of Jews in England owed their existence to Cromwell and not to any dramatic change in Christian attitudes. Menasseh had failed to alter public opinion to any significant extent, and, except for some personal friendships that he had made in England, he did little to change the anti-Jewish prejudices that had been building up over the centuries.

In the years ahead the Jews of England were to continue to be viewed with curiosity and scorn. Zealous clerics would pray for their conversion, and mystics would view them as harbingers of the Messiah. Their commercial talents and capital would be put to good use, but for the most part they would still be haunted by the mediaeval stories told about them, and the old fears and jealousies would linger on.

SIX

THE REKINDLING OF
OLD HATREDS

From the time of the readmission
of Jews to England through the turn of the century, the image of
the Jews did not significantly change. The Jews still were viewed as
a stubborn people who refused to accept Christianity, and they
were, as in the past, the object of scorn and ridicule in many of the
conversionist tracts and sermons of the day. The stage Jew almost
disappeared from the drama, but scattered negative references to
Jews were found in Restoration plays. Mystics continued to view
them as harbingers of the end of days and fanciful accounts of
Jewish armies which were made up of descendants of the Ten Lost
Tribes and which were preparing to invade the Holy Land, were
popular. During this period theological speculations about the
coming of the messianic era were of diminishing importance.
Economic jealousies had a more profound effect upon Christian
attitudes, and they caused deep feelings of insecurity among the
leaders of the emerging Jewish community. The anti-Semitic tracts
that had been prepared during the readmission controversy were
cited by men who envied and hated the Jews for their economic
position in English society, and old theological hatreds found in
these works were revived when it proved to be financially
advantageous.

Through the efforts of Cromwell the Jews were able to establish
a synagogue and openly practice their faith in England. It was also
through the strength of his personality that those who hated the

134

Jews remained somewhat subdued. The negative reactions of the public to the establishment of a small Jewish community were limited to private correspondence and entries in personal diaries;[1] little, if anything, was stated publicly. The Jews, under Cromwell's protection, actually enjoyed certain privileges that were denied to some Christian groups like the Catholics and the Quakers. In addition to being allowed to hold their own worship services, they were given permission to purchase a cemetery and to engage freely in trade. By 1657 they were admitted as brokers on the City Exchange, a privilege that was only supposed to be granted to freemen.[2]

On the surface, the Jews seemingly enjoyed a peaceful, uneventful existence. The building in which they conducted their services was part of an ecclesiastical trust, and they paid their rent to the parish of St. Katherine. Both the tenants and their landlord were on good terms, and the Christians who came in contact with the Jewish community developed strong bonds of friendship with their neighbors. The churchwarden's record of the early burials of the congregation note that the bells of the Church of St. Katherine tolled to mark the passing of some of the early Jews of the resettlement. On the occasion of the first Jewish funeral, the church lent the Jews their pall.[3] These were simple acts of kindness and respect that were shown by the leaders of the parish.

From the beginning of the period of the resettlement, the Jews mixed freely with their Christian neighbors. Unlike their brethren on the continent, the English Jews never established a ghetto. In the absolute monarchies on the other side of the channel, the Jews who were emancipated had to adjust to a new life in an open society. To gain acceptance they had to struggle to overcome their alien character and their alien dress and social customs. The Jews of England did not isolate themselves from society; and in a relatively short period of time they assimilated themselves into the English national character. Thus, they achieved social emancipation before they attained full political freedom.[4] That there were a very small number of Jews in England at this time was an important factor in keeping down any hostile outbreaks against the newcomers. By 1656 there were only twenty-seven Jewish families in the country,[5] and most Englishmen were scarcely aware of their presence.

135

But underneath this seemingly secure existence there were undercurrents of strong hatred. The privileged status of the Jewish minority aroused the jealousies of the merchants and the city fathers of London. The animosities that had been stirred up during the debates over the readmission were not completely forgotten, and Cromwell could not completely suppress the lies and exaggerations circulated by Prynne and his disciples. As long as the Lord Protector was alive, the enemies of the Jews remained silent, and it was only after his death that they came out into the open.

Richard Baker represented the anti-Jewish interests when he presented to Richard Cromwell a petition calling for the banishment of the Jews from the country. He further suggested that they be fined for the amount of goods that they had exported that exceeded their imports.[6] Richard Cromwell took no action on the proposal, and the matter was temporarily dropped. The enemies of the Jews waited for the restoration of the monarchy to resume their anti-Jewish activities. They hoped that the new king would be more receptive to their demands.

When Charles II entered London, he was presented with a petition from the mayor and the alderman of the city protesting against the allowing of the Jews to hold public worship services that were in opposition to the Christian faith. The signers of the petition also expressed the fear that English blood would be tainted through intermarriage with these foreigners. However, the main complaints against the Jews were economic, and the city officials were primarily concerned with Jewish mercantile competition. They noted how the Jews, through nefarious means, had become so successful in trade that they "retired themselves with ye English estates to ye ruin of many good families."[7] Thus, for the safety of the Christian faith and the good and welfare of the English people, they believed that it was best that the Jews be expelled from the country permanently.

Thomas Violet, a notorious informer and exporter of contraband bullion, also tried to convince the king to punish his Jewish subjects.[8] In a petition submitted in December 1660, he claimed that it was a felony for any Jew to be in England, and that they should therefore have their estates confiscated and then be thrown into prison. He believed that they should be kept there until their

136

co-religionists would ransom them.[9] Violet copied many of Prynne's anti-Jewish prejudices that had appeared in *A Short Demurrer*. He began his bitter attack by considering the arrival of the Jews in England at the time of William the Conqueror. He tried to show how, through the years, the Jews had been a thorn in the side of the English people. He claimed that in the past they had bribed good Christians to convert to Judaism and that they had also bribed the king to side with them against the clergy. The Jews had entered into open disputations with the clerics and had done everything in their power to challenge the Christian faith. Violet believed that they would repeat their actions during the restoration when there were already a great number of atheists, heretics, and Anabaptists in the kingdom. He was also convinced that the economic crimes that the Jews commited in pre-expulsion England would be repeated during the reign of Charles II. He claimed that the present-day Jews in the country, through their devious practices, had already taken over the nation's economy at the expense of the Christian merchants. The Jews had supposedly robbed the state of 100,000 pounds in wine trade alone, and they had deliberately dumped unnecessary commodities on the English market to ruin the economy.[10]

Fortunately for the Jews, however, Charles II did not revoke the privileges that Cromwell had bestowed upon their community. Charles, like numerous gentlemen of his day, was apathetic about religion, and his theological opinions, when he bothered to express them, were deistic in tone and content. He was tolerant of differences in worship and belief, and he was bored with religious controversy.[11] Charles had been assisted by Jews on the continent during his exile, and he appreciated their role in the economy of a mercantile nation like England. Even though they might arouse the jealousies of the native merchants, their skills in foreign trade would be a definite asset to the crown. His queen, Catherine of Braganza, who had Jews in her service, may also have influenced him in favor of allowing them to live undisturbed in the country.[12] Those who petitioned the king to expel the Jews from the country failed to reckon with Charles II's personal feelings of tolerance and also with his strong interest in promoting Cromwell's mercantile policies. During Charles's lifetime, the position of the Jews in

137

England was fairly secure, and it was only after his death that the enemies of the Jews created any real trouble.

In 1685, after James II had assumed the throne, Samuel Hayne, a political writer, published a pamphlet in which he attacked the Jews for having an unfair advantage over the native merchants because of their exemption from alien duties. Hayne made particular mention of the way that the Jews had accumulated great wealth through trickery and deceit at the expense of the native Englishmen.[13] Although he was joined by the Corporation of London in his attacks upon the Jews, the king continued to allow the Jewish merchants special privileges in their mercantile dealings. Unable to change the favored commercial status of the Jews, their enemies decided to attack them on purely religious grounds. Thomas Beaumont tried to have the entire Jewish community punished for violating an old anti-Catholic law that had been passed during the reign of Elizabeth which imposed a fine of twenty pounds a month for nonattendance at church services. After considerable lobbying by the Jewish community and some well-placed gifts, the charges were dropped, and James II reaffirmed the right of the Jews to practice their religion in peace.

The leaders of the Jewish community realized that their right to exist in England hung on a very thin thread, and they did everything in their power to see that their members did nothing to antagonize either the civil or the religious authorities. Their feeling of insecurity and their awareness of undercurrents of anti-Jewish prejudice can be noted in the synagogue rules which they imposed upon their co-religionists. They specified that no Jew was to discuss religion with a Christian neighbor for fear that it would provoke ill will between the two groups and eventually affect the well being of all the members of the Jewish community.[14] To prevent overzealous clerics from blaming the Jews for trying to seduce good Christians from the faith of Jesus, the Jewish communal leaders prohibited the acceptance of converts.[15] This had caused considerable friction in the past, and the Jewish leaders wanted to avoid the possibility of its ever recurring. Having been accused for centuries of taking delight in cheating Christians, the leaders were very strict with Jews who were involved in any crimes. They made it absolutely clear that those who violated the laws of England would have to suffer the consequences of their actions without any assistance from the Jewish community.[16]

Although the leaders of the Jewish community tried to keep their members out of public scrutiny as much as they could, some Englishmen were inevitably drawn to the newly formed synagogue to see how the Jews conducted their religious services. These visitors were struck by the way the Jews prayed, by the melodies that they chanted, and particularly by the lack of decorum in the sanctuary. The Jews' physical appearance and their manner of dress also interested the observers. The reaction of these visitors to flesh-and-blood Jews at worship is a good indication of their general attitudes towards both Jews and Judaism at the time. One of the most prominent Englishmen who visited the synagogue in Creechurch Lane was Samuel Pepys. In December of 1659 he attended services which marked the conclusion of the thirty-day mourning period for Caravajal. He noted in a letter to his patron, Edward Montagu, that he had gone there "for observation sake."[17] This may have been a way of reassuring his patron that he was not one of the Puritan Judaizers who was enamored with Jewish rituals and beliefs. In any event, Pepys was sufficiently interested to return for at least one more visit. His timing was poor, and he was present at *Simchat Torah*, when traditionally a very lighthearted atmosphere fills the synagogue. He recorded the following observations in his diary:

> But, Lord! to see the disorder, laughing sporting and no attention, but confusion in all their service, more like brutes than knowing the true God, would make a man forswear ever seeing them more: and indeed I never did see so much, or could have imagined there had been any religion in the whole world so absurdly performed as this.[18]

Another visitor to the synagogue was John Greenhalgh (? –1691), a schoolmaster, who had a strong curiosity regarding the religious practices of the Jews. In a letter to his good friend, the Reverend Thomas Crompton, in April 1662 he gave a lengthy description of the services that he had observed. Greenhalgh admitted that at first ". . . the Jews with their *taleism* over their heads presented to the observer a strange, uncouth, foreign,

139

and . . . barbarous sight."[19] He was able, however, to overcome these prejudices and appreciate the deeper significance of the service. He was particularly moved by the prayers for the coming of the Messiah and the restoration of the Temple. He wrote: "I was strangely, uncouthly, unaccumstomedly moved, and deeply affected; tears stood in my eyes the while, to see those banished Sons of Israel standing in their ancient garb (veiled) but in a strange land, solemnly and carefully looking East towards their own country."[20] Near the end of the letter, much of this compassion seemed to disappear, and the "irrational reasoning against Christ" that he discovered in his conversations with the rabbi of the congregation caused him to write, "In a word the curse is upon them to the uttermost; and they have a grosser veil over the eye of the soul, than that which covers their heads." Greenhalgh was annoyed that the Jews refused to accept Christianity and that even the most convincing argument was "but an arrow shot against a wall of brass."

Later in the century another distinguished visitor, Robert Kirk (1641–1682) was particularly unkind in his description of Jewish services. He stressed the fact that the Jews were aliens and that their mode of worship was grossly inferior to that of the Protestant faith. He commented on the poor English that was spoken by the Jews, the lack of dignity that the rabbi of the congregation displayed, and the poor decorum that he found in the sanctuary. He was shocked to discover that both the rabbi and his congregants laughed and talked after each paragraph in the Torah reading was completed. Kirk claimed that "They never prayed nor discovered their heads, nor bowed the knee . . . They had no methodical worship. They were all very black men and indistinct in their reasoning as gipsies."[21]

Just as the leaders of the Jewish community could not remove their members from public view, they could also do nothing to keep the Jews out of the religious literature and the Christian sermons of the time. During the period of the resettlement, various conversionist tracts appeared which indirectly affected the image of the Jews in the eyes of the Christian population. One of these works dealt with the conversion of Eve Cohan, a Jewess, to the Protestant faith. In the preface the author stated that the main purpose of the book was to show the sincerity of converts to Christianity. However, throughout the work there was a generous sprinkling of anti-Jewish remarks which turned it into a tract that bitterly condemned the Jewish community. The Jews were pictured as a treacherous group who would stop at nothing to prevent an innocent young woman from leaving their fold and embracing Protestantism. "They betook themselves to all the Arts of Villany, in which they are so well practiced"[22] to achieve their ends—only to be stopped by a determined convert and some sympathetic Christians.

The author described how Eve Cohan, having been convinced of the validity of Christianity, left her home to be baptized. Her mother, a cruel and heartless woman, and members of the Jewish community threatened her with physical harm and used every means at their disposal to force her to renounce the Christian faith. According to the author, the Jews were motivated by a theological hatred for Christianity which went back to the time of the Crucifixion. He was convinced that "those whose ancestors in Unbelief, had with so bloody a Malice crucified our Blessed Saviour, would have spared no invention of Mischief, to execute their Revenge on one, that was now resolved to believe in Him" (p. 12). When physical force failed, the Jews tried to use the courts to achieve their purposes. In the biased eyes of the author, the Jews had the ability to pervert justice through their influence with men in high places. They were also skilled jurists who used their abilities to take advantage of the hated Christians. In this instance they were unsuccessful, and Eve Cohan managed to start a new life as Elizabeth Verboon. At the conclusion of this tale of Jewish cruelty and Christian perserverance, the author noted that "This Recital was thought necessary to let the Nation see what sort of People these Jews are whom we harbour so kindly among us" (p. 25). Not only did they persist in their idolatrous beliefs, but they "still thirst after the Blood of such of their Nation as believe in Him whom their Fathers Crucified" (p. 25). The author wanted to point out the dangers of allowing such people to live in the country. No convert was safe with them around since they would not hesitate "for little mony (to) betray a Member of Christ to be Crucified by them" (p. 27).

141

George Fox's (1624–1691) conversionist tract, *A Declaration to the Iewes*, repeated many of the classic Christian accusations against the Jewish people concerning their part in the Crucifixion. After reminding the reader how the Jews had rejected Jesus, put him to death on the cross, and cast lots for his garments, Fox tried to show that this was in fulfillment of various biblical prophesies. It was proof that Jesus was the Messiah and that the Jews should accept him as such. Although the work was not intended to be an anti-Jewish tract, Fox's description of the alleged crimes of the Jews reinforced the classic beliefs that had been taught by the church for centuries. For example, he wrote the following concerning Jewish involvement in the Crucifixion: "you would have no King but Caesar, and desired a murtherer, and crucified him; and when Pilate said to you behold your King, and washed his hands from his blood, you cried let his blood be upon us and our children."[23]

Thus, for the sake of bringing Jews closer to Jesus, they and the Christian public had to be reminded of their supposed past sins. Those who were willing to convert would no doubt be forgiven. However, men like Fox stigmatized the great majority of the Jews who resisted such attempts at conversion.

The strong feeling, stimulated by the Puritans and other religious groups, that the Jews should be converted to Christianity if they were to be accepted as part of a Christian commonwealth continued through the end of the century. The fact that the Jews stubbornly rejected the attempts to bring them into the fold made them, in the eyes of the clergy, the objects of both pity and scorn. This can be noted not only in the conversionist literature of the times but also in the many references to Jews made from the pulpits. John Evelyn noted in his diary that he was appointed as a trustee of a bequest by a certain Mr. Boyle to see to it that a minister be appointed to preach a sermon on the first Sunday of each month "expressly against Atheists, Deists, Libertins, Jews, etc. without descending to any other controversy whatever."[24]

Aside from such deliberate attempts to challenge the Jewish faith and to attack the Jewish people, there were numerous derogatory remarks made against Jews and Judaism in sermons which were devoted to the central concerns of the Anglican preachers, including "the rise of infidelity, the danger of scoffing at religion, the problem of justifying faith, and the question of obedience to spiritual guides."[25] On one hand, the clergy had to combat the Puritanism that still remained in the country, and, on the other, they had to deal with deism, which was becoming increasingly popular among those Englishmen who were sick of the strife caused by organized religion. The Jews who had rejected Jesus and his teachings were the classical adversaries of Christianity, and preachers like Isaac Barrow (1630–1677) could use them to illustrate the sins of the modern day enemies of the church. In one popular sermon, Barrow listed the different kinds of infidelity that existed in society. He noted that they stemmed from "stupidity or dullness of apprehension... a stupidity rising from mists of prejudice, from steams of lust and passion."[26] He then pointed out, "This is that, which is so often charged on the Jews as cause of their infidelity; who did hear but not understand, and did see but not perceive; because their heart was gross, and their ears were dull of hearing, and their eyes were closed." Another source of infidelity was perverseness of will, which was a stubborn desire to maintain an opinion in the face of convincing contrary evidence. Barrow noted that "such was the temper of the Jews whom St. Stephen therefore called a stiff-necked people, uncircumcised in heart and ears," who would not yield to "the most winning discourse that ever was uttered." He continued to show how infidelity arose from "Blind zeal grounded upon prejudice" and from corruption of mind by any kind of brutish lust, any irregular passion and bad inclination. In each case he used the Jews as examples to illustrate this sinfulness.

The preachers of the Restoration often repeated the old clichés concerning the Jews, and, like their predecessors, they perpetuated the story of the Crucifixion and the barbaric way that this "cursed people" had supposedly put Jesus to death. Good Friday was always a popular time for such sermons, and Evelyn noted in his diary that on this day in 1689 the Bishop of St. Asaph devoted his talk to the "cruelty and malice of the stubborn Jewes" and how they "crucifie him still by their sins."[27] Advent was another popular time to discuss the Jewish involvement in the Crucifixion. In a sermon delivered in November 1697 at St. Clements, the

143

preacher, a Mr. Adams, discussed how when Jesus came to his people (the Jews), they rejected him. He believed that the Scribes and the Pharisees had poisoned the minds of their countrymen and that when Jesus tried to point out their hypocrisy, they not only persuaded the people to reject him, but they did not rest until they "murdered the Lord of Life which was their utter destruction."[28]

A few preachers of the time tried to reinterpret the Crucifixion, but the slurs against the Jews endured. For example, Dr. Jeane, a divinity professor at Oxford, delivered a sermon at Whitehall during Lent in which he mentioned how "the most wicked Tyrants and men did frequently bring about God Almightys purposes for the good of his children defeating their intentions."[29] He considered the malice that the Jews displayed towards Jesus to be the "instruments of the greatest blessing that ever was bestowed upon mankind."[30] But if the Jews were part of a divine plan, their malicious behavior was still inexcusable. As another preacher so aptly put it, "God determined the death of his sonn, but the Jews did wickedly to put him to death."[31]

In their attempts to stress what they considered were the superior qualities of Christianity, many preachers downgraded Judaism and encouraged anti-Jewish prejudices. For example, one cleric based a sermon on the verse in the Sermon on the Mount which contained the words "resist not evil." He noted that a true Christian should not revenge himself by word or deed upon his neighbor for every slight injury that he might suffer. The Jews, whom he referred to as "a very malicious and revengeful people," had permission to take an eye for an eye and a tooth for a tooth. Jesus came to perfect this law, and he prohibited "all these Jewish revenges and severitys, persuading and requiring meekenesses, and patience, Charity and mercy after his owne blessed Example."[32] Another cleric admitted that Jesus' commandment of loving one another was not really new and was a part of Jewish tradition. However, it was so "worn out and forgotten among the Envious and uncharitable Jewes, that it needed renewing."[33]

Beginning with the Restoration and persisting through the end of the century, the past prejudices against the Jews continued to be echoed from the pulpits of England. The language of the preachers was more refined, and the coarse mediaeval stories were omitted, but the classic attitudes towards Jews and Judaism were virtually unchanged. The Jews were still guilty of contempt and blasphemy. They were a malicious people who failed to appreciate the truth and who had to pay the price for their rejection of Jesus. In what appeared to be an era of greater social acceptance of the Jew in English society, the pulpit orators clung stubbornly to their anti-Jewish doctrines. Of all the molders of public opinion, they were the most reactionary and the most bigoted. This can best be appreciated when their utterances against the Jews are compared with those of playwrights of their day. In the past the theater had been as rich a source of anti-Jewish sentiments as the religious press and the pulpit. This was no longer the case when the playhouses reopened during the reign of Charles II.

Although there had been a number of Jewish characters in English drama during the Elizabethan and Jacobean eras, they were usually ignored by the Restoration dramatists. Perhaps the fact that Charles II gave the Jews his protection when they were threatened by their enemies discouraged the writers under royal patronage from publicly attacking them. It is also possible that these playwrights had such an abundance of source materials for their plays that they did not need the stage Jew to enliven their works.[34] Certainly, during the Restoration, the church had less of an influence upon public opinion than it had enjoyed in the past, and the old religious themes found in earlier plays were not very popular with the playgoers.

It is difficult to locate any significant Jewish characters in Restoration plays. In John Dryden's (1631–1700) *Love Triumphant* (1694) an apostate Jew named Sancho appeared as a minor character. The references made to his Jewish ancestry and personality reflect some of the milder anti-Jewish prejudices of the time. For example, he was referred to as follows by one of his enemies: "His outside's Tawdry, and his inside's Fool. He's an Usurer's Son, and his Father was a Jew" (1.1). Although Sancho had converted to Christianity, he was never allowed to forget his Jewish ancestry. When he was advised not to fight with a Christian lest blood be spilled, Sancho remarked, "Well to save Christian Blood, I will. His opponent replied, "And to save Jewish Blood, that's your Blood Sirrah, I am contented too" (3.1). Sancho was

145

portrayed as a rascal with few scruples, and yet his morals were no better or worse than those of the other Christian characters in the play. This dramatic work, which was the last that Dryden wrote, was a failure; both the play and its Jewish character were quickly forgotten.

A more popular play that contained some minor Jewish characters was *Belphegor, or the Marriage of the Devil* (1691), written by John Wilson (? –1696). The Jews in this particular work were bailiffs who seized furniture that had been sold on credit to some Christians. A few negative remarks were directed to them, but their roles in the play were unimportant. In another work written by Wilson, *The Cheats* (1663), the word "Jew" was used in a derogatory sense to describe a Scotsman, Alderman Whitebroth. When he was referred to as "a Jew indeed" (1.2), he was being described as a stingy, hard-hearted individual. This was the general connotation of the word for the average member of the audience, and it was a part of the everyday speech of the time.

The Jews were considered to be shady individuals with a disreputable past, but there seemed to be no conscious attempt to spread anti-Jewish sentiments from the stage. Jews were not prominent in the mind of the average Englishman, and playwrights did not need to portray them in depth. This was true of other writers of the period. Dryden mentioned the Jews in his work *Absalom and Achitophel* (1681), a biting satire on the political conditions of the country. However, the use of biblical names and places was merely a vehicle to convey the author's political sentiments, and it is doubtful if Dryden had any desire to cast aspersions on either ancient or modern Jewry. He was referring to internal problems in English society when, for example, he wrote:

The Jews, a Headstrong, Moody Murmuring race,
As ever try'd th' extent and stretch of grace;
God's pamper'd people whom, debauch'd with ease,
No King could govern, nor no God could please.
[45–48]

The same can be said for references to Jews in works written in answer to the poem.[35]

Although the native Jews of England were almost ignored by the writers of the period, their brethren on the continent and in Asia Minor continued to interest the public. As in the past, travelers included descriptions of Jewish communal life, customs and ceremonies, and such in their accounts of voyages. In addition, those mystics who anxiously awaited the end of days still believed that the Jews would be instrumental in bringing about this great event. Like their predecessors in Puritan England, they circulated in pamphlet form any accounts of Jewish activities abroad, no matter how fanciful, that would support their views.

In 1665 a short pamphlet, *The Restauration of the Jews: Or a True Relation of Their Progress and Proceedings in Order to the Regaining of their Ancient Kingdom,* appeared. It consisted of excerpts of letters written from Antwerp, Leghorn, and Florence that described how the Jews were supposedly preparing for the conquest of Israel and the reestablishment of their national state. The author did not identify any of the correspondents, but they all had very vivid imaginations and believed the rumors and half-truths about Jewish armies that were being organized to conquer the Holy Land.

In the first letter, sent from Antwerp and dated October 20 1665, the correspondent described how a band of Jews carrying swords, spears, and bows and arrows was being led by a miracle-working holy man on a mission of conquest. He noted that "They had many encounters with people in the way and have taken some places, none being able to withstand them; they put all to the sword except Jews."[36] The writer further claimed that these warriors were all descendants of the ten tribes, whose ancestors did not know Jesus and who now wanted to receive the gospel. They supposedly felt that the church in its present state was corrupt and that their task was to purify it so that the reign of Jesus and his saints could be established. He believed that in the year 1666 the prophesies of both the Old and New Testaments would be fulfilled and that a new era would begin.

In the second letter in the pamphlet, sent from Leghorn, the correspondent described how a group of Jews miraculously defeated a large force of Turkish troops. He claimed that the arrows shot against the Jews turned around in flight and struck down the

147

archers who had aimed them. An equally fanciful tale was told in the next letter in the pamphlet, one sent from Florence. It described a battle between the Jews and the Turks where some eight thousand of the latter group had been killed when their swords and muskets turned against them.[37]

Many mystics in England were drawn to the supposed miraculous deeds of the pseudo-messiah, Sabbetai Zevi (1626–1676), whose meteoric rise to fame occurred at about the time they expected to witness the "end of days." Any news about this "King of the Jews" was eagerly sought after by them and by a great many Englishmen who wanted to know more about this exotic personality. In 1666 a letter sent by the French ambassador at Constantinople to his brother, a resident of Venice, was translated and distributed in London. It disclosed that the ambassador took the stories of Sabbetai Zevi's miracles quite seriously. He repeated the tales that the "King of the Jews" was able to predict the time of death of people and that he could walk through fire without damaging his clothes or singeing a hair on his head. He quoted Sabbetai Zevi as promising "that in the month of June next, the Redemption of Israel will be published through the whole World."[38]

Henry Oldenburg, (1615?–1677) secretary of the Royal Society, was so interested in the stories and half-truths he had heard regarding the pseudo-messiah that he wrote to Benedict Spinoza and asked if it were true that the Jews would soon be returning to Israel. He noted in the letter that "Few in this place believe it, but many wish it." Oldenburg seemed in favor of a return of the Jews, but he was also concerned about the implications of such an event. "I should like to know what the Jews in Amsterdam have heard about the matter," he asked Spinoza, "and how they are affected by such an important announcement which if it were true would seem to bring a crisis in the whole world."[39]

The following entry in Pepys's *Diary* for February 19, 1665, sums up the intensity of the messianic fervor of the time and illustrates how both Jew and Christian sensed that dramatic events were about to unfold:

> I am told for certain what I have heard once or twice already, of a Jew in town, that in the name of the rest do offer to give any man ten

pounds to be paid 100 pounds if a certain person now at Smyrna . . . is the true Messiah. One named a friend of his that had received ten pieces of gold upon this score, and says that the Jew hath disposed of 1100 pounds in this manner, which is very strange; and certainly this year of 1666 will be a year of great action; but what the consequences of it will be, God knows.

[5:212]

Although several Jews in England continued to believe in Sabbetai Zevi even after he renounced his faith, the Christian community soon lost interest in him, and it is doubtful if he had any lasting effect upon Christian-Jewish relations.[40]

During the last decades of the century, the major interest in the Jews centered around their mercantile status and their growing affluence. William III, who succeeded James II in 1688, continued the friendly policies of his predecessors towards the Jewish community.[41] Because he was the ruler of both England and the Netherlands, the Jewish merchants and bankers of London and Amsterdam established even closer connections than had existed in previous decades. This connection had definite advantages for the Jews and the king, but it was detrimental to the English merchants. Although the enemies of the Jews attacked them for being both aliens and infidels, the Christians used this religious abuse to strengthen their arguments against Jewish commercial privileges and in favor of having Jews pay alien duties.[42] As in the past, jealousy over commercial success resulted in slanders against the Jewish community. Jews were blamed, for example, for the miserable condition of the English subjects who were enslaved in Algiers and for the difficulties encountered in arranging for their ransom. In addition, the city fathers of London were always anxious to discover any petty breach of the law involving Jews. Eventually, high officials from the Lord Mayor on down received gifts from the Jews of the city to maintain their good will.

But more important considerations than this bribery persuaded the authorities to allow the Jews to remain in the country unmolested. Economic writers advocated liberty of conscience as a means of attracting foreign immigrants, discouraging emigration, and improving trade. Those who studied the commercial success of the Netherlands appreciated the financial benefits of religious

149

toleration and urged that it become part of the English way of life. As early as 1669 a parliamentary committee dealing with the decay of trade that England was experiencing advised that "some ease and relaxation in ecclesiastical matters would be a means of improving the trade of this Kingdom."[43]

In 1685, when Louis XIV revoked the Edict of Nantes, English industry benefited from the immigration of thousands of Huguenot craftsmen, many of whom were skilled in the weaving of silk. Realizing the advantages that his country would gain over her commercial rivals, Sir Joshua Child (1630–1699), president of the East India Company, urged that Jews and other foreign merchants be allowed to become citizens of England. He believed that although they might hurt a few native traders, they would nevertheless benefit the country as a whole. Jewish thriftiness would also set a good example for the English to follow. He advocated that the Jews be granted internal autonomy as an incentive to settle in the country.[44] This hope, expressed by men like Joshua Child, of ultimately emancipating the Jew was in keeping with the spirit of the emerging capitalism of the time, which stressed the need for individual freedom so that each person would have the maximum opportunity to develop his economic potential and that of society as well.[45] The acceptance of the Jew as an equal was part of this new freedom that went beyond the realm of economics and which touched upon the religious toleration of all dissenting groups. John Locke (1632–1704) was one of the most persuasive spokesmen for those who advocated religious liberty. He firmly rejected the idea that church and state were integrally linked and that membership in one involved membership in the other. The role of the state was to preserve order, settle disputes, and protect life and property. The church, in contrast, was concerned with the worship of God and with the salvation of souls. Neither should have the right to interfere with the affairs of the other. Locke viewed toleration in terms of the extent of power that the civil magistrates had in religious affairs.[46] He believed that only for the sake of preserving the peace did the government have the authority to restrict the practices of any group. Locke considered the few Jews who lived in the country to be members of a community who, unlike the Catholics, were no threat to the civil government. They were, therefore, entitled to be treated as equals with other law abiding citizens.

> Those whose doctrine is peaceable, and whose manners are pure and blameless, ought to be upon equal terms with their fellow subjects .... If we may openly speak the truth, and as becomes one man to another, neither pagan nor Mahometan, nor Jew, ought to be excluded from the civil rights of the commonwealth because of his religion.[47]

In his personal attitudes Locke may have been able to shake off anti-Jewish prejudices inherited from the past. Yet they persisted not only in religious and secular literature, but in Parliament as well. As late as 1689 the House of Commons passed a resolution ordering a bill to be introduced that would place an additional tax of 100,000 pounds on the Jewish community. The bill, despite its defeat, showed that for some Englishmen the mediaeval approach of squeezing the Jew for needed revenue was not dead.

By the turn of the century the Jews in England were in a much better situation than were their brethren elsewhere in Europe. Economically, they were secure, and their right to live in peace and to practice their faith was established. They were not restricted to a ghetto, and there were no government sanctioned anti-Jewish outbreaks. Zealous churchmen were still concerned about saving the Jews' souls and keeping Christians out of their clutches. Jews still were objects of scorn for those who needed an outlet for their frustrations. However, the decline of the authority of the church, the growth of industry and trade with its stress upon the need for individual freedom, and the social philosophies of men like John Locke all contributed to a greater toleration of the Jews in England. The progress that the Jewish community of England had made up to the end of the century was to be consolidated in the years ahead. Complete economic, social, and political emancipation would ultimately be theirs.

SEVEN

CONCLUSIONS

Anti-Jewish attitudes in England during the four centuries that elapsed from the time of the expulsion through the period of the reestablishment of a small Jewish community in England, quite clearly originated from, and were nurtured by, the fundamental teachings of the church. The clerics believed that if Christianity was indeed the true faith and its followers were the new Israel, then Judaism had to be discredited in the eyes of the faithful. In mediaeval sermons, plays, and religious literature, the Jews were often portrayed as the adversaries of the church who from the time of the Crucifixion threatened good Christians. They were pictured as grotesque individuals, ever ready to steal consecrated wafers, murder innocent children, and mock the rituals and the beliefs of the true faith. Christianity's superior powers could ultimately defeat these demons, and the faithful were reassured that their trust in the sacraments would protect them from all harm. By constantly downgrading the Jews and their beliefs, and by linking them with the devil as an object for the projection of hostilities, the clerics hoped that the people would better appreciate the Christian faith. Whatever success the church enjoyed in enhancing its image in this manner was achieved at the expense of the Jews. While there was hardly a significant number of Jews in England after 1290, their role as scapegoat was hallowed by tradition and became part of religious teachings transcending Christian denominational lines.

152

The three major religious groups which successively exercised religious authority during these four centuries—Catholics, Anglicans, and Puritans— shared a common approach to the Jews. Whatever differences existed among them in the realm of Christian practices and beliefs disappeared when they wrote or spoke about ancient or contemporary Jewry. There was a remarkable similarity in the way that the Jews were treated in the sermons delivered by the clerics of the three groups, and, with the exception of some of the cruder stories found in the orations of the mediaeval preachers, the seventeenth-century clergymen repeated from their pulpits the stock anti-Jewish sentiments of the past. In many instances the Jews were mentioned only indirectly to emphasize the superiority of some Christian principle. Yet, the cumulative effect of these derogatory references was considerable, especially as this blended into an already rich anti-Jewish folklore. The few clerics who attempted to reinterpret the significance of the Crucifixion and to minimize the role played by the Jews were certainly not in the mainstream of Christian thought. It is doubtful if they had any meaningful effect upon attitudes.

Much has been written about the Puritan identification with ancient Israel and with the Hebraic Bible. Yet, from a theological viewpoint, in the Puritan literature and sermons the position of the Jews in relation to the Christians had not changed. Writers and preachers who urged that the Jews be treated with respect and love were motivated primarily by strong desires to convert them. Many of these Puritans had messianic dreams, and they believed that the ultimate conversion of the Jews would be an important part of the final redemption of all mankind. Scarcely any of them could accept the Jews on their own, and any attempts to read genuine religious toleration into their works is doomed to failure. The final rejection of any open readmission of the Jews on the part of the clergy is indicative of their belief that the Jewish people were a despised, accursed group who should not come into contact with good Christians. The mediaeval image which Christians had inherited and which they had willingly sustained was too much a part of them to be cast aside.

Christian teachings concerning the accursedness of the Jew radiated out into all aspects of English culture. Once the church had created a socially accepted scapegoat, the dramatist and the writer had a ready-made villain that they could exploit in their works. The hook-nosed, red-bearded Judas evolved in Elizabethan drama into the characters of Barabbas and Shylock. Their very features were enough to remind the audience of the connection that existed between these men and the Jew who betrayed Jesus for thirty pieces of silver. The church had done its job well; whenever the Jew appeared on the stage, he was haunted by the demonic image that had been perpetuated through the centuries. In Restoration drama; the Jewish villain almost disappeared, yet, the mention of the word "Jew" carried connotations of scorn and contempt. The same can be said of the evolution of the Jew in fiction, where old prejudices lingered on, nurtured by the teachings of the church.

The Jew, long associated in Christian teachings with the devil, was the logical person to be branded as a subversive. Along with the witch and the Catholic, he was the focus of the irrational fears of the multitudes. Yet, with the exception of the Lopez trial and a few less dramatic incidents, the actual Jews living in England were left in peace. Perhaps the main reason why England never had an organized anti-Jewish policy after the expulsion was that there were too few Jews in the country to pose a serious threat to the religious establishment. Thus, scattered Jewish families were not disturbed, even though theoretically they were forbidden to live in the country. There is evidence that on a number of occasions both their neighbors and the authorities knew of their presence. Only when undue attention was focused on individual Jews was any action taken. The mind of the English people was such that a group of strangers could be tolerated in their midst as long as they remained small in number and did not disturb the status quo.

During Cromwell's time the thought that a large number of Jews might swarm into the country aroused the ire of religious leaders and of the common citizen as well. In addition to being objectionable in a religious sense, the Jews were viewed as a group of foreigners who owed their prime allegiance to a nation in exile.

They were strangers not only in a religious sense, but also in a national and ethnic one. An occasional Jewish trader who sought freedom from Spanish oppression could be tolerated and even protected in the law courts. However, the thought that the country could be flooded with many such individuals who had connections with their co-religionists all over the world was unacceptable to the people, particularly to the native merchants. The rulers of England saw the value of Jewish mercantile connections, and men like Cromwell appreciated their potential value to the country. However, the masses, having been exposed to the classic Christian approach to the Jews, the mediaeval folklore concerning their mysterious rites and barbaric customs, and the image of the usurous stage Jew, were not sympathetic to the readmission. The fact that a man like William Prynne could amass in such a short time so much anti-Jewish material is indicative of the covert hatred that existed in English society during the Commonwealth.

The Jews of the Restoration were able to live undisturbed because of the protection they received from the crown in exchange for their economic services and because of the tact that their leaders displayed in keeping them out of the public eye. Although Jews appeared in a negative light in conversionist tracts and their observers both at home and abroad viewed them through glasses tinted with centuries of prejudice, the small number of Jews in the country was important in minimizing hostility towards them. Periodically, the hatred spawned in the past came to haunt the Jews. Men like Thomas Violet and Samuel Hayne, for example, claimed that in addition to their economic crimes the Jews were a threat to Christianity; clearly the teachings of the church could be used for any number of purposes by the hate-monger or by the charlatan who was seeking financial gain.

Ultimately, the increasing secularism of the age, the spirit of emerging capitalism, and the new social philosophies pushed many of these anti-Jewish attitudes into the background. It was not any significant change in Christian doctrine that encouraged the eventual toleration of the Jew in society. Instead, in the years that followed, forces beyond the realm of organized religion brought this goal to fruition, and they eventually made England a haven for Jews seeking refuge from persecution.

NOTES

PREFACE

1. Nicholas Berdyaev, *Christianity and Anti-Semitism* (Sussex, England: Ditchling Press, 1952), p. 9.

CHAPTER 1

1. Salo W. Baron, *The Jewish Community–Its History and Structure to the American Revolution* (Philadelphia: Jewish Publication Society, 1948), 2: 246. (Hereafter Jewish Publication Society will be referred to as J.P.S.)
2. Letter to Lady Margaret de Quincy from Robert Grosseteste as cited by Lee M. Friedman, *Robert Grosseteste and the Jews* (Cambridge, Mass.: Harvard University Press, 1934), p. 13.
3. Ibid., p. 15.
4. Joshúa Trachtenberg, *The Devil and the Jews: The Medieval Conception of the Jew and its Relation to Modern Anti-Semitism* (New York: Harper & Row, 1966), p. 7.
5. Thomas of Monmouth was a monk in the Benedictine monastery of Norwich who lived at the time of the ritual murder accusations of 1144. For a full account of the alleged crime committed by the Jews, see his work, *The Life and Miracles of Saint William of Norwich*.
6. Mathew of Paris (1200–1259) was a noted chronicler who recorded in his *Chronica Majora* the supposed role of the Jews in the murder of Hugh of Lincoln.
7. Cecil Roth, "The Medieval Conception of the Jew," in Cecil Roth, ed., *Personalities and Events in Jewish History* (Philadelphia: J.P.S., 1962), p. 67.
8. As Harold Fisch points out, "It is no accident that the revival of the blood libel has always been associated with actual outbreaks of violence against the Jews: The myth is clearly produced to justify by anticipation the crime already meditated in the unconscious." *The Dual Image: The Figure of the Jew in English and American Literature* (New York: Ktav Publishing House, 1971), p. 23.
9. Trachtenberg, p. 140.
10. Langmuir notes that this was due to the newness of the Jews in the country and the people's relative unfamiliarity with them. This situation, combined with the Jews' theological status as deicides made them a much more suitable object for fantasies in England than on the Continent. (From Gavin Langmuir, "Rumours Spread," unpublished ms., Department of History, Stanford University.)
11. Harry Lowenfeld, in discussing the importance of the belief in the Devil, points out

156

that: "he [the devil] arises from the ambivalence of the drives, from the need to preserve the love object and to protect it from hostile feelings and from the resulting necessity of finding an object for one's hatred. The projection of one's hostile wishes onto the adversary—the evil fiend—is critical in this mechanism. It serves to remove the burden of guilt, since all guilt can be ascribed to the Evil one." "The Decline in the Belief in the Devil," *Psychoanalytic Quarterly* 38 (1969): 457.

12. Homer G. Pfander, "The Popular Sermon of the Medieval Friar in England," unpublished Ph.D. dissertation, Department of English, New York University, 1937, pp. 3–5.

13. According to Gerould these legendary anecdotes in praise of the Virgin "contain very much that is sordid, a great deal that is frivolous, and not a little that seems to us immoral and blasphemous." Gordon Hall Gerould, *Saints' Legends* (Boston: Houghton Mifflin Co., 1916), pp. 149–50.

14. Keith Thomas, *Religion and the Decline of Magic: Studies in Popular Beliefs in Sixteenth and Seventeenth Century England* (London: Weidenfeld and Nicolson, 1971), pp. 26, 49.

15. Katherine Lee Bates, *The English Religious Drama* (1893; rpt. Port Washington, New York: Kennikat Press, 1966), p. 21.

16. Ezekial Kaufman, *Golah Venechar* (Tel Aviv: Dvir Ltd., 1930), 2: 461.

17. H. R. Trevor-Roper, "The European Witch-Craze of the Sixteenth and Seventeenth Centuries," in his *The European Witch-Craze of the Sixteenth and Seventeenth Centuries and Other Essays* (1956; rpt. New York and Evanston: Harper Torchbook, 1969), p. 114.

CHAPTER 2

1. Gavin Langmuir, "Anti-Judaism as the Necessary Preparation for Anti-Semitism," *Viator* 2 (1971): 388.

2. M. J. Landa, *The Jew in Drama* (New York: William Morrow & Co., 1927), p. 9.

3. Wolfgang S. Seiferth, *Synagogue and Church in the Middle Ages: Two Symbols in Art and Literature* (New York: Frederick Ungar Publishing Co., 1970), p. 80.

4. Landa, pp. 10–11.

5. Maurice Hussey, ed., *The Chester Mystery Plays* (New York: Theatre Arts Books, 1957), p. 99.

6. Williams notes that "the attempt to excuse Pilate as far as possible began very early and is probably a reflection of early Christianity's turning from the Jews to the Gentiles. The development of a sympathetic attitude towards Pilate can be traced even in the canonical gospels." He states that in the Chester Cycles in addition to the competition from characters like Annas, Caiaphas, Judas, and Herod, Pilate is portrayed as a weak individual who was pushed by the Jews to condemn Jesus. See Arnold Williams, *The Characterization of Pilate in the Towneley Plays* (East Lansing: Michigan State University Press, 1950), pp. 2, 19.

7. Hijman Michelson, *The Jew in Early English Literature* (Amsterdam: H. J. Paris, 1926), pp. 59–60.

8. Edward H. Weatherly, ed., *Speculum Sacerdotale* (London: Oxford University Press, 1936), pp. 104–5.

9. *The Northern Passion* was a lengthy poem composed in the north of England between the close of the thirteenth century and the beginning of the fourteenth. It was written to give religious instruction to the masses in a popular form. Minstrels incorporated it into

their repertoires, and the work became source material for playwrights. Selections from the poem also found their way into the Northern Homily Collection, a kind of sermon manual for parish priests. Thus, its message was heard from both the stage and the pulpit. The fairly large number of extant manuscripts of the poem is a good indication of the popularity of the work. Francis A. Foster, ed., *The Northern Passion* (Oxford: Oxford University Press, 1916), pp. 1–2.

10. Richard Morris, ed., *Legends of the Holy Rood: Symbols of the Passion and Cross-Poems in Old English of the Eleventh, Fourteenth and Fifteenth Centuries* (London: N. Trubner & Co., 1871), p. 84.

11. Eugen Kolbing and Mabel Day, eds., *The Siege of Jerusalem* (London: Oxford University Press, 1932), pp. xix–xxix.

12. Cited in part in G. R. Owst, *Literature and Pulpit in Medieval England* (Oxford: Oxford University Press, 1961), p. 339.

13. Thomas Wimbledon, *Wimbledon's Sermon Redde Rationem Villicationis Tue: A Middle English Sermon of the Fourteenth Century*, ed. Ione Kemp Knight (Pittsburgh: Duquesne University Press, 1967), lines 1051–54.

14. John Mirk, the author of this work, was canon of Lilleshall in Shropshire. He lived sometime in the fifteenth century. See *Mirk's Festial: A Collection of Homilies*, ed. Theodore Erbe (London: Kegan Paul, Trench, Trubner & Co., 1905), pp. 108–09.

15. Ibid., pp. 248–49.

16. Mary Macleod Banks, ed., *An Alphabet of Tales: An English 15th Century Translation of the Alphabetum Narrationum of Etienne de Besancon, Parts I and II* (London: Kegan Paul, Trench, Trubner & Co., 1904–05), p. 159.

17. Mirk, pp. 14–15.

18. *Middle English Sermons Edited from British Museum MS. Royal 18B xxiii*, ed. Woodburn Ross (Oxford: Oxford University Press, 1960), pp. 63–65.

19. G. R. Owst, *Preaching in Medieval England–An Introduction to Sermon Manuscripts of the Period 1350–1450* (Cambridge: Cambridge University Press, 1926), p. 185.

20. *Alphabet of Tales*, pt. 2, pp. 277–78.

21. Ibid., pp. 176–77.

22. The legend of Theophilus was probably the most popular legend in the mediaeval world and it exists in several different versions. He was the Vicedominus of the bishop of Cilia in the sixth century. This was confused by later writers with Sicily and in the *North English Homily Collection* it appears as Cizile. Gordon Hall, *The North English Homily Collection: A Study of the Manuscript Relations and of the Sources of the Tales* (Oxford, 1902), p. 76.

23. Trachtenberg, pp. 142–43.

24. *Alphabet of Tales*, pp. 110–12.

25. Arthur Brandeis, ed., *Jacob's Well: An English Treatise on the Cleansing of Man's Conscience* (London: Oxford University Press, 1900), p. 177.

26. *Speculum Sacerdotale*, p. 10.

27. Ibid., pp. 187–88.

28. Mirk, pp. 149–54.

29. J. J. Bagley, *Historical Interpretation: Sources of English Medieval History, 1066–1540* (London: Penguin Books, 1965), p. 174.

30. Ibid., p. 171.

31. Juliana of Norwich, *Sixteen Revelations of Divine Love*, ed. Grace Warrack (London: 1972), p. 68.

32. *The Book of Margery Kempe*, ed. W. Butler-Bowdon (London: Jonathan Cape Ltd., 1963), p. 274.
33. Edgar Rosenberg, *From Shylock to Svengali—Jewish Stereo-Types in English Fiction* (Stanford, Calif.: Stanford University Press, 1960), p. 24.
34. Richard J. Schoeck, "Chaucer's Prioress: Mercy and Tender Heart," in *Chaucer Criticism*, ed. Richard Shoeck and Jerome Taylor (Notre Dame, Ind.: University of Notre Dame Press, 1960), pp. 246, 253.
35. *The Prioress and the Critics* (Berkeley: University of California Press, 1965), pp. 1, 35. See also Edwin J. Howard, *Geoffrey Chaucer*, Twayne's English Author Series 1 (New York: Twayne Publishers, Inc. 1964), p. 168.
36. See, for example, Shoeck, p. 255.
37. Paul Franklin Baum, "The Mediaeval Legend of Judas Iscariot," *PMLA* 21 (1916), p. 483.
38. James Parkes, "Jewish Christian Relations in England," *Three Centuries of Anglo-Jewish History*, ed. V. D. Lipman (Cambridge: Jewish Historical Society of England, 1961), p. 151. (Hereafter Jewish Historical Society of England will be referred to as J.H.S.E.)
39. It should be noted the chroniclers such as Richard Grafton and John Fortesque, who wrote about the events in England after 1290, did not mention the presence of Jews in the country. One exception was John Capgrave (1393–1464), who made a vague reference to some Jews who were put to death in 1318 for assisting in the poisoning of some wells. See his *The Chronicle of England*, ed. Francis Charles Hingeston (London: Longman, Brown, Green, Logmans and Roberts, 1858), p. 186.
40. E. Nathan Adler, *History of the Jews in London* (Philadelphia: J.P.S., 1930), p. 73.
41. E. Nathan Adler, *Auto da Fé and the Jew* (London: H. Frowde, 1908), p. 20.
42. Cecil Roth, "Sir Edward Brampton, Alias Duarte Brandao Governor of Guernsey 1482–1485," in Roth's *Essays and Portraits in Anglo-Jewish History* (Philadelphia: J.P.S., 1962), p. 68.
43. Ibid., p. 79.
44. Lucien Wolf, "Jews in Tudor England," in *Essays in Jewish History*, ed. Cecil Roth (London: J.H.S.E., 1934), p. 74.
45. Ibid.
46. Adler, *Auto da Fé*, p. 19.
47. Levit. 18:16 states, "Thou shalt not uncover the nakedness of thy brother's wife: it is thy brother's nakedness." Deut. 25:5 seems to contradict this. "If brethren dwell together, and one of them die, and have no child, the wife of the dead shall not be married abroad unto one not of his kin; her husband's brother shall go in unto her and take her to him to wife and perform the duty of a husband's brother unto her."
48. R. Weiss, "Learning and Education in Western Europe from 1470–1520," in *The Cambridge Modern History*, 1: *The Renaissance 1493–1520*, ed. G. R. Potter (Cambridge: Cambridge University Press, 1961), p. 120.
49. Hans Brown, "Fifteenth Century Civilization and the Renaissance," in *The Cambridge Modern History*, 1: 56.
50. H. P. Stokes, "The Jews in Cambridge from the Expulsion to the Return," in *Studies in Anglo-Jewish History* (Edinburgh: Ballantyne, Hanson & Co., 1913), pp. 209–10. Stokes does not give the full citation of this letter.
51. Cecil Roth, *A History of the Jews in England* (Oxford: Clarendon Press, 1964), p. 148.
52. Wolf, "Jews in Tudor England," pp. 89–90.

CHAPTER 3

1. E.M.W. Tillyard, *The Elizabethan World Picture* (New York: Vintage Books,), p. 4.
2. S. Ettinger, "The Beginnings of the Change in the Attitude of European Society Towards the Jews," in *Scripta Hierosolymitana*, ed. Alexander Fuks and Israel Halpern (Jerusalem: Hebrew University Press, 1961), 3: 195.
3. *Execution of Justice in England*, cited by Godwin Smith, *A History of England* (New York: Charles Scribner's Sons, 1966), p. 261.
4. Hersch L. Zitt, "The Jew in the Elizabethan World Picture," *Historia Judaica* 14 (1952): 53–54.
5. *D'Ewes Journals*, pp. 508–9, as cited by Sidney Lee, "Elizabethan England and the Jews," *Transactions of the New Shakespeare Society* (1887–90), p. 155.
6. C. J. Sisson, "A Colony of Jews in Shakespeare's London," *Essays and Studies* 23 (1938): 41, 45, 51. Sisson does not give the source of the last two statements.
7. "Jews in Elizabethan England," *Transactions of the Jewish Historical Society of England* 11 (1928): 33–35. In this lengthy article Wolf gives a full listing of all the known Jews who lived in England at the time of Elizabeth. (Hereafter *Transactions of the Jewish Historical Society of England* will be referred to as T.J.H.S.E.)
8. Letter to Rodrigo Lopez as cited by Wolf, "Jews in Elizabethan Society," p. 20.
9. Ibid., 11: 21.
10. Albert M. Hyamson, *A History of the Jews in England* (London: Methuen & Co., 1928), p. 116.
11. Wolf, *T.J.H.S.E.* 11: 22.
12. Norman F. Cantor, *The English: A History of Politics and Society to 1760* (New York: Simon & Shuster, 1967), p. 396.
13. Martin Hume, "The So Called Conspiracy of Dr. Ruy Lopez," *T.J.H.S.E.*, 6(1908):37.
14. Lee, p. 162. Lee does not give any direct citation for this poem other than the fact that it was found in *Popish Plots and Treasons from the Beginning of the Reign of Queen Elizabeth*.
15. Thomas, *Religion and the Decline of Magic*, p. 271.
16. George Lyman Kittredge, *Witchcraft in Old and New England* (Cambridge, Mass.: Harvard University Press, 1929), pp. 195, 68.
17. Thomas, p. 295.
18. "European Witch-Craze," p. 110.
19. D. W. Davies describes the Sherley family as follows: "Like so many of their contemporaries they were gentlemen on the make. Chicanery, larceny, adultery, heroism, and treachery figured in their story. Such peccadilloes were to be found in the lives of many of their peers, but the Sherleys possessed a talent for carrying such matters to extremes." *Elizabethans Errant: The Strange Fortunes of Sir Thomas Sherley and His Three Sons* (Ithaca, N.Y.: Cornell University Press, 1967), p. 1.
20. Ibid., pp. 181–82.
21. Sir Thomas Sherley the Younger to James I, 1607. H.M.C. Salisbury Mss., 19 (1965), cited by Davies, p. 182.
22. E. R. Samuel, "Portuguese Jews in Jacobean London," *T.J.H.S.E.* 18 (1953–55): 183, 187.
23. Fernando de Mercado, one of the secret Jews who started the trouble, was able to bribe the Earl of Suffolk not to "discover" his Judaism. He thus remained in England unmolested. Francisco Pinta de Britto, another secret Jew who was well known on the Royal Exchange, remained in England until his death in 1618.

NOTES

24. "Two Jews Before the Privy Council and an English Law Court in 1614–15," *Jewish Quarterly Review* 14 (1902): 354. (Hereafter the *Jewish Quarterly Review* will be referred to as *J.Q.R.*)

25. "Fruitfull Lessons Upon the Passion," in *Writings and Translations of Myles Coverdale*, ed. George Pearson (Cambridge: Cambridge University Press, 1844), p. 311.

26. "An Homily or Sermon Concerning the Nativity of our Saviour Jesus Christ," in *Certain Sermons Appointed by the Queen's Majesty*, ed. G. E. Corrie (London: John W. Parker, 1850), p. 407.

27. Bishop Pilkington, "An Homily Against Excess of Apparel," ibid., p. 316.

28. Bishop Pilkington, "An Homily of the Right Use of the Church or Temple of God and the Reverence Due Unto the Same," ibid., p. 569.

29. "An Homily Against Disobedience and Willful Rebellion," ibid., p. 569.

30. "A Sermon Preached before the King's Majestie at White-Hall on the VI of April, MDCIII, Being Good Friday," in *Sermons*, ed. G. M. Story (Oxford: Clarendon Press, 1967), p. 159.

31. Lee, p. 143.

32. Robert Wilson, *The Three Ladies of London*, in *A Select Collection of Old English Plays*, ed. W. Carew Hazlett (London: Reeves & Turner 1874), 6: 397.

33. Arthur Bivins Stonex, "The Usurer in Elizabethan Drama," *PMLA* 31 (1916): 195.

34. Douglas Cole, *Suffering and Evil in the Plays of Christopher Marlowe* (Princeton, New Jersey: Princeton University Press, 1962), p. 123.

35. G. K. Hunter, "The Theology of Marlowe's The Jew of Malta," *Journal of the Warburg and Courtauld Institutues* 27 (1964): 214.

36. Ibid., p. 234.

37. David Philipson, *The Jew in English Fiction* (Cincinnati: Robert Clarke & Co., 1889), p. 27.

38. Hunter, p. 235. Cole states that "the Christians come in for criticism, either directly through the words of Barabbas or indirectly through the implications of their actions, to the degree that they betray their faith and approach the absolute 'Jewishness'—the avarice and the egoism—of Barabbas, to the degree that they substitute gold for God" (p. 135).

39. J. B. Steane, *Marlowe: A Critical Study* (Cambridge: Cambridge University Press, 1964), pp. 168–69.

40. "The Jew of Malta," in *Marlowe: A Collection of Critical Essays*, ed. Clifford Leech (Englewood Cliffs, N.J.: Prentice Hall, 1964), p. 156.

41. Hyam Maccoby believes that this is very significant and claims that "The Jew is the Man in Possession, who possesses both the Treasure and the Daughter. The Christians whose power over the Jews was actually limitless, never lost the feeling that they were dispossessed. They identified themselves with the Young Man, who comes to the rich Father and carries off his material and sexual treasure." He suggests that the plays reveal that Christian hatred of the Jews was oedipal in nature. They viewed the Jew as the bad father and identified him with the angry Christian Father-God. See Maccoby's "The Delectable Daughter," *Midstream* 16 (Nov. 1970): 51.

42. Fisch, p. 35.

43. Nevill Coghill, "The Basis of Shakespearian Comedy," in *Essays and Studies III*, ed. Rostrevor Hamilton (London: John Murray, 1950), p. 21. See also Barbara K. Lewalski, "Biblical Allusion and Allegory in The Merchant of Venice," *Shakespeare Quarterly* 13 (1962): 331.

44. Lewalski, pp. 328–29.
45. Ibid., pp. 331, 338.
46. A. D. Moody, "An Ironic Comedy," in *Twentieth Century Interpretations of The Merchant of Venice*, ed. Sylvan Barnet (Englewood Cliffs, N.J.: Prentice-Hall, 1970), p. 101.
47. *The Truth About Shylock* (New York: Random House, 1962), p. 34.
48. The two sides of Shylock, i.e., being a sinner and also being sinned against, prompted Arye Ibn Zahav to propose the theory that the personality of Shylock is actually a composite picture of two different characterizations of the man written at different times. He believes that Shakespeare first pictured the Jew in bleak terms in a work of his, *The Jew of Venice*. Later, after the Lopez incident, Shakespeare realized the human qualities of the Jew, Shylock, and added to his original work a new dimension to his personality. Ibn Zahav attempts to prove this by showing how in *The Merchant of Venice* there is contradiction between the man who supposedly lends Bassanio money in the hope of teaching him a lesson in humility, and the hate-filled usurer who is willing to kill the Christian for the sake of revenge. Although his whole theory is based on the flimsiest evidence, it does point out that Shylock is much more than a simple villain without any trace of humanity. See his "Demuto Shel Shylock Mehasocher Mevenetzia," *Tarbiz* 13 (1942): 178–90.
49. Cary B. Graham, "Standards of Value in The Merchant of Venice," *Shakespeare Quarterly* 4 (1953): 147.
50. William Shakespeare, *The Merchant of Venice*, ed. Arthur Quiller-Couch and John Dover Wilson (Cambridge: Cambridge University Press, 1962), p. xviii.
51. "Shakespeare, the Jews and *The Merchant of Venice*," *Shakespeare Quarterly* 20 (1969): 4.
52. "Love's Wealth and the Judgement of *The Merchant of Venice*." in *Twentieth Century Interpretations of The Merchant of Venice*, ed. Sylvan Barnet (Englewood Cliffs, N.J.: Prentice Hall, 1970), p.89.
53. Modder, pp. 28–29.
54. In 1652, when there was talk of readmitting the Jews to England, a special edition of *The Merchant of Venice* was published. At the time the theaters had been closed by the Puritans, and it is possible that it was printed to sway public opinion against the readmission.
55. *The Unfortunate Traveller*, in *The Works of Thomas Nashe*, ed. Ronald B. McKerrow, Vol. 2 (London: Sidgwick and Jackson, 1910), p. 310.
56. G. R. Hibbard, *Thomas Nashe: A Critical Introduction* (Cambridge, Mass.: Harvard University Press, 1962) pp. 172–73.
57. Fisch, *Dual Image*, p. 38.
58. Montague Frank Modder, *The Jew in the Literature of England to the End of the Nineteenth Century* (1939; rpt. Philadelphia: J.P.S., 1944), p. 19.
59. *Chronicles of England, Scotland and Ireland* (New York: AMS Press, 1965), 3: 492.
60. Henry Blunt, the author of *A Voyage to the Levant*, which described his travels in the early part of the seventeenth century, noted in the opening pages that one of the objects of his journey was "In some measure to acquaint my selfe with those other sects which live under the Turkes, as Greekes, Armenians, Freinks, and Zinganaes, but especially the Iewes; a race from all others so averse both in nature and institution, as glorying to single selfe out of the rest of mankinde remaines obstinate contemptible and famous." Blunt's *A Voyage to the Levant* (1636) is cited by Albert Hyamson, "The Lost Tribes and the Return to England," *T.J.H.S.E.* 5 (1902–1905): 128.

61. *Coryat's Crudities* (London: Printed for W. Cater, 1786) 1: 298. (This is a reprint of the edition of 1611.) Page numbers for future citations from this work are given in the text.

62. The caption for this picture on the frontpiece of the work was: "In vaine doth Coryate pipe and dispute,/ His wench was, Iewes will not be caught with his flute." or "Thy Cortizan clipt thee, ware Tom I advise thee,/ And flie from the Iewes lest they circumcise thee."

63. Cited by Lee, p. 150.

64. *Shakespeare's Europe—Unpublished Chapters of Fynes Moryson's Itinerary.* Cited by A. Cohen, *An Anglo-Jewish Scrapbook 1600–1840* (London: M. L. Cailingold, 1943), p. 143.

65. *The Travels of John Sanderson in the Levant (1584–1602).* Cited by Cohen, p. 15.

66. *The Present State of the Jews: More Particularly Relating to Those in Barbury.* Cited by Cohen, p. 330.

67. Louis Wright, *Middle Class Culture in Elizabethan England* (Ithaca: Cornell University Press, 1958), p. 326.

68. These books are: *The Scepter of Ivoah* (London: Printed by N. Newton and A. Hatfield for Iohn Wright, 1584); *The Coronation of David* (London: Printed by Thomas Orwin for Thomas Gubbin and John Perin, 1588); and *Of The Headstone: By Builders Still Over Much Omitted* (London: Printed by W. Iaggard, 1611).

69. Broughton's arguments for this project can be found in *A Petition to the King (and the Lord's of the Council) to hasten allowance for Ebrew institution of Ebrewes* (London: 1608).

70. *A Require of Agreement to the Groundes of Divinitie Studie: Wherin great scholars falling, and being caught of Iewes disgrace the gospel and trap them to destruction* (No place or publisher given, 1611), p. 1. See also, Broughton, *Two Epistles unto Great men of Britanie in the year 1599 requesting them to put their neckes unto the work of theyr Lord . . .* (No place or publisher given, 1606), pp. Aii–Aiii.

71. *Daniel with a Brief Explication* (Hanaw: Printed by Daniel Aubri, 1607), p. 128.

72. Leon da Modena to Sir William Boswell, 1615, in Cecil Roth, *Anglo-Jewish Letters (1158–1917)* (London: The Soncino Press, 1938), pp. 44–45.

73. Cecil Roth, "Leon da Modena and His English Correspondents," *T.J.H.S.E.* 11 (1924–27): pp. 206–7.

74. "An Early Stuart Judaising Sect," *T.J.H.S.E.* 5 (1939–45): 65.

75. B. D., *A Brief Refutation of John Traske Iudaical and Novel Fancyes* (1618), p. A 2. Another critic of Traske was E. Norici, who wrote a similar tract in 1638 entitled *A Briefe Refutacyon of John Traske.*

76. The speech is cited from the Pagitt Collection in Phillips, p. 67.

77. For the full account of the reason for this statement, see *Calendar State Papers Domestic,* 1627–28, p. 281.

78. *Society and Puritanism in Pre-Revolutionary England* (New York: Schocken Books, 1964), p. 204.

79. Franz Kobler, "Sir Henry Finch (1558–1625) and the First English Advocates of Restoration of the Jews to Palestine," *T.J.H.S.E.* 16 (1945–51): 105.

80. See, for example, Thomas Draxe, *The Worlde's Resurrection* (London: 1608).

81. *The World's Great Restauration or The Calling of the Jews. . . .* (1621), pp. 3–6. Cited by Mordecai Wilensky, *Shivat Hayehudim L'Angliah* (Jerusalem: Reuven Mas, 1943), p. 5.

82. Kobler, p. 116.

83. Wallace Notestein, Helen Francis Relf, and Hartley Simpson, *Commons Debates 1621*

(New Haven: Yale University Press, 1935), 3: 299. (The debate was held on May 24, 1621.)
84. Notestein, *Commons Debates* 2: 70. (The debate was held on May 28, 1621.)
85. Wilensky, p. 1.
86. Leonard Busher, *Religious Peace or a Plea for Liberty of Conscience* (London: Printed for John Sweeting, 1646), p. 2.
87. Ibid., p. 33.

CHAPTER 4

1. Hyamson, *History of the Jews in England*, pp. 135–36.
2. *A Challenge for Beauty*, cited by Modder, *The Jew in the Literature of England to the End of the Nineteenth Century*, p. 28.
3. John Evelyn, *Diary*, ed. E.S. de Bear (Oxford: Clarendon Press, 1955), 2: 293 (Jan. 15, 1645).
4. Letter to Dr. B in James Howell, *Familiar Letters or Epistolae Ho-Elianae* (London: J. M. Dent & Co., 1903), 2: 114.
5. *The Rise of Puritanism or The Way to the New Jerusalem As Set Forth in Pulpit and Press From Thomas Cartwright to John Milton* (New York: Harper Torch Books, 1957), p. 117.
6. W. B. Selbie, "The Influence of the Old Testament on Puritanism," in *The Legacy of Israel*, ed. Edwyn R. Bevan and Charles Singer (Oxford: Clarendon Press, 1953), p. 407–8.
7. Paul Knell, *Israel and England Paralelled, In a Sermon Preached Before the Honorable Society of Grayes-Inne, Upon Sunday in the Afternoon, April 16, 1648* (London, 1648), pp. 14–15. The preacher referred to himself as "Sometimes Chaplain to a Regiment of Curiasiers in his Majesties Army." The text quotation is from p. 16.
8. Robert Johnson, *Lux and Lex or the Light and the Law of Jacob's House: Held Forth in a Sermon Before the Honorable House of Commons March 31, 1647* (London: Printed by A. Miller, 1647), pp. 1–2.
9. J. G., "A Severe Sentence Against Secure Citizens. A Sermon Preached at St. Maries in Oxford," in *The Sage Senator* (London: Printed by J. Cottrel for Sam Speed, 1660), p. 155. The sermon was delivered in 1644.
10. *A Sermon Against False Prophets Preached in St. Maries Church in Oxford, Shortly After the Surrender of that Garrison* (1646), p. 8.
11. *The Devilish Conspiracy, Hellish Treason, Heathenish Condemnation and Damnable Murder Committed, and Executed by the Jews Against the Anointed of the Lord Christ their King* (London: 1648), p. 2. In the copy that I used in the British Museum, the date was altered in ink to read 1649. Either officially or unofficially, the same person who changed the date noted that the author of this printed sermon was the Bishop of Rochester.
12. Ibid., p. 23.
13. Ibid., p. 38.
14. Lithgow cited in Cohen, *Scrapbook*, p. 324.
15. (Newcastle: Printed for William London, 1653), p. 13.
16. John Clare, *The Converted Jew of Certaine Dialogues Between Micheas a Learned Jew and Others Touching Divers Points of Religion, Controverted Between Catholics and Protestants* (MDCXXX), p. 2.
17. One exception to this occurred when a group of freeholders protested against their

tithes. They claimed that such a custom was limited in the Bible to the Land of Judea and after several quotations from scriptures they noted, "And it is the opinion of the Jews at this day (as it is reported by most men that have been amongst them) that if they should come again into the land of Canaan, it were not lawfull for any of them to receive tithes: because they could have no lawfull priesthood, there being none can prove themselves to be of the tribe of Levi." *The Husbandman's Plea Against Tithes* (London: 1647), p. 49.

18. *History of Zionism 1600–1918* (London: Longman's Green & Co., 1919), 1: 40.

19. *Israel's Redemption or the Prophetical History of our Saviours Kingdom on Earth* (London: Printed for Daniel Frere, 1642), pp. 5–6.

20. Robert Maton, *Gog and Magog or the Battle of the Great Day of God Almightie* (Printed by R. Cotes for Daniel Frere, 1642), p. 113. No place of publication given.

21. (London: 1647), pp. 1–2.

22. Wilensky, *Shivat Hayehudim*, p. 32.

23. *The Blessed Jew of Marocco or a Blackmoor Made White* (York: Thomas Broad. 1649), pp. 132–33. Further page references to this work are given in the text.

24. *A Word for the Armie and Two Words to the Kingdome To Cleare the One and Cure the Other* (London: Printed by M. Simmons for Giles Calvert, 1647), p. 11.

25. *The Necessity of Toleration*, p. 265. Cited by Wilensky, *Shivat Hayehudim*, p. 13.

26. Johanna and Ebenezer Cartwright's family settled in Holland during the persecutions of "Bloody Mary." It was there that they came in contact with Jews who told them of the persecutions that their ancestors had suffered in England at the time of Richard and Edward. See *The Petition of the Jewes for the Repealing of the Act of Parliament for their Banishment Out of England* (London: Printed for George Roberts, 1649), p. 3.

27. *Treatise of the Foure Degenerate Sonnes* . . . (London:1636), pp.335–42. The material that follows is from this section.

28. Ibid., pp. 339–40.

29. Ibid., p. 341.

30. Wilensky, p. 7.

31. *The Bloudy Tenent of Persecution, for cause of Conscience, discussed, in A Conference betweene Truth and Peace* (1644), p. 1 of the preface.

32. Ibid., chap. 56.

33. Ibid., pp. 37–38.

34. *Considerations Tending to the Happy Accomplishment of England's Reformation in Church and State* (London: 1647), pp. 23–24.

35. Vernon is difficult to identify. See W. K. Jordan, *The Development of Religious Toleration in England*, vol. 4: *Attainment of the Theory and Accommodations in Thought and Institutions 1640–1660* (1932; rpt. Gloucester, Mass.: Peter Smith, (1964), p. 332.

36. *The sword's abuse asserted: or a word to the army: shewing the weakness of carnal weapons in spiritual warfare etc.* (London: 1648), pp. 13–14. Cited by Jordan, *Religious Toleration*, 4: 335.

37. Nicholas (1593–1669) was a privy councillor and secretary of state to Charles I. See Nicholas's *An apology for the honourable nation of the Jews and all the sons of Israel* (London: 1649). Nicholas quoted Jeremiah 30:16, "Therefore all who devour you shall be devoured, etc."

38. Ibid., pp. 8, 6.

39. Ibid., p. 15.

40. *Anatomy of Melancholy*, ed. Floyd Dell and Paul Jordan Smith (New York: Tudor

Publishing Co. 1938), pt. 3, sec. 4. The following text citations are to this section of the book.

41. Burton viewed the Koran as a "gallimaufry of lies, tales, ceremonies, traditions, precepts, stole from other sects, and confusedly heaped up to delude a company of rude and barbarious clowns." Ibid.

42. William Parncy Dunn, *Sir Thomas Browne, A Study in Religious Philosophy* (Minneapolis: University of Minnesota Press, 1950), p. 14.

43. *Commons Journals*, 5: 512. Cited in Israel Abrahams and C. E. Sayle, "The Purchase of Hebrew Books by the English Parliament in 1647," *T.J.H.S.E.* 8 (1915–17): 70.

44. *Ervbhin or Miscellanies Christian and Judaicall and Others* (London: G. Miller, 1629), p. 103. Page numbers for further citations from this work are given in the text.

45. Selden lived through the reigns of Elizabeth, James I, Charles I, and Cromwell (1584–1659). He was a noted jurist, scholar, and statesman. Some of his works relating to Judaica included, *Dissertatio de anno civili et calendario reipublicae Judaicae* (1644) and *Uxor Ebraica* (1646). For source of the quotation, see Robert Waters, *John Selden and His Table Talk* (New York: Eaton and Mains, 1899), p. 112. Further citations from this work are noted by page numbers in the text.

46. Sheringham (1602–1678) was a royalist clergyman who was educated at Cambridge. Deprived of his office during the time of Cromwell, he fled to the Netherlands where he taught Hebrew and Arabic in Rotterdam.

47. Israel Abrahams, "Isaac Abendana's Cambridge Mishnah and Oxford Calendars," *T.J.H.S.E.*, 8 (1915–17): 116–17.

48. *Foure Degenerate Sonnes*, p. 303.

49. *Diary*, 2: 377 (Feb. 25, 1645).

CHAPTER 5

1. H. N. Brailsford, *The Levellers and the English Revolution* (Stanford: Stanford University Press, 1961), p. 55.

2. Wilbur Cortez Abbott and Catherine D. Crane, *The Writings and Speeches of Oliver Cromwell with an Introduction, Notes and Account of His Life* (Cambridge: Harvard University Press, 1937–39), 2: 182–83.

3. *Proposals for the Propagation of the Gospel, Offered to Parliament* (March 20, 1651), p. 17.

4. For example, Norwood stated, "Why fear not, if you and your doctrines have their foundation in and upon Christ, they shall, they must stand, let the windes blowe, the floods beat. Why man, Christ is a Rock." Ibid., pp. 18–19.

5. Letter to Col. Hammond dated Nov. 6, 1648. Cited by Abbott and Crane, 1: 697.

6. *Seventh Report of the Royal Commission on Historical Manuscripts*, p. 401b. Cited by Mordecai Wilensky, "The Royalist Position Concerning the Readmission of Jews to England," *J.Q.R.* 41 (1951): 398.

7. Carlyle, *Cromwell's Letters and Speeches*, 1: 148. Cited by Lucien Wolf, *Menasseh ben Israel's Mission to Oliver Cromwell* (London: *J.H.S.E.*, 1901), p. xxix.

8. Hyamson, *History of Jews in England*, p. 140. For a detailed account of Jewish aid see Lucien Wolf, "Cromwell's Jewish Intelligencers," in *Essays in Jewish History*, ed. Cecil Roth (London: *J.H.S.E.*, 1934), pp. 91–114.

9. D. Patimkin, "Mercantilism and the Readmission of the Jews to England," *Jewish Social Studies* 7 (1946): 177.

10. Brailsford, p. 395.

NOTES

11. *Judaeorum Memorabilia,* pp. 189–91. Cited by Wilensky, *Shivat Hayehudim,* p. 69.
12. *I Proclaim From the Lord of Hosts the Returne of the Jewes From Their Captivity, and the Building of the Temple in Glory in Their Owne Land* (London: Printed by Charles Sumpter for Giles Calvert, 1650). This is a one page proclamation that was probably handed out to anyone who would read it.
13. Tany explained his Jewishness in the following way, "I am a Iew. My Jesus is the Iews Iehovah, the Iews Iehovah my Jesus, these two are but the names of the same intended thing." See Tany's *His Aurora Tranlagorum in Salem Gloria* (London: Printed for S. B. by Henry Hills, 1655), p. 11. Also see, for example, the criticisms he made against the faculties of Oxford and Cambridge. "You say that you are called and sent of Christ; it must be then messengers of his second coming, that is, to restore the captive Iewes according to the promise." Tany's *Theaurau Iohn High Priest of the Iewes His Disputive Challenge to the Universities of Oxford and Cambridge and the Whole Hirach of Roms Clargical Priests* (London: 1651), p. 3.
14. Cecil Roth, *A Life of Menasseh ben Israel* (Philadelphia: J.P.S., 1945), pp. 64–66.
15. Wolf, *Menasseh ben Israel's Mission,* p. xxiv.
16. *Jews in America* (London: Printed for Henry Brown, 1660), p. 36.
17. Cecil Roth, "New Light on the Resettlement," *T.J.H.S.E.,* 12 (1927): 113–14.
18. Wolf, *Menasseh ben Israel's Mission,* p. xxvi.
19. (London: 1650), p. A 3.
20. Ibid., p. 9.
21. Roth, "New Light on the Resettlement."
22. Menasseh ben Israel, "Humble Addresses." Cited by Wolf, p. 78. Page numbers for additional citations from this work are given in the text.
23. *William Prynne: A Study in Puritanism* (Cambridge, Mass.: Harvard University Press, 1931), pp. 185–86.
24. The book was issued in two parts, the first completed in December 1655 and the second in February 1656.
25. *A Short Demurrer to the Jewes Long Discontinued Barred Remitter into England* (London: Printed for Edward Thomas, 1656). The quotations in this paragraph in the text are all from preface of the book, "To the Christian Reader." Citations from other sections of the work are noted by page number.
26. Mordecai Wilensky, "The Literary Controversy in 1656 Concerning the Return of the Jews to England," *Publications of the American Academy for Jewish Research* 20 (1951): 360.
27. *A View of the Jewish Religion* (London: Printed by T. M. for E. Brewster and S. Miller, 1656). The last page of "To the Reader." Further citations are given by page number in the text.
28. Osterman believes that Ross wrote the pamphlet. Wilensky feels that it reflects his spirit but will not commit himself. See Nathan Osterman, "The Controversy Over the Proposed Readmission of the Jews to England," *Jewish Social Studies,* 3 (1941): 308, and Wilensky, *Shivat Hayehudim,* p. 177.
29. *The Case of the Jewes Stated: Or the Jewes Synagogue Opened* (London: Printed by Robert Ibbitson, 1656), pp. 1–2.
30. *Anglo-Judaeus, or the History of the Jews Whilst Here in England* (London: Printed by T. N. for Thomas Heath, 1656), p. 2 in the "Epistle Dedicatory." Further citations from this work are noted by page number in the text.
31. Wilfred Samuel, "The Strayings of Paul Isaiah in England (1651–1656)," *T.J.H.S.E.* 16 (1945–51): 82.

32. Paul Isaiah, *A Brief Compendium of the Vain Hopes of the Jewish Messias. The Ignorant Fables of their Rabbies and the Confusing of the Jewish Religion* (London: 1652), p. 2.

33. Ibid., pp. 9–10.

34. *The Messias of the Christians, and the Jewes Held Forth in a Discourse Between a Christian and a Jew Obstinately Adhering to his Strange Opinions and the Forced Interpretations of Scripture* (London: Printed by William Hunt, 1655), To the Christian Reader, no pagination.

35. *Israels Condition and Cause Pleaded or Some Arguments for the Jews Admission into England* (London: Printed by P. W. for William Larmar and Jonathan Ball, 1656), p. 4. Further citations from this work are given by page number in the text.

36. *A Brief Answer to Some of the Objections and Demurs Made Against the Coming In and Inhabiting of the Jews in This Commonwealth etc.* (London: 1656). Reprinted in Occasional Papers English Series, no. 3, p. 25. Further citations are made in the text.

37. *The Resurrection of Dead Bones or the Conversion of the Jewes* (London: Printed for Giles Calvert, 1655), pp. 3–4. See text for further citations.

38. *A Case of Conscience, Whether it be Lawful to Admit Jews into a Christian Commonwealth?* (London: Printed for Richard Wodenothe, 1656), p. 3. See text for further citations.

39. Thomas Barlow was the chief librarian at the Bodleian Library from 1642–1660 and the Bishop of Lincoln from 1675–1691.

40. Although the pamphlet was circulated in manuscript form prior to the Whitehall Conference of 1656, it was not printed until 1692. It appeared in a collection of his works entitled *The Case of the Jews in Several Miscellaneous and Weighty Cases of Conscience* (London: 1692), p. 9. See text for further citations.

41. Osterman suggests that men like Barlow insisted upon these unfavorable conditions out of fear that "material propserity would render conversion difficult." He further claims that, "It was important to make the Jew realize that there were definite disadvantages to remaining a Jew." Certainly, the particular restrictions that were chosen also reflect the hatred that was felt by the writers and the degree of anti-Semitic prejudice that was present in society. He seems to oversimplify a very complex problem. See Osterman, *Jewish Social Studies*, 3: 315.

42. *A Narrative of the Late Proceeds at White-Hall Concerning the Jewes* (London: Printed for Giles Calvert, 1655), "To the Reader," p. A. See text for further citations.

43. Roth, *Menasseh ben Israel,*, p. 241.

44. Menasseh ben Israel, *Vindiciae Judaeorum* (London: Printed by R. D., 1656), p. A 2.

45. Lucien Wolf, "Crypto Jews Under the Commonwealth," *T.J.H.S.E.* 1 (1895): 66–76.

46. Ibid., p. 66.

47. "Petition of London Jews, March 1656." Cited in full by Wolf, "Crypto Jews Under the Commonwealth," p. 76.

CHAPTER 6

1. For example, a Scotsman named Brodie recorded in his diary on Jan. 15, 1657, the following, "I heard of the Jewish Synagogue at London, and mentioned that to the Lord: we are sure to hear that blessed name that we believe on blasphemed: a false worship set up, and this shall be done without grief? May the Lord bring forth good out of it! For I know not what to say on it." Cited by Cohen,, *Scrapbook*, p. 260.

2. Lucien Wolf, "Status of the Jews in England after the Resettlement," *T.J.H.S.E.* 4 (1899–1901: 180–81.

3. Wilfred Sampson Samuel, *The First London Synagogue of the Resettlement* (London: Spottiswoode Ballantyne & Co., 1924), p. 25.

4. Howard Brotz, "The Position of the Jews in English Society," *The Jewish Journal of Sociology* 1 (Apr. 1959): 94.

5. Lucien Wolf, "The Jewry of the Restoration: 1660–1664," *T.J.H.S.E.* 5 (1902–1905): 5.

6. Richard Baker, *The Marchants Humble Petition and Remonstrance* (London: 1659), p. 17.

7. Guildhall Archives Remembrancer 9, no. 44, fols. 1–18. Cited by Wolf, "Status of the Jews after Resettlement," p. 189.

8. For a full description of his dealings, see *The Great Trappaner of England, Discovered, Being a True Narrative of Many Dangerous and Abominable Practices of One Thomas Violet Goldsmith, to Trappan the Jews, etc.* (London? 1660).

9. *A Petition Against the Jewes* (London? 1661), p. 8.

10. Ibid., p. 5.

11. George Clark, *The Later Stuarts 1660–1714* (Oxford: Oxford University Press, 1965), p. 19.

12. When Catherine was on her way to become queen, she was stricken with erysipelas. Antonio Mendes, a secret Jew and the physician to King John IV of Portugal, was sent for, and he successfully cured the disease. He became a member of her household, and his brother Andrea became her chamberlain. These two men and a third brother accompanied Catherine to England where they openly proclaimed themselves as Jews. The queen insisted on keeping them in her service and, according to Piciotto, "it is not at all improbable that the Queen may have exercised influence in favor of the Jews." James Picciotto, *Sketches of Anglo-Jewish History* (London: Trubner & Co., 1875), p. 44.

13. Hayne complained: "That the alien made denizen here continued his co-partnership with his former partner who was a denizen in some foreign part and one owing the goods here and the other there past as free denizens on both sides by which they could undersell either English or alien who are necessitated to pay alien duty either here or there." *An Abstract of All the Statues Made Concerning Alliens Trading in England* (London: 1685), pp. 5–6, 9.

14. The exact wording of the rule is as follows: (Escama 34) "No Jew shall hold dispute or argument on matters of religion with Guim, nor urge them to follow our Holy Law, nor may offensive words be spoken to them against their profession, because to do otherwise is to disturb the liberty which we enjoy and to make us disliked." Lionel Barnett, *El Libro de los Acuerdos—Being the Records and Accounts of the Spanish Portuguese Synagogue of London from 1663–1681* (Oxford: University Press, 1931), p. 12.

15. The prohibition was stated as follows: (Escama 32) "No person who is of our nation, Portuguese and Spaniards, may be circumcised, and no mohel shall be allowed to circumcise them under pain of herem; . . . and under the said penalty is incured anyone who may bathe a foreign woman, because it is not meet that they be admitted into our congregation." Ibid.

16. They stated: (Escama 35) "If it should be that the law seize any Jew for evil deeds, such as robberies, frauds or other untoward things . . . no money shall be wasted upon such a one nor shall the Mahamad endeavor to liberate him but they shall consent that he be punished by law according to his crimes." Ibid.

17. Wilfred Samuel, "Caravajal and Pepys," *Miscellanies of the Jewish Historical Society of*

England 2 (1935): 29. Hereafter the *Miscellanies of the Jewish Historical Society of England* will be referred to as *M.J.H.S.E.*

18. *The Diary of Samuel Pepys*, ed. Henry B. Wheatly (London: Harcourt Brace & Co., 1924), 3: 284. The entry was made for Oct. 14, 1663.

19. Letter to Thomas Crompton, Apr. 22, 1662, cited in Roth, *Anglo-Jewish Letters (1158–1917)*, p. 63.

20. Ibid.

21. Robert Kirk, *The Commonplace Book of the Rev. Robert Kirk of Aberfoyle*. Cited by Donald MacLean and Norman G. Brett-James, "London in 1689–90," *Transactions of the London and Middlesex Archeological Society*, 7, pt. 1, p. 151.

22. William, Lord Bishop of St. Asaph, *The Conversion and Persecution of Eve Cohann* (London: Printed by J. D. for Richard Chiswell, 1680), p. 2. Page numbers for further citations of this work are given in the text.

23. (London: Printed for John White, 1661), p. 11. For additional references made by Fox to the Jewish involvement in the Crucifixion, see George Fox, *An Answer to the Arguments of the Iewes* (London? Printed for M. W., 1661), pp. 3, 8, 11.

24. *Diary*, ed. E. S. de Berr, vol. 5 (Oxford: Clarendon Press, 1955), p. 88 (Feb. 13, 1692).

25. Irene Simon, *Three Restoration Divines: Barrow, South, Tillotson, Selected Sermons* (Paris, Société d'Édition les Belles Lettres, 1967), p. 228.

26. The following quotations are from Barrow's sermon, "Of the Evil and Unreasonableness of Infidelity," in Simon, *Three Restoration Divines*, pp. 381–92.

27. Evelyn, *Diary*, 4: 630 (Mar. 29, 1689).

28. Ibid., 5: 276–77 (Nov. 28, 1697).

29. Ibid., 4: 571 (Mar. 16, 1688).

30. Ibid.

31. Ibid., p. 648 (Sept. 1, 1689).

32. Ibid., 5: 425. The sermon was delivered on Sept. 8, 1700. Evelyn does not mention the name of the preacher.

33. Ibid., p. 231. The sermon was delivered by a Mr. Wye at Wotton on Feb. 23, 1696. It was based on John 13:34.

34. Landa adds one more theory to explain why the playwrights did not revive the hideous tradition of the stage Jew when the theaters were reopened during the Restoration. He claims that the very small number of Jews in England may have been a factor. This reasoning is questionable, because there were even fewer Jews present in England during the Elizabethan period than during the Restoration. He fails to appreciate that the actual Jew had nothing to do with the portrayal of his people on the stage, and that such portrayals were primarily determined by the intensity of mediaeval prejudices which were often sustained by the church. See Landa's *Jew in Drama*, pp. 105–6.

35. See, for example, Elkanah Settle, *Absalom Senior or Achitophel Transpos'd, A Poem* (London: Printed for S. E., 1682); Samuel Pordage, *Azaria and Hushai, A Poem* (London: Printed for Charles Lee, 1682); and *Poetical Reflections on a Late Poem Entitled Absalom and Achitophel* (London: 1681).

36. R. R., *The Restauration of the Jewes: Or a True Relation of Their Progress and Proceedings in Order to the Regaining of their Ancient Kingdom* (London: Printed by A. Maxwell, 1665), p. 3.

37. Ibid., p. 5.

38. *A New Letter Concerning the Jewes Written by the French Ambassador at Constantinople* (London: Printed by A. Maxwell, 1666), p. 5.

39. Roth, *Anglo-Jewish Letters,*, p. 69.

40. The English preoccupation with messianism lasted through the end of the century. John Evelyn recorded in his diary for Apr. 26, 1694, that John Mason (1646–1694), a famous preacher, had roused the people of Buckinghamshire with the news that Jesus had appeared to him on the sixteenth of the month and had told him that the millenium was about to start and that Jew and Christian alike would be led to Jerusalem. Evelyn, *Diary*, 5: 177–78.

41. For example, William III was very careful to place a watch on all people arriving or departing from England who did not have the necessary passes. Jews, however, seemed to be above suspicion, and when Moses Dejaco and his party were stopped at Margate in May 1692 without the necessary papers, they were allowed to continue on to London because they were "all Jews and in no way disaffected to the Government." Israel Abrahams, "Passes Issued to Jews in the Period 1689–1696," *M.J.H.S.E.* (1925): xxiv.

42. See for example, Samuel Hayne, *The Manifesto of Near One Hundred and Fifty Knights, and Eminent Merchants and Citizens of London Against the Jews Now in England* (London: 1697).

43. Clark, p. 35.

44. Ettinger, "Change in the Attitude Towards the Jews," p. 215.

45. For an analysis of the effect of capitalism upon the emancipation of the Jew in England and on the continent, see Ellis Rivkin, *The Shaping of Jewish History: A Radical New Interpretation* (New York: Charles Scribner's Sons, 1971), pp. 159–64.

46. J. W. Gough, *John Locke's Political Philosophy* (Oxford: Oxford University Press, 1950), p. 176.

47. *The Works of John Locke* (London: Printed for Thomas T. Egg, 1823; rpt. Scientia Verlag Aalen, 1963), 4: 52.

BIBLIOGRAPHY

PRIMARY SOURCES

ABBOTT, WILBUR CORTEZ, AND CRANE, CATHERINE D., eds. *The Writings and Speeches of Oliver Cromwell With an Introduction, Notes and an Account of His Life.* Vol. 1: *1599–1649.* Vol. 2: *The Commonwealth 1649–1653.* Cambridge: Harvard University Press, 1937–38.

ANDREWES, LANCELOT. *Sermons.* Ed. G. M. Story. Oxford: Clarendon Press, 1967.

BAKER, RICHARD. *The Marchants Humble Petition and Remonstrance.* London, 1659.

BANKS, MARY MACLEOD, ed. *An Alphabet of Tales: An English 15th Century Translation of the Alphabetum Narrationum of Étienne de Besançon.* Parts 1 and 2. London: Kegan Paul, Trench, Trubner & Co., 1904–05.

BARNETT, LIONEL D., trans. *El Libro de los Acuerdos—Being the Records and Accounts of the Spanish Portuguese Synagogue of London From 1663 to 1681.* Oxford: Oxford University Press, 1931.

BREREWOOD, EDWARD. *Enquiries Touching the Diversity of Languages and Religions Through the Chiefe Parts of the World.* London: Printed for John Bill, 1614.

A Brief Answer to Some of the Objections and Demurs Made Against the Coming in and the Inhabiting of the Jews in this Commonwealth. London: Printed by Henry Hills, 1656. *Pamphlets Relating to the Jews in England During the Seventeenth and Eighteenth Centuries.* Prepared by the personnel of the Works Progress Administration, P. Radin, Editor. San Francisco: California State Library, 1939.

BROUGHTON, HUGH. *Daniel with a Brief Explication.* Hanaw: Printed by Daniel Aubri, 1607.

————. *Two Epistles Unto Great Men of Britanie in the Yeare 1599 Requesting Them to Put Their Neckes Unto the Work of Theyr Lord.* 1606.

————. *A Require of Agreement to the Groundes of Divinitie Studie: Wherin Great Scholars Falling, and Being Caught of Jewes Disgrace the Gospel and Trap Them to Destruction.* 1611.

BROWNE, SIR THOMAS. "Hydriotaphia." Vol. 1: *The Works of Thomas Browne.* Ed. Geoffrey Keynes. Chicago: University of Chicago Press, 1964.

————. "Pseudodoxia Epidemica." Vol. 2: *The Works of Sir Thomas Browne.* Ed. Geoffrey Keynes. Chicago: University of Chicago Press, 1964.

————. "Religio Medici." Vol. 1: *The Works of Sir Thomas Browne.* Ed. Geoffrey Keynes. Chicago: University of Chicago Press, 1964.

BURTON, ROBERT. *The Anatomy of Melancholy.* Ed. Floyd Dell and Paul Jordan Smith. New York: Tudor Publishing Co., 1938.

BIBLIOGRAPHY

BUSHER, LEONARD. *Religious Peace or a Plea for Liberty of Conscience*. London: Printed for John Sweeting, 1646.

BUTLER-BOWDON, W., ed. *The Book of Margery Kemp*. London: Jonathan Cape Ltd., 1936.

Calendar of State Papers (Domestic), 1649–1660.

CALVERT, THOMAS. *The Blessed Jew of Marocco or a Blackmoor Made White*. York: Thomas Broad, 1649.

CAPGRAVE, JOHN. *The Chronicle of England*. Ed. Francis Charles Hingeston. London: Longman, Brown, Green, Longmans, and Roberts, 1858.

CARTWRIGHT, JOANNA AND EBENEZER. *The Petition of the Jewes For the Repealing of the Act of Parliament for their Banishment out of England*. London: Printed for George Roberts, 1649.

The Case of the Jewes Stated: Or The Jewes Synagogue Opened. London: Printed by Robert Ibbitson, 1656.

CHAUCER, GEOFFREY. "The Prioress's Tale." *The Complete Works of Geoffrey Chaucer*. Ed. F. N. Robinson. Boston: Houghton Mifflin Co., 1933.

CHEAUMONT, DE. *A New Letter Concerning the Jewes Written by the French Ambassador at Constantinople to his Brother the French Resident at Venice*. London: Printed by A. Maxwell, 1666.

CHILD, FRANCIS JAMES, ed. *The English and Scottish Popular Ballads*.. Vols. 1 and 3. New York: The Folklore Press, 1956.

CLARE, JOHN. *The Converted Jew or Certaine Dialogues Betweene Micheas a Learned Jew and Others Touching Divers Points of Religion, Controverted Betweene Catholics and Protestants* (1630).

CLARK, HENRY. *The Wise Taken in Their Craftiness and Their Wisdom Made Manifest to be Foolishness With God*. London: Printed for Giles Calvert, 1656.

COHEN, ABRAHAM. *An Anglo-Jewish Scrapbook 1600–1840*. London: M. L. Cailingold, 1943.

CORRIE, G. E., ed. *Certain Sermons Appointed by the Queen's Majesty*. London: John W. Parker, 1850.

CORYAT, THOMAS. *Coryat's Crudities*. Vol. 1. London: Printed for W. Cater, 1786.

COVERDALE, MYLES. *Writings and Translations of Myles Coverdale*. Ed. George Pearson. Cambridge: Cambridge University Press, 1844.

D. B. *A Briefe Refutation of John Traskes Judaical and Novel Fancyes*. 1618.

DAY, JOHN. *The Travels of the Three English Brothers*. *The Works of John Day*. Ed. A. H. Bullen. London: Chiswick Press, 1881.

DAY, MABEL, ed. *The Wheatley Manuscript*. London: Oxford University Press, 1921.

The Devilish Conspiracy, Hellish Treason, Heathenish Condemnation and Damnable Murder Committed, and Executed by the Jewes Against the Anointed of the Lord Christ their King. London, 1648. (In the copy that I used at the British Museum the date was altered in ink to read 1649. Either officially or unofficially, the same person who changed the date noted that the author of this work was the Bishop of Rochester.)

Doomesday: Or the Great Day of the Lords Judgement. London, 1647.

DRYDEN, JOHN. *Love Triumphant*. *The Works of John Dryden*. Vol. 8. Ed. George Saintsbury. Edinburgh: William Paterson, 1884.

DRYDEN, JOHN. *Absalom and Achitophel*. *The Poems and Fables of John Dryden*. Ed. James Kinsley. London: Oxford University Press, 1962.

DURY, JOHN. *A Case of Conscience, Whether it be Lawful to Admit Jews into a Christian Commonwealth?* London: Printed for Richard Wodenothe, 1656.

An Endevor After the Reconcilement of that Long Debated Much Lamented Difference Between the Godly Presbyterians and Independents; About Church-Government. In a Discourse Touching Jews Synagogues. London, 1648. (In the copy that I used in the British Museum, the date was altered in ink to read 1647.)

EVELYN, JOHN. Diary. Ed. E.S. de Berr. 6 vols. Oxford: Clarendon Press, 1955.

A False Jew: Or a wonderful Discovery of a Scot, Baptized at London for a Christian, Circumcized at Rome to Act a Jew, Rebaptized at Hexham for a Believer, But Found out at Newcastle to be a Cheat. Newcastle: Printed for William London, 1653.

FELL, M. For Menasseth Ben Israel the Call of the Jewes Out of Babylon. London: Printed for Giles Calvert, 1656. (In the copy that I used in the British Museum the date was altered in ink to read 1655.)

FOSTER, FRANCES A., ed. The Northern Passion. London: Oxford University Press, 1916.

FOX, GEORGE. Christ's Parable of Dives and Lazarus For all Call'd Christians and Others to consider. 1677.

_____. An Answer to the Arguments of the Iewes. London: Printed for M. W., 1661.

_____. A Declaration to the Jews For Them To Read Over, In Which They May See That the Messiah is Come. London: Printed for John White, 1661.

_____. The Spirit of Man, the Candle of the Lord: The Candle of the Wicked Often Put out. 1677.

FURNIVALL, F. J., ed. The Minor Poems of the Vernon Manuscript Part II. London: Kegan Paul, Trench, Trubner & Co., 1893.

GREENE, ROBERT. The Tragical Reign of Selimus. Ed. Alexander B. Grosart. London: J. M. Dent & Co., 1898.

GOWER, JOHN. Confessio Amantis. The English Works of John Gower. Ed. G. C. Macaulay. London: Oxford University Press, 1900.

_____. Vox Clamantis. The Major Latin Works of John Gower. Ed. and trans. Eric W. Stockton. Seattle: University of Washington Press, 1962.

H. W. Anglo-Judaeus, or the History of the Jews Whilst here in England. London: Printed by T. N. for Thomas Heath, 1656.

HARTLIB, SAMUEL. Considerations Tending to the Happy Accomplishment of England's Reformation in Church and State. London, 1647.

HAYNE, SAMUEL. An Abstract of All the Statutes Made Concerning Alien Trading in England.. London, 1685.

HICKES, G. A. Peculium Dei A Discourse About the Jews as the Peculiar People of God in a Sermon Preached Before the Honorable the Alderman and Citizens of London. London: Printed for Walter Kettilby, 1681.

HOLINSHED, RAPHAEL. Chronicles of England Scotland and Ireland. Vol. 2, New York: AMS Press Inc., 1965.

HOLMES, NATHANIEL. "A Brief Cronology Concerning the Jews From the Year of Christ 1650 to 1666." Memorable Remarks Upon the Ancient and Modern State of the Jewish Nation. Boston: Printed by B. Jackson, 1786.

_____. An Essay Concerning the Sabbath. London, 1673.

HORSTMANN, CARL, ed. The Early South-English Legendary or Lives of Saints. London: N. Trubner & Co., 1887.

_____, ed. The Minor Poems of the Vernon Manuscript Part I. London: Kegan Paul, Trench, Trubner & Co., 1892.

HOWELL, JAMES. Familiar Letters or Epistolae Ho-Elianae. 4 vols. London: J. M. Dent and Co., 1903.

174

BIBLIOGRAPHY

The Husbandmans Plea Against Tithes. London, 1647.

HUSSEY, MAURICE, ed. *The Chester Mystery Plays.* New York: Theatre Arts Books, 1957.

ISAIAH, PAUL. *A Brief Compendium of the Vain Hopes of the Jewish Messias. The Ignorant Fables of their Rabbies and the Confuting of the Jewish Religion.* London, 1652. (The copy that I used in the British Museum lists the author of this work to be Eleazar Bargishai. This is one of the names that Paul Isaiah used.)

――――. *The Messias of the Christians, and the Jewes Held Forth in a Discourse Between a Christian and a Jew Obstinately Adhering to his Strange Opinions and the forced interpretations of Scripture.* London: Printed by William Hunt, 1655.

ISRAEL, MENASSEH BEN. *The Hope of Israel.* Lucien Wolf, *Menasseh ben Israel's Mission to Oliver Cromwell.* London: Macmillan & Co., 1901.

――――. "Humble Addresses," Lucien Wolf, *Menasseh ben Israel's Mission to Oliver Cromwell.* London: Macmillan & Co., 1901.

――――. *Vindiciae Judaeorum.* London: Printed by R. D., 1656.

Israels Condition and Cause Pleaded or Some Arguments for the Jews Admission into England. London: Printed by P. W. for William Larmar and Jonathan Ball, 1656.

J. G. "A Severe Sentence Against Secure Citizens. A Sermon Preached at St. Maries in Oxford," in *The Sage Senator.* London: Printed by J. Cottrel for Sam Speed, 1660.

JESSE, HENRY. *A Narrative of the late Proceeds at White-Hall Concerning the Jews.* London: Printed for L. Chapman, 1656.

JOHNSON, ROBERT. *Lux and Lex or the Light and the Law of Jacobs House: Held Forth in a Sermon Before the Honorable House of Commons March 31, 1647.* London: Printed by A. Miller, 1647.

JUDAEUS, PHILO. *The Resurrection of Dead Bones or the Conversion of the Jewes.* London: Printed for Giles Calvert, 1655. (In the copy that I used in the British Museum, the date was altered to read 1654.)

JULIANA OF NORWICH, *Sixteen Revelations of Divine Love.* Ed. Grace Warrack. London, 1927.

KNELL, PAUL. *Israel and England Paralelled, In a Sermon preached before the honorable society of Grayes-Inne, upon Sunday in the afternoon, April 16, 1648.* London, 1648.

LIGHTEFOOTE, JOHN. *Ervbhin or Miscellanies Christian and Judaicall and Others.* London: G. Miller, 1629.

LOCKE, JOHN. "A Letter Concerning Toleration." *The Works of John Locke,* vol. 4. London: Printed for Thomas T. Egg, 1823. (Reprinted by Scientia Verlag Aalen, 1963.)

MACLURE, MILLAR. *The Paul's Cross Sermons 1534–1642.* Toronto: University of Toronto Press, 1958.

MAIME, JASPER. *A Sermon Against False Prophets Preached in St. Maries Church in Oxford, Shortly After the Surrender of that Garrison,* 1646.

MARLOWE, CHRISTOPHER. *The Jew of Malta. English Drama 1580–1642.* Ed. C. F. Tucker Brooke and Nathaniel Burton Paradise. Boston: D. C. Heath & Co. 1933.

MARVELL, ANDREW. "To His Coy Mistress." *Seventeenth Century Prose and Poetry.* Ed. Witherspoon and Warnke. New York: Harcourt, Brace & World, Inc., 1963.

MATON, ROBERT. *Gog and Magog or the Battle of the Great Day of God Almightie.* London: Printed by R. Cotes For Daniel Frere, 1642.

――――. *Israels Redemption or the Propheticall History of our Saviours Kingdom on Earth.* London: Printed for Daniel Frere, 1642.

MIRK, JOHN. *Mirk's Festial: A Collection of Homilies.* Ed. Theodore Erbe. London: K. Paul, Trench, Trubner & Co., 1905.

MORRIS, RICHARD. *Legends of the Holy Rood; Symbols of the Passion and Cross Poems in Old English of the Eleventh, Fourteenth and Fifteenth Centuries.* London: N. Trubner & Co., 1871.

NASHE, THOMAS. *The Unfortunate Traveller. The Works of Thomas Nashe.* Vol. 2. Ed. Ronald B. Mckerrow. London: Sidgwick & Jackson, 1910.

A New Letter Concerning the Jewes Written by the French Ambassador at Constantinople to his Brother the French Resident at Venice. London: Printed by A. Maxwell for Robert Boulter, 1666.

NICHOLAS, EDWARD. *An apology for the honourable nation of the Jews and all the sons of Israel.* London, 1649.

NORWOOD, ROBERT. *Proposals for the Propagation of the Gospel, Offered to the Parliament.* March 20, 1651. (In the copy of this work that I used in the British Museum, the date that was inked in is March 20, 1651. Wilensky has it listed as 1652.)

NOTESTEIN, WALLACE; RELF, HELEN FRANCIS; AND SIMPSON, HARTLEY. *Commons Debates 1621.* Vols. 2 and 3. New Haven: Yale University Press, 1935.

PEEL, ALBERT, AND CARLSON, LELAND, eds. *Cartwrightiana.* London: George Allen and Unwin Ltd., 1951.

PENINGTON, ISAAC. *Some Considerations Propounded to the Jews.* (Roth suggests that the work was printed in London in 1660. The copy that I used in the British Museum gave neither the place nor date of publication.

PETERS, HUGH. *A Word for the Armie and Two Words to the Kingdome To Cleare the One and Cure the Other.* London: Printed by M. Simmons for Giles Calvert, 1647.

The Play of the Sacrament in Chief Pre-Shakespearean Dramas. Ed. Joseph Quincy Adams. Cambridge: The Riverside Press, 1924.

PRYNNE, WILLIAM. *A Short Demurrer to the Jewes.* London: E. Thomas, 1656. This edition contains both parts 1 and 2.

PYNCHON, WILLIAM. *A Treatise of the Sabbath.* London: Printed for Thomas Newberry, 1654.

R. R. *The Restauration of the Jewes: Or a Relation of Their Progress and Proceedings in order to the Regaining of their Ancient Kingdom.* London: Printed by A. Maxwell, 1665.

ROSS, ALEXANDER. *A View of the Jewish Religion.* London: Printed by T. M. for E. Brewster and S. Miller, 1656.

ROSS, WOODBURN, ed. *Middle English Sermons Edited from British Museum MS. Royal 18 B. xxiii.* Oxford: Oxford University Press, 1960.

ROTH, CECIL. *Anglo-Jewish Letters 1158–1917.* London: The Soncino Press, 1938.

SHAKESPEARE, WILLIAM. *The Merchant of Venice.* Ed. Arthur Quiller-Couch and John Dover Wilson. Cambridge: Cambridge University Press, 1962.

SMITH, HENRY. *Twelve Sermons Preached by Mr. Henry Smith.* London: Printed by John Haviland for George Edwards, 1629.

ST. ASAPH, WILLIAM, LORD BISHOP OF. *The Conversion & Persecutions of Eve Cohan.* London: Printed by J. D. for Richard Chiswell, 1680.

The Siege of Jerusalem. Ed. E. Kelbing and Mabel Day. London: Oxford University Press, 1932.

TANY, THOMAS. *His Aurora Tranlagorum in Salem Gloria.* London: Printed for S. B. by Henry Hills, 1655.

———. *"I Proclaime From the Lord of Hosts the Returne of the Jewes From Their Captivity, and the Building of the Temple in Glory, in Their Owne Land."* London: Printed by Charles Sumpter for Giles Calvert, 1650.

———. *Theauraujohn High Priest to the Jewes His Disputive Challenge to the Universities of Oxford and Cambridge and the Whole Hirach of Roms Clargical Priests.* London, 1651.

THOROWGOOD, THOMAS. *Jews in America.* London: Printed for Henry Brome, 1660.

TILLOTSON, JOHN. *Sermons Preached Upon Several Occasions.* London: Printed for Brabazon Aylmer, 1685.

Two Conferences: One Betwixt a Papist and a Jew, The Other Betwixt a Protestant and a Jew: In Two Letters From a Merchant in London, to His Correspondent in Amsterdam. London, 1678.

VALENTINE, THOMAS. *A Charge Against the Jews and the Christian World For Not Coming to Christ Who Would Have Freely Given Them Eternal Life. Delivered in a Sermon Before the Right Honorable House of Peers.* London: Printed by M. S., 1647.

VIOLET, THOMAS. *Petition Against the Jewes, Presented to the King's Majesty and the Parliament.* London, 1661.

W. S. *An Epistle From the Spirit of Love and Peace Unto all the Upright Israelites, Who are Born of the Seed that is Blessed for Evermore.* 1663.

WALL, MOSES. *Considerations Upon the Point of Conversion of the Jews.* London, 1652. Lucien Wolf, *Menasseh ben Israel's Mission to Oliver Cromwell.* London: Jewish Historical Society of England, 1906.

WATERS, ROBERT. *John Selden and His Table Talk.* New York: Eaton & Mains, 1899. The full text of John Selden's *Table Talk* can be found between pp. 67 and 215.

WEATHERLY, EDWARD H., ed. *Speculum Sacerdotale.* London: Oxford University Press, 1936.

WEEMSE, JOHN. *A Treatise of the Four Degenerate Sonnes: the Atheist, the Magician, the Idolater and the Jew.* London, 1636.

WILLIAMS ROGER. *The Bloudy Tenent of Persecution, for Cause of Conscience discussed, in A Conference betweene Truth and Peace,,* 1644.

WILLIAMS, ROGER. *The Fourth Paper, Presented by Major Butler, To the Honourable Committee of Parliament, for the Propagating the Gospel of Christ Jesus.* London: Printed for Giles Calvert, 1652. *The Complete Writings of Roger Williams.* Vol. 3. Ed. Perry Miller. New York: Russell & Russell, 1963.

WILSON, J. DOVER, AND DOBELL, BERTRAM, eds. *The Resurrection of our Lord.* Oxford: Oxford University Press, 1912.

WILSON, JOHN. *Belphegor: or, The Marriage of the Devil. The Dramatic Works of John Wilson.* Ed. James Maidment and W. H. Logan. Edinburgh: William Paterson, 1874.

WILSON, JOHN. *The Cheats. The Dramatic Works of John Wilson.* Ed. James Maidment and W. H. Logan. Edinburgh: William Paterson, 1874.

WILSON, ROBERT. *The Three Ladies of London. A Select Collection of Old English Plays.* Vol. 6. Ed. W. Carew Hazlett. London: Reeves & Turner, 1874.

WIMBLEDON, THOMAS. *Wimbledon's Sermon Redde Rationem Villicationis Tue. A Middle English Sermon of the Fourteenth Century.* Ed. Ione Kemp Knight. Pittsburgh: Duquesne University Press, 1967.

SECONDARY SOURCES

ABRAMS, ISRAEL. *Jewish Life in the Middle Ages.* New York: Meridan Press, 1958.

ADLER, E. NATHAN. *Auto da Fé and the Jew.* London: M. Frowde, 1908.

———. *History of the Jews in London.* Philadelphia: J.P.S., 1930.

ASHLEY, MAURICE. *The Greatness of Oliver Cromwell.* New York: The Macmillan Co., 1958.

BAGLEY, J. J. *Historical Interpretation: Sources of English Medieval History, 1066–1540.* London: Penguin Books, 1965.

BARON, SALO W. *A Social and Religious History of the Jews.* Vol. 4: *Meeting of East and West.* Vol. 10: *On the Empire's Periphery.* Vol. 11: *Meeting of East and West.* Philadelphia: J.P.S., 1957–67.

————. *The Jewish Community—Its History and Structure to The American Revolution.* Vol. 1. Philadelphia: J.P.S., 1948.

BATES, KATHARINE LEE. *The English Religious Drama,* 1893; rpt. Port Washington, N.Y.: Kennikat Press, 1966.

BERDYAEV, NICHOLAS. *Christianity and Anti-Semitism.* Sussex, Eng.: The Ditchling Press, 1952.

BOYD, BEVERLY. *The Middle English Miracles of the Virgin.* San Marino, Calif.: The Huntington Library, 1964.

BRAILSFORD, H. N. *The Levellers and the English Revolution.* Stanford: Stanford University Press, 1961.

BRANDEIS, ARTHUR, ed. *Jacob's Well: An English Treatise on the Cleansing of Man's Conscience.* London: Oxford University Press, 1900.

CALISCH, EDWARD N. *The Jew in English Literature, As Author and as Subject.* 1909; rpt. Port Washington, N.Y.: Kennikat Press, 1969.

CANTOR, NORMAN F. *The English: A History of Politics and Society to 1760.* New York: Simon and Schuster, 1967.

CARDOZO, J. L. *The Contemporary Jew in the Elizabethan Drama.* Amsterdam: H. J. Paris, 1925.

CLARK, GEORGE. *The Later Stuarts 1660–1714.* Oxford: Oxford University Press, 1965.

COLE, DOUGLAS. *Suffering and Evil in the Plays of Christopher Marlowe.* Princeton, N.J.: Princeton University Press, 1962.

COLEMAN, EDWARD D. *The Jew in English Drama—An Annotated Bibliography.* New York: New York Public Library, 1943.

COLLIS, LOUISE. *Memoirs of a Medieval Woman: The Life and Times of Margery Kempe.* New York: Thomas Y. Crowell, 1964.

CORSA, HELEN STORM. *Chaucer: Poet of Mirth and Morality.* Notre Dame, Ind.: University of Notre Dame Press, 1964.

DAVIES, D. W. *Elizabethans Errant: The Strange Fortunes of Sir Thomas Sherley and His Three Sons.* Ithaca, N.Y.: Cornell University Press, 1967.

DUNN, WILLIAM PARMLY. *Sir Thomas Browne, A Study in Religious Philosophy.* Minneapolis: University of Minnesota Press, 1950.

FIRTH, CHARLES. *Oliver Cromwell and the Rule of the Puritans in England.* London: Oxford University Press, 1953.

FISCH, HAROLD. *The Dual Image: The Figure of the Jew in English and American Literature.* New York: Ktav Publishing House, 1971.

————. *Jerusalem and Albion: The Hebraic Factor in Seventeenth-Century Literature.* New York: Schocken Books, 1964.

FLETCHER, HARRIS FRANCIS. *Milton's Rabbinical Readings.* Urbana, Ill.: University of Illinois Press, 1930.

FRIEDMAN, LEE M. *Robert Grosseteste and the Jews.* Cambridge, Mass.: Harvard University Press, 1934.

GEROULD, GORDON HALL. *Saints' Legends.* Boston: Houghton Mifflin Co., 1916.

GRAETZ, HEINRICH. *History of the Jews.* Vol. 4. Philadelphia: J.P.S., 1894.

GREBANIER, BERNARD. *The Truth About Shylock.* New York: Random House, 1962.

BIBLIOGRAPHY

HALLER, WILLIAM. *The Rise of Puritanism or The Way to the New Jerusalem As Set Forth in Pulpit and Press From Thomas Cartwright to John Milton, 1570–1643*, 1938; rpt. New York: Harper Torch Books, 1957.

HENRIQUES, H.S.Q. *The Return of the Jews to England.* London: Macmillan & Co., 1905.

HIBBARD, G. R. *Thomas Nashe: A Critical Introduction.* Cambridge, Mass.: Harvard University Press, 1962.

HILL, CHRISTOPHER. *Reformation to Industrial Revolution.* New York: Random House, 1967.

HOWARD, EDWIN J. *Geoffrey Chaucer.* Twayne's English Author Series 1. New York: Twayne Publishers, Inc., 1964.

HYAMSON, ALBERT M. *A History of the Jews in England.* London: Methuen & Co., 1928.

———. *The Sephardim of England: A History of the Spanish and Portuguese Jewish Community 1492–1951.* London: Methuen & Co. Ltd., 1951.

JACOBS, JOSEPH. *The Jews of Angevin England.* London: David Nutt, 1893.

JORDAN, W. K. *The Development of Religious Toleration in England.* Vol. 3: *From the Convention of the Long Parliament to the Restoration, 1640–1660.* Vol. 4: *Attainment of the Theory and Accommodations in Thought and Institutions, 1640–1660.* 1932; rpt. Gloucester, Mass.: Peter Smith, 1965.

KAUFMAN, EZEKIAL. *Golah Venechar.* Vol. 2. Tel Aviv: Dvir Ltd., 1930.

KIRBY, ETHYN WILLIAMS. *William Prynne: A Study in Puritanism.* Cambridge, Mass.: Harvard University Press, 1931.

KITTREDGE, GEORGE LYMAN. *Witchcraft in Old and New England.* Cambridge, Mass.: Harvard University Press, 1929.

LANDA, M. J. *The Jew in Drama.* New York: William Morrow & Co., 1927.

LEHMANN, RUTH P. *Nova Bibliotheca Anglo-Judaica.* London: Jewish Historical Society of England, 1961.

MACFARLANE, A.D.J. *Witchcraft in Tudor Stuart England.* New York: Harper & Row, 1970.

MICHELSON, H. *The Jew in Early English Literature.* Amsterdam: H. J. Paris, 1926.

MITCHELL, FRASER W. *English Pulpit Oratory from Andrews to Tillotson.* New York: Russell & Russell, Inc., 1962.

MODDER, MONTAGUE FRANK. *The Jew in the Literature of England to the End of the Nineteenth Century.* 1939; rpt. Philadelphia: J.P.S., 1944.

NOTESTEIN, WALLACE. *A History of Witchcraft in England from 1558 to 1718.* 1911; rpt. New York: Thomas Y. Crowell Co., 1968.

OWST, G. R. *Literature and Pulpit in Medieval England.* Oxford: Blackwell, 1961.

———. *Preaching in Medieval England—An Introduction to Sermon Manuscripts of the Period 1350–1450.* Cambridge: Cambridge University Press, 1926.

PARKES, JAMES. *The Jew in the Medieval Community.* London: Soncino Press, 1938.

PICCIOTTO, JAMES. *Sketches of Anglo-Jewish History.* London: Trubner & Co., 1875.

PFANDER, HOMER G. "The Popular Sermon of the Medieval Friar in England." Unpublished Ph.D. dissertation, New York University, 1937.

PHILIPSON, DAVID. *The Jew in English Fiction.* Cincinnati: Robert Clarke & Co., 1889.

POLIAKOV, LEON. *The History of Anti-Semitism.* New York: The Vanguard Press, 1965.

POTTER, G. R., ed. *The New Cambridge Modern History.* Vol. 1: *The Renaissance 1493–1520.* Cambridge: Cambridge University Press, 1961.

RIDLEY, FLORENCE H. *The Prioress and the Critics.* Berkeley and Los Angeles: University of California Press, 1965.

RIVKIN, ELLIS. *The Shaping of Jewish History: A Radical New Interpretation.* New York: Charles Scribner's Sons, 1971.

ROBERTSON, D. B. *The Religious Foundations of Leveller Democracy*. New York: King's Crown Press, Columbia University, 1951.

ROSENBERG, EDGAR. *From Shylock to Svengali—Jewish Stereotypes in English Fiction*. Stanford: Stanford University Press, 1960.

ROTH, CECIL. *A History of the Jews in England*. Oxford: Clarendon Press, 1964.

————. *A History of the Marranos*. Philadelphia: J.P.S., 1932.

————. *A Life of Menasseh ben Israel*. Philadelphia: J.P.S., 1945.

————. *Magna Bibliotheca Anglo-Judaica*. London: Jewish Historical Society of England, 1937.

ROWSE, A. L. *Christopher Marlowe: His Life and Work*. New York: Harper & Row, 1964.

SAMUEL, WILFRED SAMPSON. *The First London Synagogue of the Resettlement*. London: Spottiswoode, Ballantyne & Co., 1924.

SEIDEN, MORTON IRVING. *The Paradox of Hate: A Study in Ritual Murder*. South Brunswick, N.J.: Thomas Yoseloff, 1967.

SEIFERTH, WOLFGANG S. *Synagogue and Church in the Middle Ages: Two Symbols in Art and Literature*. New York: Frederick Ungar Publishing Co., 1970.

SIMON, IRENE. *Three Restoration Divines: Barrow, South, Tillotson. Selected Sermons*. Paris: Société d'Édition les Belles Lettres, 1967.

SINSHEIMER, HERMAN. *Shylock: The History of a Character*. London: Victor Gollancz Ltd., 1947.

SOKOLOW, NAHUM. *History of Zionism 1600–1918*. 2 vols. London: Longmans Green & Co., 1919.

STEANE, J. B. *Marlowe: A Critical Study*. Cambridge: Cambridge University Press, 1964.

STOKES, H. P. *A Short History of the Jews in England*. New York: Macmillan, 1921.

TANNENBAUM, SAMUEL A. *Shakespeare's The Merchant of Venice (A Concise Bibliography)*. New York: Samuel A. Tannenbaum, 1941.

THOMAS, KEITH. *Religion and the Decline of Magic: Studies in Popular Beliefs in Sixteenth and Seventeenth Century England*. London: Weidenfeld and Nicolson, 1971.

TILLYARD, E. M. *The Elizabethan World Picture*. New York: Vintage Books, n.d.

TRACHTENBERG, JOSHUA. *The Devil and the Jews: The Medieval Conception of the Jew and Its Relation to Modern Anti-Semitism*. 1943; rpt. New York: Harper & Row, 1966.

TREVELYAN, GEORGE MACAULAY. *History of England*. London: Longmans, Green & Co., 1929.

WILLIAMS, ARNOLD. *The Characterization of Pilate in the Towneley Plays*. East Lansing: Michigan State University Press, 1950.

WOLF, LUCIEN. *Menasseh ben Israel's Mission to Oliver Cromwell*. London: Jewish Historical Society of England, 1901.

WRIGHT, LOUIS. *Middle Class Culture in Elizabethan England*. Ithaca: Cornell University Press, 1958.

WILENSKY, MORDECAI. *Shivat Hayehudim L'Angliah*. Jerusalem: Reuvan Mas, 1943.

WYNNE, ARNOLD. *The Growth of English Drama*. 1914; rpt. Freeport, N.Y.: Books For Libraries Press, 1968.

ESSAYS AND ARTICLES

ABRAHAMS, ISRAEL. "Isaac Abendana's Cambridge Mishnah and Oxford Calendars." *T.J.H.S.E.* 8 (1915–17): 98–121.

————. "Passes Issued to Jews in the Period 1689–1696." *M.J.H.S.E.*, Part 1 (1925): xxiv–xxxiii.

_____. "A Mining Incident in the Reign of Queen Elizabeth." *T.J.H.S.E.* 4 (1899–1901): 83–101.

ABRAHAMS, ISRAEL, AND SAYLE, C. E. "The Purchase of Hebrew Books by the English Parliament in 1647." *T.J.M.S.E.* 8 (1915–17): 63–77.

ABRAHAMS, LIONEL BARNETT. "Menasseh ben Israel's Mission to Oliver Cromwell." *J.Q.R.* 14 (1902): 1–25.

_____. "Two Jews Before the Privy Council and an English Law Court in 1614–15." *J.Q.R.* 14 (1902): 354–58.

ADLER, E.N. "The Hebrew Treasures of England." *T.J.H.S.E.* 8 (1915–17): 1–18.

ALTMANN, ALEXANDER. "William Wollaston English Deist and Rabbinic Scholar." *T.J.H.S.E.* 16 (1945–51): 185–211.

BARNETT, R. D. "The Correspondence of the Mahamad of the Spanish and Portuguese Congregation of London during the Seventeenth and Eighteenth Centuries." *T.J.H.S.E.* 20 (1959–61): 1–50.

BAUM, PAULL FRANKLIN. "The English Ballad of Judas Iscariot." *PMLA* 31 (1916): 181–89.

_____. "The Mediaeval Legend of Judas Iscariot." *PMLA* 31 (1916): 481–632.

BOWMAN, JOHN. "A Seventeenth Century Bill of Rights for Jews." *J.Q.R.* 39 (1949): 379–95.

BOX, G. H. "Hebrew Studies in the Reformation Period and After: Their Place and Influence," in *The Legacy of Israel.* Ed. Edwyn R. Bevan and Charles Singer. Oxford: Clarendon Press, 1953. Pp. 315–75.

BRONSTEIN, HERBERT. "Shakespeare, the Jews and The Merchant of Venice." *Shakespeare Quarterly* 20 (1969): 3–10.

BROTZ, HOWARD. "The Position of the Jews in English Society." *The Jewish Journal of Sociology* 1 (1959): 94–113.

BROWN, CARLETON. "Chaucer's Prioress's Tale and Its Analogues." *PMLA* 31 (1906): 486–518.

BROWN, JOHN RUSSELL. "Love's Wealth and the Judgement of the Merchant of Venice." *Twentieth Century Interpretations of The Merchant of Venice.* Ed. Sylvan Barnet. Englewood Cliffs, N.J.: Prentice-Hall, 1970. Pp. 81–90.

COGHILL, NEVILL. "The Basis of Shakespearian Comedy." *Essays and Studies III.* Ed. Rostrevor Hamilton. London: John Murray, 1950. Pp. 1–29.

ETTINGER, S. "The Beginnings of the Change in the Attitude of European Society Towards the Jews," *Scripta Hierosolymitana.* Ed. Alexander Fuks and Israel Halpern. Jerusalem: Hebrew University Press, 1961. Vol. 7, pp. 193–219.

FINES, JOHN. "Judaising in the Period of the English Reformation—The Case of Richard Bruern." *T.J.H.S.E.* 21 (1962–76): 323–26.

FIRTH, C. H. "Some Historical Notes, 1648–1680." *T.J.H.S.E.* 4 (1903): 194–201.

GOLLANCZ, HERMAN. "A Contribution to the History of the Readmission of the Jews." *T.J.H.S.E.* 6 (1908–1910): 189–204.

_____. "Anglo-Judaica: A Description of a Collection of Pamphlets and Books Illustrative of the Interest in Hebrew Studies and of the Progress of the Jewish Cause in Christian England." *T.J.H.S.E.* 6 (1908–10): 56–87.

GRAHAM, CARY B. "Standards of Value in The Merchant of Venice." *Shakespeare Quarterly* 4 (1952): 145–51.

HENRIQUES, H. S. Q. "Proposals for Special Taxation of the Jews after the Revolution." *T.J.H.S.E.* 9 (1918–20): 39–50.

_____. "Reflections on the History of the Anglo-Jewish Community." *T.J.H.S.E.* 9 (1918–20): 131–42.

HIRSCH, S. A. "Presidential Address Before the Jewish Historical Society of England, December 1909." *T.J.H.S.E.* 7 (1911–14): 1–18.

HUME, MARTIN. "The So-Called Conspiracy of Dr. Ruy Lopez." *T.J.H.S.E.*, 6 (1908): 32–55.

HUNTER, G. K. "The Theology of Marlowe's The Jew of Malta." *Journal of the Warburg and Courtauld Institutes* 27 (1964): 211–40.

HYAMSON, ALBERT. "The Lost Tribes and the Return of the Jews to England." *T.J.H.S.E.* 5 (1902–05): 115–47.

——. "The Lost Tribes and the Influence of the Search for Them on the Return of the Jews to England." *J.Q.R.* 15 (1903): 640–76.

IBN ZAHAV, ARYE. "Demuto Shel Shylock Behasocher MeVenetzia." *Tarbiz* 13 (1942). 178–90.

KOBLER, FRANZ. "Sir Henry Finch and the First English Advocates of the Restoration of the Jews to Palestine." *T.J.H.S.E.* 16 (1945–51): 101–20.

LANGMUIR, GAVIN. "Anti-Judaism as the Necessary Preparation for Anti-Semitism." *Viator* 2 (1971): 383–89.

LEE, SIDNEY. "Elizabethan England and the Jews." *Transactions of the New Shakespeare Society* (1887–1900): 143–66.

LEVY, S. "Anglo-Jewish Historiography." *T.J.H.S.E.* VI (1908–10), 1–20.

——. "Bishop Barlow on the Case of the Jews." *T.J.H.S.E.* 3 (1899): 151–56.

——. "English Students of Maimonides." *M.J.H.S.E.*, Part 4 (1942): 61–84.

——. "John Dury and the English Jewry." *T.J.H.S.E.* 4 (1899–1901): 76–82.

LEWALSKI, BARBARA K. "Biblical Allusions and Allegory in *The Merchant of Venice*." *Shakespeare Quarterly*, 13 (1962): 327–43.

LEWIS, L., AND ROTH, CECIL. "New Light on the Apostasy of Sabbatai Zevi." *J.Q.R.* 53 (1963): 219–25.

LOWENFELD, HENRY. "The Decline in Belief in the Devil: The Consequences for Group Psychology." *Psychoanalytic Quarterly*, 38 (1969): 455–62.

MACCOBY, HYAM. "The Delectable Daughter." *Midstream* 16 (Nov. 1970): 50–59.

——. "The Figure of Shylock." *Midstream* 16 (Feb. 1970): 56–69.

MOODY, A. D. "An Ironic Comedy." *Twentieth Century Interpretations of the Merchant of Venice.* Ed. Sylvan Barnet. Englewood Cliffs, N.J.: Prentice-Hall, 1970. Pp. 100–108.

OSTERMAN, NAHUM. "The Controversy on the Proposed Readmission of the Jews to England." *Jewish Social Studies* 3 (1941): 301–28.

PARKES, JAMES. "Jewish Christian Relations in England." *Three Centuries of Anglo-Jewish History.* Ed. V. D. Lipman. Cambridge: Jewish Historical Society of England, 1961. Pp. 149–67.

PATINKIN, D. "Mercantilism and the Readmission of the Jews to England." *Jewish Social Studies* 7 (1946): 171–78.

PHILLIPS, HENRY E. I. "An Early Stuart Judaising Sect." *T.J.H.S.E.* 15 (1939–45): 63–72.

REINER, JACOB. "The English Yosippon." *J.Q.R.* 58 (1967): 126–42.

ROTH, CECIL. "The Background of Shylock." Roth, *Personalities and Events in Jewish History*. Philadelphia: J.P.S., 1962. Pp. 237–47.

——. "An English Account of the Jews of Jerusalem in the Seventeenth Century." *M.J.H.S.E.* Part 2 (1935): 99–104.

——. "Leon da Modena and England." *T.J.H.S.E.* 11 (1924–27): 206–27.

——. "Leon da Modena and his English Correspondents." *T.J.H.S.E.* 17 (1951–52): 39–43.

——. "The Medieval Conception of the Jew." Roth, *Personalities and Events in Jewish History*. Philadelphia: J.P.S., 1962. Pp. 53–68.

——. "The Middle Period of Anglo-Jewish History Reconsidered." *T.J.H.S.E.* 19 (1956): 1–12.

BIBLIOGRAPHY

———. "The Mystery of the Resettlement." Roth, *Essays and Portraits in Anglo-Jewish History.* Philadelphia: J.P.S., 1962. Pp. 86–107.

———. "New Light on the Resettlement." *T.J.H.S.E.* 12 (1927): 112–42.

———. "Perkin Warbeck and His Jewish Master." *T.J.H.S.E.* 9 (1922): 145–59.

———. "Philo-Semitism in England." Roth, *Essays and Portraits in Anglo-Jewish History.* Philadelphia: J.P.S., 1962. Pp. 10–21.

———. "Proselytes of Righteousness." Roth, *Personalities and Events in Jewish History.* Philadelphia: J.P.S., 1962. Pp. 143–71.

———. "Sir Edward Brampton, Alias Duarte Brandae, Governor of Guernsey 1482–1485." Roth, *Essays and Portraits in Anglo-Jewish History.* Philadelphia: J.P.S. 1962. Pp. 68–85.

RUBENS, ALFRED. "Portrait of Anglo-Jewry, 1656–1836." *T.J.H.S.E.*, 19 (1955–59): 13–52.

SAMUEL, E. R. "Portuguese Jews in Jacobean London." *T.J.H.S.E.*, 18 (1953–55): 171–230.

———. "Carvajal and Pepys." *M.J.H.S.E.* Part 2 (1935): 24–29.

———. "The Jewish Oratories of Cromwellian London." *M.J.H.S.E.* Part 3 (1937): 46–55.

———. "The Strayings of Paul Isaiah in England (1651–1656)." *T.J.H.S.E.* 16 (1945–51): 77–87.

———. "Sir William Davidson, Royalist (1616–1689) and the Jews." *T.J.H.S.E.* 14 (1935–59): 39–79.

SCHECHTER, FRANK I. "The Rightlessness of Medieval English Jewry." *J.Q.R.* 4 (1913–14): 121–51.

SCHOECK, RICHARD J. "Chaucer's Prioress: Mercy and Tender Heart." *Caucer Criticism* Ed. Richard Schoeck and Jerome Taylor. Notre Dame, Ind.: Notre Dame University Press, 1965. Pp. 245–58.

SCHOEPS, HANS-JOACHIN. "Philo-Semitism in the Baroque Period." *J.Q.R.* 47 (1956): 139–44.

SELBIE, W. B. "The Influence of the Old Testament on Puritanism." *The Legacy of Israel.* Ed. Edwyn R. Bevan and Charles Singer. Oxford: Clarendon Press, 1953. Pp. 407–31.

SISSON, C. J. "A Colony of Jews in Shakespeare's London." *Essays and Studies* 23 (1938): 38–51.

STERN, ALFRED. "Menasseh ben Israel et Cromwell." *Revue des Etudes Juives* 6 (1883): 96–111.

STONEX, ARTHUR BIVINS. "The Usurer in Elizabethan Drama." *PMLA.* 31 (1916): 190–210.

TREVOR-ROPER, H. R. "The European Witch-Craze of the Sixteenth and Seventeenth Centuries." H. R. Trevor-Roper. *The European Witch-Craze of the Sixteenth and Seventeenth Centuries and Other Essays.* 1956; rpt. New York: Harper Torch Books, 1969. Pp. 90–192.

WILENSKY, MORDECAI. "Dalid Kontrosim Angleem Al HaTenuah HaShabtait." *Zion* 17 (1952): 157–72.

———. "The Literary Controversy in 1656 Concerning the Return of the Jews to England." *Publications of the American Academy for Jewish Research* 20 (1951): 357–93.

———. "The Royalist Position Concerning the Readmission of the Jews to England." *J.Q.R.* 41 (1951): 397–409.

———. "Thomas Barlow's and John Dury's Attitude Towards the Readmission of the Jews to England." *J.Q.R.* 50 (1959–60): 165–75, 256–68.

WOLF, LUCIEN. "Cromwell's Jewish Intelligencers." *Essays in Jewish History.* Ed. Cecil Roth. London: Jewish Historical Society of England, 1934. Pp. 93–114.

———. "Jews in Tudor England." *Essays in Jewish History.* Ed. Cecil Roth. London: Jewish Historical Society of England, 1934. Pp. 71–90.

———. "Crypto-Jews Under the Commonwealth." *T.J.H.S.E.* 7 (1895): 55–88.

———. "Jews in Elizabethan England." *T.J.H.S.E.* 11 (1928): 1–91.

————. "Josippon in England." *T.J.H.S.E.* 6 (1908–1910): 277–88.

————. "The Jewry of the Restoration: 1660–1664." *T.J.H.S.E.* 5 (1902–05): 5–33.

————. "Status of the Jews in England After the Resettlement." *T.J.H.S.E.* 4 (1899–1901): 177–93.

ZITT, HERSCH L. "The Jew in the Elizabethan World-Picture." *Historia Judaica* 14 (1952): 53–60.

INDEX

Aaron of Lincoln, 14–15
Abraham and Isaac (mystery play), 23
Absalom and Achitophel, 146
Addison, L. A., 75
Aliens: tolerance of, 54
Almanac, 59
Anatomy of Melancholy, The, 99–100
Andrewes, Lancelot, 63, 83
Anglo-Judaeus, 119–21, 123
Antichrist, 18, 67
Anti-Judaism. *See* Anti-Semitism
Anti-Semitism: church policy of, 15–16, 152–53, effect on readmission question, 117–18, 121; European, 49, 50; in acts of Parliament, 151, in *A Short Demurrer to the Jewes*, 114–16; in ballads, 43–44; in Banns, 24; in conversionist tracts, 141; in drama, 22–24, 51, 63–72 passim; in folklore, 43–44; in literature, 36, 72, 89, 99–100; in sermons, 18, 21, 62, 87–89, 142–44; in travelers' accounts of Jews, 73–76; in visual arts, 35–36; origins in church teachings, 41, 153–54

Baker, Richard, 136
Ballad of Geruntus, The, 44
Ballad of Judas Iscariot, The, 44
Ballads: anti-Semitism in, 43–44
Barabbas, 65–67
Barlow, Thomas, 127, 128
Barrow, Isaac, 143
Beaumont, Thomas, 138
Belphegor, or the Marriage of the Devil, 145–46
Bible. *See* Old Testament Jews
Blood libel, 17, 118, 120; denied, 93–131

Blunt, Henry, 162n60
Boswell, Sir William, 77
Brampton, Edward (Duarte Brandao), 45–46
Brightman, Thomas, 80
Bristol Jews, 47–48
Broughton, Hugh, 76–77
Browne, Sir Thomas, 100–1
Bunny, Edmund, 76
Burton, Robert, 98–100
Busher, Leonard, 82

Caceres, Simon de, 84
Calvert, Thomas, 93–94
Canterbury Tales, 37–40 passim
Caravajal, Antonio Fernandez, 84, 139
Cartwright, Ebenezer and Johanna, 95, 165n26
Catherine of Braganza, 137, 169n12
Catholics: and Jews, as subversives, 89–90
Charles I: and Jews, 84–105
Charles II. mercantile policies, 137–38
Chaucer, Geoffrey, 37–40 passim
Child, Joshua, 150
Christ's Passion (mystery play), 22
Chronicles (Hollinshed), 72
Church: forbade money lending, 14; policy toward Jews, 15–16, 152–53
City Exchange: Jews admitted as brokers, 135
"Clippers and forgers," 114, 120
Cohan, Eve (Elizabeth Verboon), 140–41
Collier, Thomas, 123
Confessio Amantis, 40–41
Converted Christians: Jews' rejection of, 138. *See also* Judaizers

185

Bernard Glassman is rabbi of Tifereth Israel Synagogue in New Bedford, Massachusetts. He teaches in the History Department of Southeastern Massachusetts University. A graduate of Brooklyn College (1957), he holds advanced degrees from Old Dominion University (M.A. in history, 1969) and Jewish Theological Seminary of America (B.H.L., 1958; M.H.L., 1961; D.H.L., 1971).

The manuscript was edited by Linda Grant. The book was designed by Selma R. Tenenbaum. The typeface for the text is Caledonia designed by W. A. Dwiggins about 1938; and the display face is Futura Display designed by Paul Reuner about 1927.

The text is printed on Nicolet text paper and the book is bound in Columbia Mills Llamique cloth over binders' boards. Manufactured in the United States of America.